Action
and
Purpose

Action
and
Purpose

Richard Taylor

HUMANITIES PRESS
ATLANTIC HIGHLANDS, N.J.

Reprinted 1973 by Humanities Press
by Arrangement with the Author

Library of Congress Cataloging in Publication Data

Taylor, Richard, 1919–
  Action and purpose.

  Reprint of the ed. published by Prentice-Hall,
Englewood Cliffs, N. J.
    1. Act (Philosophy) 2. Agent (Philosophy)
3. Philosophical anthropology. I. Title.
[BD450.T28 1973]   128'.3   73-9918
ISBN 0-391-00318-6

To *Hylda*

Preface

I have here exhibited a somewhat novel approach to some very old problems upon which modern philosophy seems to me to have shed more darkness than light. I call this approach novel only because it is not one that philosophers nowadays customarily take, though it is by no means new to philosophy. It emphasizes the ideas of action and purpose rather than, say, cause and effect, as instrumental to an understanding of human nature. I have not, however, tried to defend any philosophical system, nor to uphold any familiar theory that I happen to cherish. Ever since I began thinking on these things I have realized, more and more, that wisdom does not consist in the mastery of theories and skill in beating down objections to them, but rather in seeing the difficulties that beset one at every turn of his thinking, difficulties that slowly impress upon one the complexity and mystery of human nature, and gradually unfold more and more for one to see but less and less to understand.

I began thinking about these things several years ago in London. Returning, and having no place to live and no teaching to claim my energy, I tried to think through what is involved in the idea of a man's sometimes having it within his power to do various alternative things. This idea seemed to me crucial to philosophy, but my only conviction was that what I had been taught in the matter, by men of undoubted philosophical genius, was basically false, though I knew not where the truth lay. At intervals thereafter for several years I kept working out this and related notions, quite inconclusively, until at last I had a drawerful of manuscript, all in such fragmentary and chaotic condition that I despaired of trying to make anything useful of it.

I then thought I must find out more about psychology. There was certainly an abundance of books on this subject, and I thought that if any people actually know something about human nature they must surely be found among the authors of those books. I found, however, that the questions that interested me were simply ignored by these writers, that ever so many interesting things were said about brains and nerves and glands, all the names of these being duly given, and about conditioning and reflexes and the like, but nothing whatever about things so elementary as, say, a voluntary act of choice. It seemed almost as if there were a conspiracy in this branch of psychology to pretend that such things do not exist; or at least, not unless they could be twisted to resemble the model of an electrical circuit or exhibited in the perfectly comprehensible picture of a stimulus and a response. Psychological works, on the other hand, which dealt with practical problems of human motivation, with neurosis and the like, far from pretending that the questions that interested me did not exist, simply took them all for granted, speaking unabashedly of goals, freedom, the ego, and so on, with hardly the least hint of an attempt to connect these things with what was described in the aforementioned books. It seemed that these diverse approaches had almost nothing whatever in common except the name of them, that between them there yawned an abyss of human ignorance, and that, alas! it was in that vast *terra incognita* that all my philosophical torments lay.

The philosophical problems I have dealt with in this book are therefore essentially original, and my purpose has been positive. I have not, in other words, found my subject matter by gleaning from philosophical books theories to criticize or authors to refute. Some of the things I have discussed, and particularly the idea of action, have nevertheless come very much to the forefront of philosophical thought in recent years, and the influence upon me of such writers as A. I. Melden, Gilbert Ryle, G. E. M. Anscombe, and J. L. Austin will be quite apparent. My keen interest in the concept of purposeful behavior arose many years ago from a controversy with the late Dr. Norbert Weiner and some of his associates. This controversy was published in *The Philosophy of Science,* 1950, but none of it has been reproduced here, for I have long since decided that both their positions and mine were substantially wrong. I hope here to have finally set forth at least some of the truth concerning this terribly important but neglected concept.

Part I of the book is mainly critical and, in places, fairly technical. Its main purpose is to demolish a whole spectrum of theories, of which Hume's philosophy is the remote ancestor of most, and modern physical science their guardian. This cannot be done by trite observations and declamation but only by the most careful analysis. The general point of Part I may, however, be obtained from its concluding chapter, for those who may want to skip to Part II, which is not very technical and contains my positive answers. It is largely exploratory, and while I have tried to be fastidious I have not needed much technical machinery to work out there the teleological conception of behavior which is the main objective of the book.

I express here my gratitude to my former colleagues, Roderick Chisholm and C. J. Ducasse, for planting in my mind the seeds of many of the ideas I have developed here, though neither is likely to approve of all that I have nourished from them. My original manuscript was begun on a sabbatic leave from Brown University, during which time I was sustained by a grant from the George A. and Eliza Gardner Howard Foundation, to the trustees of which I am most grateful. I began thinking of these things in London, where I went on a travel grant from the American Philosophical Society, to which also is due my grateful thanks.

The revised substance of four of the chapters of this book have been previously published. Much of Chapter 4 was published under the title " 'I Can' " in the *Philosophical Review,* Vol. 69 (1960). Much of Chapter 3 appeared in *The Monist,* Vol. 47 (1963), under the title "Causation," but has since been substantially modified. A considerable part of Chapter 11 is a revision of my paper, "The Stream of Thoughts *vs.* Mental Acts," which appeared in the *Philosophical Quarterly*, Vol. 13 (1963). Parts of Chapter 12 were published in *The American Philosophical Quarterly*, Vol. 1 (1964), under the title "Deliberation and Foreknowledge." To the editors of these journals are due my thanks for permission to incorporate that material into the present book. I wish finally to thank Dr. Keith Lehrer and Random House, Inc., for permission to incorporate Chapter 13, much of which was read at a conference on the problem of free will at the University of Rochester in May, 1964, and which has appeared in *Freedom and Determinism*, edited by Dr. Lehrer and published by Random House.

Contents

Part One

Causation
and
Action

1

Introduction

A man who is at all reflective, whose attention is not, like that of an animal, perpetually absorbed in external things, cannot but wonder sooner or later at *himself*. He cannot but be struck, not merely by the apparent mystery of living things generally, but particularly by the existence of such a being as himself, who not only thinks, but who acts, creates, brings about the realization of ends, and sometimes chooses for better or worse. People generally are so common in one's experience that it is natural to take them for granted, as presenting no puzzle or mystery, and to think only of such practical problems as arise in one's relationships to them, much as fish must take other fish for granted, or as we take for granted the air around us and the stones at our feet. The vast majority of mankind, certainly, not excluding even some who are distinguished for their intellects, are not reflective. They shun even the most elementary philosophical questions as they would a discomfort, and one upon which, moreover, no practical issue can turn. They thus go to their graves with the most childlike conceptions of themselves and of human nature generally, never confronting anything in the physical world, from which their practical concepts are derived, that clashes with these conceptions or forces any revision of them. There are, for instance, intelligent and even learned men who assume that *thinking* consists simply in "having" things called "thoughts," or even of saying words to oneself, that *reasoning* and *deliberating* are physical processes in the brain, that human *activity* is simply the internally caused motions of the body, and so on. But some philosophic spirits, sometimes, are overwhelmed by a seeming discontinuity between themselves and the rest of physical nature, and they are sufficiently tormented by this apparent contrast to want to understand it and see what it implies. It is to these that my ideas are directed.

The history of thought exhibits a certain pattern, wherein certain general ideas one after another become dominant, each of them tending to persist long after those forces which gave rise to it have waned, eventually becoming dislodged by another general conception having the same power to persist by its own inertia. The earliest speculative thinkers, for example, were obsessed with the idea of substance; they thought the world could be made intelligible simply by finding out what this substance was. That there might be no elemental substance was an idea they simply resisted. Gradually the idea evolved that the world, or "reality," is composed of nothing but "matter," and that matter has the form of "atoms," incredibly hard, tiny particles. This idea took such firm hold in men's minds that it formed the basis of physical science for centuries. Following the emergence of this notion, philosophers became obsessed with the idea of ends or purposes, supposing that the "why" of things could be expressed only in these terms. This idea, central to Aristotelian philosophy, and later to theology, was, like the theory of atoms, not the product of inquiry and discovery, but rather the more or less arbitrary foundation of inquiry. Theological conceptions, in their turn, served as the basis of speculation and inquiry for a very long period. Again, of course, these were not the fruit of investigation, but rather the foundation of thought, the framework within which men sought the solutions to problems. In the seventeenth century, the Cartesian conception of man, as consisting of two wholly distinct substances, mind and matter, came to dominate philosophy and psychology, and it is only with great difficulty that even contemporary philosophers can shake themselves free of that model, despite its more or less arbitrary character. The model itself is, like its predecessors, not so much a theory that has resulted from the observation and interpretation of data, but rather a framework within which the data themselves are interpreted—a general conception which determines a priori what shall be considered as data, what shall be construed as problems, and what shall count as solutions.

Now I do not mean here to review the history of thought, but only to call attention to the manner in which certain conceptions tend to become fixed, requiring time and the labors of men of great originality and genius merely to dislodge them. The thinking of past generations often seems dogmatic; we wonder how they could have become so attached to certain general conceptions which appear to us totally groundless. Yet to their adherents these conceptions seemed quite obvious. They were what gave life and meaning to their thoughts. I believe, moreover, that we of this age are by no means emancipated from the general conception; if we look closely and sceptically at contemporary thought we shall find that it, too, proceeds within a certain framework, no less arbitrary than those it has displaced. It is usually called, misleadingly, the framework of scientific explanation. The thing to stress, however, is that scientific explanation usually does not now mean simply explanation based upon and verifiable by observation, but rather, explanation that fits into a certain general conception of what reality ought to be like. The framework is, in other words, not simply a method of discovery, but rather a fairly large metaphysical hypothesis. It is, for example, quite uncritically thought to be "scientific" to *hold* that men are ("ultimately") very like machines and that their behavior can ("ultimately," as we are always told) be understood in terms of the same principles by which the behavior of inanimate things is understood. Or, again, it is somehow deemed "scientific" to deny that men ever act freely. Hence arguments in favor of the causal determinism of human behavior are always received with the keenest interest and guaranteed an audience, while arguments casting doubt upon this hypothesis are generally met with scepticism and even hostility. Arguments of the former kind need not even be very good, philosophically. They can be question-begging, or even quite irrelevant, like so many of the speculations of psychologists. They are nevertheless sensed to be somehow "on the right track"— scientific in spirit if not in content. Of course, their being on the right track does not in the least entail their being cogent, objective, undogmatic, or philosophically perceptive. Instead, it results from their seeming somehow to fit more or less into the general conception of what reality must be like, a conception which was borrowed from physical science, and which thus inherited the honorific appellative "scientific." To give another example, it is generally deemed scientific to interpret human behavior that is purposive or creative along the same lines that the behavior of inanimate things, such as machines, is interpreted; to reduce, as is said, the former to the latter, giving much emphasis to *conditions* and little to reasons. Obviously the mere observation of human behavior does not point to such a conception. On the contrary, such an idea would not have been possible had men been guided from the start only by observations of human behavior, without any science of inanimate things. The reason such speculations find ready acceptance is, rather, that they fit into the general conception of the world that has been derived from physical science—that they fit, in other words, into a very general, metaphysical framework which contemporary thinkers find congenial, and which they are fond of assuming must, "ultimately," prove all-encompassing.

I am not, of course, suggesting that science and philosophy have not progressed, that the present generation does not know more than previous ones. What I am suggesting, however, is that contemporary thought is hardly less dogmatic than that of our predecessors. The general conceptions and prevailing ideas change, but are no less stubbornly clung to, and—what is rarely appreciated—are no less arbitrary than the ones they have replaced. We find it quaint that earlier thinkers should have wanted to interpret physical nature anthropomorphically, that they should have wanted to explain everything, including the existence of the world itself, in terms of such ideas as efficient and final causes. Yet even learned men of today see no similar quaintness in the notion that human behavior must *not* be interpreted anthropomorphically, that is, in terms of a framework appropriate for the understanding of human behavior. What seems obvious to one age seems dogmatic and arbitrary to another. It seems to me naïve to suppose that men today have suddenly ceased being arbitrary and dogmatic in the general conceptions which they have embraced, or to suppose that contemporary general conceptions are somehow more obviously correct than those of past ages. Such general conceptions do not, at any rate, become less dogmatic by being baptized "scientific." I am moreover convinced that, as philosophers, men become wiser, *not* by trying to force their experience into a preconceived framework which dictates what is and what is not allowable, but rather by trying to see the implications, whatever these may be, of what we do actually experience. If these implications sometimes seem to run contrary to what we had supposed and fondly hoped was the general truth of things, then it is no step in the direction of wisdom to pretend otherwise and fall back upon what we say will "ultimately" and "in principle" turn out to be so.

Now if we take the point of view of external observers, that is, the point of view experimental science necessarily restricts itself to, we cannot but regard men as natural objects differing only in complexity from physical objects and other living things, and governed by the same natural laws and principles that physical science presupposes. There will, for example, be nothing in our observations, experiments, or data to convey such notions as purpose or creativity, except insofar as these notions can somehow be reduced to empirical concepts and thus made applicable, at least in principle, to all objects of observation, and at the same time rendered superfluous to any inquiry into human nature. Indeed, from the point of view of an observer it is even possible to wonder, as philosophers have long since pointed out, how we can know that men are conscious, sensitive beings—a problem that cannot possibly arise for one who considers human nature, not as it exhibits itself to observation, but as it exists in himself.

For this reason, plus the fact that the problems I want to consider can only arise from reflections upon oneself, my subject of inquiry is human nature as I find it exhibited in myself. This does not mean that I proceed by "introspection"—it is not even clear what that is—but rather that the most important test of any philosophical theory we shall consider will consist in its application to oneself. Any theory which would render doubtful some distinction of which each of us is already certain will be regarded as doubtful. To illustrate this with just one example: One sometimes has no certain knowledge, when he observes a simple bodily motion on the part of another man, whether that motion was an act of that man, or simply a motion that occurred, caused perhaps by the wind or a moving object. If it is a motion of his own body, however, he usually knows, without being able to say exactly *how* he knows, whether he made the motion or whether it resulted from some extraneous cause, such as a spasm, a reflex, or an impact with some thing. Any theory, therefore, which obliterates the distinction between these two kinds of fact, or implies that no distinction can be drawn between them, must be rejected, simply on the basis of what each of us already knows about himself.

It is for this reason, too, that I shall in some places use the stylistically objectionable first personal pronoun to state what I know of myself in cases in which I cannot in the same way know certain facts about others. The reader will understand, however, that my purpose is not thus to convey miscellaneous autobiographical data, but rather to lead him to the consideration of himself. As I use the word "I," then, the reader is to suppose that the thoughts thus expressed are his own, and that he is the subject of those reflections.

I shall begin, then, with the subject of causation, my initial purpose being the negative one of showing that, while everyone knows what causation is, no one can say what it is. The importance of this is that, since David Hume's reflections on human nature and the accompanying and subsequent development of physical science, ever so many ideas that are crucial to an understanding of human nature have been analyzed or "reduced" in one way or another to concepts of cause and effect. Examples are such ideas as those of voluntary action, purposeful behavior, and the like. Since it has generally been assumed —erroneously, I maintain—that causation is not an ultimate philosophical category, but rather one that can be analyzed in terms of the constancy of conjunction of events, laws of nature, and the like, the result has been some perfectly bizarre conceptions of human nature and, in particular, of human action and purpose. To see this, we need to look rather closely at the concept of causation and then, hopefully freed from misconceptions that are still very prevalent, we can turn more positively to the ideas of action and purpose which are the main themes of these reflections.

2

The
Original
Idea
of a Cause

An efficient cause was once generally thought of as something which *produces* something. That which was produced, according to this idea, was either some new substance, such as ashes from wood, or simply a change in some previously existing substance. This is obviously only a relative distinction, however, for outside Christian theology philosophers have usually taken for granted that no new substance can be produced by a cause out of nothing. Ashes, for example, result from imposing changes on something that already exists. The most general idea of an efficient cause, then, was traditionally that of something which produces, and thus accounts for, some *change*. If the change was sufficiently striking to warrant applying a new name to what resulted, then the effect was spoken of as a new substance, and the process by which it was produced was called "generation." If the change was less drastic it was simply referred to as a "motion" or change in a continuing substance. A moth, for example, is simply the result of change in a pre-existing caterpillar, but the change is so striking that the result can be thought of as a new being, whereas a leaf which turns from green to red is still thought of as a leaf, and even as "the same" leaf. Aristotle drew this distinction in terms of essential and accidental properties, but it seems rather to be a distinction which is relative only to vocabulary and to methods of classification. It need not, in any case, detain us.

Five Archaic
and Important Ideas

There are, however, five important ideas that stand out in the metaphysical speculations involving causation developed prior to the rise of experimental science. One is that the original idea of an efficient cause had no necessary connection with the ideas of uniformity, constancy, or law. It was always supposed that, given the cause, the effect must follow, but this was not usually understood to mean that, given the same cause, the same effect must always follow. A particular sculptor, for example, was considered the efficient cause of a particular statue, but it was not supposed that this sculptor could do nothing but make statues. It is for this reason that the problem of free will first arose, not at all as a consequence of the idea of causation, but rather as a consequence of the ideas of God's invariable will or knowledge.

The second important idea is that an efficient cause was almost always thought of as an object or substance—typically, as a person, human or divine—rather than as an event, process, or state. Thus the sun was thought of as a cause of light, a sculptor as the cause of a statue, a soldier the cause of his enemy's death, and God, of course, the cause of the world. It was thus very natural for philosophers to suppose that any series or chain of causally connected events must have some source, must originate in some first or initiating cause, that this must be some substance or "thing" rather than just another event, and that only this could be properly spoken of as the cause of any of those changes.

The third and most important idea is that a cause was always thought of as something that exerted *power*, as something that originated something or brought it into being by virtue of its power to do so. The necessity of an effect, given its cause, was thought to be a consequence of the power of that cause to compel it or bring it about, and not a consequence of any supposed invariance between that cause and that effect. Thus, if a sculptor has the power to make a statue, and exercises that power upon marble, then the marble cannot help becoming a statue; the effect must follow, given the exercise of that power by its cause. It was thus that there arose the idea, so clear to our predecessors but so obscure to us, that a cause must be as great or greater than its effect. It was also this idea of the power of a cause to produce its effect that gave rise to the common distinction between acting and being acted upon, and the kindred distinctions between agent and patient, action and passion. A sculptor acts in creating, or causing, a statue, but the marble upon which he acts does not act; it is a purely passive recipient of changes imposed by an active being.

A fourth idea, closely connected with that of causal efficacy or power, is that of *necessity* in the causal relationship. An efficient cause, it was always thought, necessitates its effect in the sense that, given the former, the latter *cannot* (and not merely *does* not) fail to occur. There was never thought to be any necessitation in the reverse direction, however; that is, an effect was never thought of as necessitating the occurrence of its cause, even in those cases in which neither preceded the other in time, and this, despite the fact that the cause could often be as certainly inferred from the effect as the effect from the cause. Thus, a man vanquishes his foe by making him die, that is, by doing something which renders it *impossible* for him to live. But despite the fact that one might quite certainly infer such a cause from such an effect, given an adequate description of the latter and its attending circumstances, it was never thought that the effect necessitated the occurrence of the cause. Similarly, a man, in raising his arm, makes it move upward, the arm being the passive recipient of changes wrought by an active cause. Or, to take an example from inanimate nature, the sun warms a stone, or makes it become warmer, but in a manner in which it cannot be said that the stone, in becoming warmer in just the way that it does, makes the sun shine (or be shining) upon it.

And finally, there is in this notion of causal efficacy an idea which was never doubted and is still a part of everyone's conception of causation; namely, the idea that the power of an efficient cause never extends to things past. This temporal priority of an efficient cause to its effect was not, moreover, thought to result merely from conventions of speech, but to be a metaphysical necessity. The power of a cause to produce an effect has always been thought to have a fixed temporal direction from its very nature as an efficient cause. Aristotelians might express this by saying that the past contains no potentialities or real possibilities; everything past can only be what it actually is. Things present, on the other hand, are usually thought of as capable of becoming a variety of things, depending on what they are converted to by the causes that act upon them. It is in this sense, according to this way of looking at things, that the future, unlike the past, contains alternative and mutually incompatible possibilities, and is thus within the power of men or other efficient causes to determine in this way or that. There has been to date insufficient appreciation of the dreadful problems, shortly to be elicited, to which this supposition gives rise.

The idea of efficient causation that I have thus far adumbrated is, of course, one that eventually came to be condemned, along with that of "final" causes, as "anthropomorphic"; so determined have natural scientists been to rid their thought of both ideas that even still there are many who prefer to avoid even the *word* "cause." Men of open minds are continually discovering, however, that we are never so learned as to derive nothing from our predecessors; here we have, I believe, a striking confirmation of this. What I propose to do in this chapter, then, is to elicit the idea of *power* or *efficacy* once thought essential to the understanding of causation. In the following chapter I shall show that it is still essential to that idea and that, partly as a consequence of this, causation is an ultimate philosophical category, or one that has not been, and evidently cannot be, analyzed in terms of any other philosophical ideas. In subsequent chapters I shall defend the claim that *purpose* is another such ultimate philosophical category —that it too is a concept that has not been and evidently cannot be analyzed or understood in terms either of causation or of any other philosophical ideas. Since, moreover, as I shall show, *both* concepts are necessary for the understanding of even some of the simplest facts of human nature, it will follow that some of the simplest facts of human nature must remain forever unintelligible to those who endeavor to eschew these original and allegedly archaic concepts of efficient causation and purpose.

Efficient Causation and Power

Until scientific workers came to concentrate their attention upon the impersonal relations of events and states to each other, and to rest content with "explanations" which consisted simply of descriptions of

such relations and the expression of these in the form of universal pro-
positions called "laws of nature," it was usually *substances* that were
thought of as causes, properly so called. Thus fire was thought of as
the cause of heat, the sun the cause of sunlight and moonlight, and
a man the cause of his own thoughts and deeds and of artifacts generally, and so on. Nor is it hard to see *why* causation was thought of
in this way, for every man, before he learns any philosophy, still thinks
of *himself* as just such a cause.

Thus, when I think and act—as distinguished from merely having
thoughts occur to me, as in reveries and dreams, or having motions
occur in my body, as in the case of my heartbeats or the growth and
shedding of my hair—I seem to be *making something happen,* initiating something, or bringing it about. I do not in this case just passively
undergo changes, whether of body or of thought, but seem actively to
produce those very changes in myself and, consequently, in my environment. Now here is why Aristotle spoke of men, and of animals generally, as "self-moving," or as things which sometimes, not literally
moved by other things, initiate motions and changes within themselves.
That men are sometimes the masters, creators, or originators of their
own thoughts has been a fairly common idea, the implications of which
have not always been obvious. Sometimes it has even been conjectured
that thoughts may be created out of nothing.

Believing themselves to be—as indeed, without speculating upon it,
men still believe—the efficient causes of some of their own motions
and thoughts, it was almost inevitable that they should think of God
as the source of thoughts and ideas transcending their own—as a being
who "thinks himself," in Aristotle's scheme—and also as the source of
all those cosmic motions with which men have nothing to do. These
ideas are as old as Plato, to whom it seemed that if there were no
God, and hence no original source of motion, the universe would be
perfectly static. In the philosophy of Aristotle and the Scholastics, God
became pre-eminently the "prime" or "unmoved" *mover.* Modern
students, to whom the classical arguments for a supreme cause seem so
immensely naïve and implausible, quite fail to realize that since these
arguments were invented the concept of causation has radically
changed. Until one thinks of a cause as a being which produces certain
states or events—which is how men in fact think of themselves as
causes—rather than as an event or state related in some special way
to another event or state, these ancient arguments for a first cause are
not even remotely intelligible.

Moreover, as I have noted, the idea of an efficient cause was inseparably linked with the idea of *active power,* such that a cause was always thought of as something that *acted,* as contrasted with being *acted upon.* So-called "secondary" causes need not, to be sure, be thought of as "acting" upon anything in a strict sense; these intermediate causes were always thought of as *means* by which some primary cause, such as a man, achieved a certain effect by acting first upon them. The idea of a secondary cause thus had no meaning apart from the idea of a primary cause, the distinction being in terms of the active source of change versus the merely passive recipient or transmitter of change. Thus arose the distinction between action and passion and such obvious correlates as agent and patient—words that now retain almost nothing of their original sense, and which have all but disappeared from the conceptual apparatus of philosophy. It is noteworthy, however, that they keep creeping back, and somehow find their way even into those disquisitions in which every effort is made to be "scientific" and to avoid metaphysical notions. Thus, it is not uncommon to find the authors of works on physiological psychology speaking of the brain, nerves, and muscles as *doing* various things, of the nerves as conveying "messages" up to the brain, and so on, as if these bodily parts were veritable persons or agents in their own right. An *agent* was originally, as the etymology of the word (cf. Lat. *agere*) suggests, something which acts to bring about changes, either in itself or in something else, rather than simply undergoing or transmitting such a change originating elsewhere, as does a secondary cause. A *patient,* accordingly, was something "passive," something acted upon, something in which changes are wrought by some being other than itself. This distinction is still imperfectly preserved in the use of active and passive verbs. The *power* of anything was thus its ability to bring about such changes. The idea of "passive power" therefore seemed to most philosophers to be an utterly incongruous notion, no *power* being needed to undergo a change wrought by something else. The class of things, moreover, possessed of such active power, and thus capable of being efficient causes, was generally thought to be quite limited. It was usually ascribed to animals, as "self-moving" beings, and hence to men and, pre-eminently, to God, but it was often denied of inanimate matter. Thus arose part of the apparent absurdity in the supposition, once much debated, whether matter might think. Descartes in effect denied power to animals, Spinoza and others were willing to ascribe it only to God, and subsequent thinkers have wanted to avoid the idea altogether. What were once thought of as "secondary" causes, or as things through which changes are merely transmitted, are now generally given sole title to the name of cause, so that a distinction between "primary" and "secondary" causes is rarely even drawn any more.

This notion of the active power of a cause was not, it should be stressed, peculiar only to archaic peripatetic and scholastic philosophies and psychologies. It was also assumed to be a basic philosophical category by writers only barely removed from the contemporary scene. Witness, for instance, Locke's long and labored discussion of the idea of power, wherein he tries, unsuccessfully, to reconcile it with the idea of "power" embodied in the infant science of his day. This discussion of Locke's is the longest in his *Essay,* but it is hardly ever referred to, simply because the problems he was wrestling with are seldom any longer felt or even quite understood. Berkeley, similarly, appeals to the principle that neither inanimate, passive substances (if such existed), nor ideas, could ever be the *causes* of sensations, or of anything else, simply because they *are* passive, and thus lack power to cause anything. The force of this repeated appeal is almost lost to modern readers who, having dissociated the idea of a cause from that of active power, are apt to regard it as utterly quaint and unsophisticated. Hume, finally, virtually buried the concept of active power, taking it as one of his first tasks to divorce it from the idea of a cause. But Hume, oddly, mixed the idea of necessitation, which is involved in that of active power—that is, the idea of *making* something happen—with the necessity which is involved in the relations of certain ideas—that is, with logical necessity—and imagined (as have nearly all his successors) that by divorcing causation from the latter he had thereby also rendered obsolete the idea of active power. Yet the suggestions made by Hume have been so useful for the analysis of the sort of causal relationship that exists between *events* that they have quite obscured the fact that they have no apparent bearing at all on the original and traditional concept of an efficient cause.

An Insufficiently Noted Change in the Meaning of " Cause "

It is no part of my purpose to deal at great length with the *history* of this notion, but there is one rarely noticed development in the history of thought that needs describing, if only because such large numbers of philosophers standing in the tradition of Hume seem to have been victimized by it. I have in mind a certain gradual shift of meanings without an accompanying shift in terminology, which can be seen as follows.

The concept of causal efficacy or power was, I believe, long regarded as basic, and as both obvious and more clear than any concepts by means of which one might try to describe or define it. Philosophers were, however, as I have noted, accustomed to speaking of such power as the power of a being to *cause* things to happen, such that men, for instance, having the power to act in certain ways, were also thought of as the causes of some of their own motions. Indeed philosophers, like others, often speak that way still. Now Hume addressed himself to the analysis of causation and showed, he thought, that it is a complex relationship between changes or events, analyzable in terms of other familiar relations such as constant conjunction and not, in any case, one that can be understood only in terms of some further primitive notion of active power, or the power to *make* things happen. It can, of course, be doubted whether the familiar relations of succession and so forth to which Hume reduced causation are adequate, but it has seldom been doubted that, so long as causation is thought of as a relation between states and events, no concept of *power*, at any rate, need be introduced into the description.

The thing to note, however, is that if we adopt this conception of causation—namely, that of a (perhaps complex) relation between states or events—then, significantly, it is no longer possible to speak of *men*, for example, as literally causing things to happen, for a man is plainly an object rather than an event in the usual sense. In the light of this obvious fact it is usual for philosophers, in speaking of men as causing things to happen, to assume that such a locution must be really an *elliptical* way of expressing a relationship between events—between, for instance, certain inner "volitions" or "acts of will," regarded as causes, and certain bodily motions, regarded as their effects; for a man cannot be related to anything as one *event* to another.

What has happened, in short, is that virtually all of Hume's successors have assumed—because the idea of active power had long been associated with that of an efficient cause, and then this had been reduced to other familiar notions such as constant conjunction and the like—that the idea of active power had *itself* been dispensed with in favor of more familiar "scientific" and less metaphysical concepts. In fact, however, *all* that has been accomplished is that the relation between events, *nowadays* spoken of as a causal relation, has been shown to be not a basic, ultimate, or unanalyzable relation; and I shall shortly cast doubt on the claim to having proved this much. Nothing, in any case, has happened to show that the relation between a certain kind of object—namely, a man—and certain events—namely, the voluntary motions of his body—which we sometimes still express by saying that he is "the cause" of those motions, is not a basic, clear, and unanalyzable concept. It can, of course, be assumed that this relation is *not* one between an object and an event, but rather just another instance of the kind of causal relation that obtains between certain events—that it is, for example, a relation between internal volitions and external motions. But that assumption is certainly not *obviously* true, and does not even *seem* true to common sense. In any case, the mere fact that the *word* "cause" has undergone this change of meaning in philosophical literature, which seems to be only a historical accident, does nothing whatever to show that the original idea of an efficient cause might not be exactly what is exemplified in human voluntary activity.

3

The Metaphysics of Causation

The ancient idea of efficient causation that I have very loosely sketched is generally considered by contemporary philosophers to be metaphysical and obscure, and quite plainly erroneous. Scientists too, insofar as they permit themselves to think about causation at all, share this disdain—though it is worth noting that both continue to *speak* quite unguardedly and unabashedly in terms of the very concepts that are involved in this ancient conception, employing quite freely the ideas of making certain things happen, of this or that agent's control over this or that state of affairs, and so on. It has become almost a commonplace in philosophy that we have officially got rid of such esoteric concepts as power and necessitation, reducing causation to such simple and discoverable relationships as invariant succession between states, processes, and events.

I believe, on the contrary, that the older metaphysical idea of an efficient cause is superior to and far closer to the truth of things than the conceptions of causation that are now usually taken for granted. Indeed, I believe that if we did not *already* have precisely the idea of an efficient cause that once played such a significant role in philosophical thought, we would not even *understand* the conceptions of causation with which modern philosophy has tried to supplant it, and that it is therefore quite idle to dream of *reducing* the former to the latter.

It is the aim of this chapter to defend this claim. I shall do so by showing that the attempts of modern philosophy to expurgate from causation the ideas elicited in the previous chapter, and particularly those of power and necessity, and to reduce causation to constancy of sequence, have failed. Many philosophers are now apparently agreed that causation cannot be described without in one way or another introducing modal concepts, which amounts to re-establishing the necessity which Hume was once thought to have gotten rid of; but hardly anyone, apparently, has noticed that we need also the idea of power or efficacy. If, as I believe, both these ideas are indispensable, then it will be found that the advance of contemporary philosophy over that of our predecessors is much less impressive than we had supposed.

Some Causal Statements

Statements like, "That window was shattered by a brick," "This fire was started by a cigarette," "A nail punctured that tire," and so on, express, though perhaps not accurately, the idea of cause and effect. The ideas expressed in them can also be expressed by saying, for example, "A brick *caused* that window to break," "A nail *caused* the puncture in that tire," and so on. The idea of causation involved in such examples is, in fact, so obvious that discussion is hardly needed to elicit it.

Two things about our manner of expressing such causal relationships in common speech give us pause. The first is that an object or substance seems often to be referred to as a cause. Thus, our statements above seem to say that a certain *brick,* which is an object, broke a window, that a *cigarette* started a fire, and that a *nail* punctured a tire. The second is that each of these objects seems to be alleged to have *done* something, in the same sense in which men, for example, are often described as *doing* various things. Thus, it does not seem wildly incongruous to say that the brick *flew* through the window, that the cigarette *started* a fire, that the nail *punctured* a tire; all these things can be said in answer to questions concerning what these various objects had *done*.

Such expressions of causation seem, in short, to express something very like the idea of efficient causation we were just considering, for there is at least a perfect grammatical similarity between two such statements as, say, "A man started this fire" and "A cigarette started this fire." It is certainly the consensus of contemporary thinkers, however, that no such idea is expressed, that statements of the kind we are now considering express certain relations between *events, states,* or *processes,* and that for the obscure and possibly esoteric idea of efficient causation by a substance that might at first seem to be involved in them we can substitute perfectly clear ideas of certain relationships between such events, states, or processes.

Thus, the statement, "That window was shattered by a brick," expresses the idea that the *striking* of that brick upon the window in a certain way was the cause of the latter's breaking, and both cause and effect here are events. To say simply that the *brick* broke the window is not to say something really false, but rather something incomplete; for unless this is understood as saying that the brick's impact, or some other event in which the brick was conspicuously involved, was the cause of the breaking, the statement is quite unintelligible.

Now this is doubtless true. If the statements we are now considering express the basic idea of causation, then causation is indeed a relationship between events, for each of those statements can be more precisely formulated in those terms. What, then, of such a statement as, "That window was shattered by a man," which appears to express a causal relationship between a certain being, that is, an agent, and some effect wrought by him? Is that statement elliptical in a similar way? It does not at first seem so. It might indeed suggest that there was some event in which that agent was conspicuously involved which was the cause of the window's breaking—such as the motion of his hand or, indeed, the motion of a brick which was moved by his hand—but that is not what it *means,* and that does not seem to be the idea of causation that it expresses. It might be true that the motion of his hand, or the motion of a brick which was moved by his hand, caused the window to break, without it being at all true that *he* broke it—in case it was not he, but someone else, who moved his hand, for example. This seems obvious. But how absurd it would be, on the other hand, to say that, while the brick's impact had indeed shattered the window, the brick itself really had nothing to do with it—on the ground that the brick had not moved itself through the window but had instead depended upon some agent to impel it!

The question before us now is simply this: Whether causation, as it is exemplified in the relationship between certain events, processes, or states, is the basic idea of causation, in terms of which, for example, causation of certain things by agents is to be understood; or whether, on the contrary, causation as it is exemplified in the actions of agents is the basic idea of causation, in terms of which, for example, the so-called causal relations between events, processes, or states are to be understood. It was once generally supposed that the latter was the correct view, that events, processes, and states were only "secondary causes," and that a cause in the original and proper sense had to be something, such as a man, having the power to make certain things happen. It is now generally supposed, on the other hand, that the former view is the correct one, and that the causation of events by agents—by men, for example—can be understood only in terms of a causal relationship between certain events, processes, or states. It is in terms of this that men are quite generally thought to cause certain things to happen only in the sense that certain things happening *inside* men—certain events, processes, or states—are the real causes of those happenings.

I want to show that, whatever grave and justified misgivings one might have concerning the older idea of efficient causation, this contemporary conception is in any case totally wrong. I think this will stand if it can be shown, *first,* that no conception of causation can possibly work unless it includes the idea of a certain kind of *necessary connection* between cause and effect, and also the idea of *efficacy* or *power* of a cause to produce its effect—the very two ideas modern philosophy has boasted it has banished from the concept of causation; *second,* that there is in the contemporary analyses of causation no basis whatsoever for affirming the temporal priority of causes to their effects apart from appealing to certain conventions of language which are, however, not a sufficient basis for affirming such priority; and *third,* that even making use of such ideas as necessitation and power, no one can *say* what causation is without involving himself in circularity or redundancy. Everyone, I maintain, *knows* what causation is—simply because, in my opinion, everyone thinks of *himself* as an efficient cause, in the traditional and generally considered archaic sense of that term.

Everyone knows what it is to make something happen and to exercise such power as he has over his body and his environment; but no one can *say* what this is, other than to say, simply, that it is causation.

Necessity *vs.* Invariable Sequence

Let the letters A, B, C ... etc., designate events, states of affairs, conditions, or substances which *have existed*. These symbols, in other words, shall designate anything we please that was ever real. This stipulation excludes from our consideration not only things future, but also things that might have existed but in fact did not exist, as well as impossible things, kinds or classes of things as distinguished from things themselves, and so on. Now I want to consider true assertions of the form, "A was the cause of B," wherein I assume that A was in fact, as asserted, the cause of B, and I want to ask just what such a statement asserts.

Let A, for example, be the beheading of Anne Boleyn, and B her subsequent death, and assume that the former was the cause of the latter. What, then, is asserted by that statement? Does it mean that A and B are constantly conjoined, B following upon A? Plainly not, for the event A, like B, occurred only once in the history of the universe. The assertion that A and B are constantly conjoined—that the one never occurs without the other—is therefore true, but not significant. Each is also constantly conjoined with every other event that has occurred only once. Nor do we avoid this obvious difficulty by saying that B must follow immediately upon A, in order to be the effect of A; for there were numberless things that followed immediately upon A. At the moment of Anne's death, for instance, numberless persons were being born here and there, others were dying, and, let us suppose, some bird was producing a novel combination of notes from a certain twig nearby, any of which events we may assume not to have happened before or since. Yet the beheading of that queen had nothing to do with these. Mere constancy of conjunction, then, even with temporal contiguity, does not constitute causation.

The Resort to Similarity

Here there is an enormous temptation to introduce classes or kinds and to say, after the fashion familiar to all students of philosophy, that

A was the cause of B, provided A was immediately followed by B, and that things similar to A are in similar circumstances always followed by things similar to B. This, however, only permits one temporarily to avoid speaking of necessary connections by exploiting the vagueness in the notion of similarity. When confronted with counter-examples one can always say that the requisite similarity was lacking, and thus avoid having to say that the necessary connection was lacking. What does "similar" mean in this context? If we construe it to mean *exactly* similar, then the class of things similar to A and the class of things similar to B each has only one member, namely, A and B, and we are back where we started. The only thing exactly similar to the beheading of Anne Boleyn, for instance, is the beheading of Anne Boleyn, and the only thing exactly similar to her death is her death. Other things are only more or less similar to these—similar, that is, in some respects, and dissimilar in others. If, however, we allow the similarity to be one of degree, then the statement that things similar to A are always followed by things similar to B is not true. A stage dramatization of the beheading of Anne Boleyn is similar—perhaps quite similar—to the beheading of Anne Boleyn, but it is not followed by anything similar to her death. Here it is tempting to introduce the idea of relevance and say that things similar to A in all relevant respects are followed by things similar to B in all relevant respects; but this just gives the whole thing away. "Relevant respects," it soon turns out, are nothing but those features of the situation that have some causal connection with each other. Or consider another example: Suppose we have two pairs of matches; the first two are similar to each other in all respects, let us suppose, except that one is red and the other blue. The other two are likewise similar in all respects, except that one is wet and the other dry. Now the *degree* of similarity between the members of each pair is the same. One of the differences, however, is "relevant" to the question of what happens when the matches are rubbed, while the other is not. Whether the match is red or blue is irrelevant, but whether it is wet or dry is not. But all this means, obviously, is that the dryness of a match is causally connected to its igniting, while its color is not.

Laws

Sometimes difficulties of the kind suggested have been countered by introducing the idea of a *law* into the description of causal connections. For instance, it is sometimes suggested that a given event A was the cause of a given event B, provided there is a law to the effect that whenever A occurs in certain circumstances it is followed by B. This appears, however, to involve the same problems of uniqueness and similarity that we have just considered. There can be no law connecting just two things. It can be no law, for example, that whenever Anne Boleyn is beheaded, *she* dies, or whenever a particular match is rubbed, *it* ignites.

One could, perhaps, overcome these difficulties by embodying in the statement of the law precisely those respects in which things must be similar in order to behave similarly under certain specified conditions, all other similarities and differences being disregarded as irrelevant. For example, there could be a law to the effect that whenever *any* match of such and such precisely stated chemical composition is treated in a certain specified way, under certain specified conditions, then it ignites. A match of that description would, of course, be similar to any other fitting the same description; other similarities and differences between them, however conspicuous, would be considered "irrelevant," that is, not mentioned in the law.

That overcomes the difficulty of specifying how similar two causes must be in order to have similar effects. They must, according to this suggestion, be exactly similar in certain respects only, and can be as dissimilar as one pleases in other respects. But here we find that, by introducing the idea of a law, we have tacitly reintroduced the idea of a necessary connection between cause and effect—precisely the thing we were trying to avoid. A general statement counts as a *law* only if we can use it to infer, not only what does or will happen, but also what *would* happen if something else were to happen, and this we can never do from a statement that is merely a true general statement.

To make this clear, assume that there is a true and perfectly general statement to the effect that any match having a certain set of specified properties ignites when rubbed in a certain specified manner under specified conditions. Now such a statement, though true, need not be a law. Suppose, for example, someone took a quantity of matches— a thousand, say—and gave them a common set of properties which uniquely distinguished them from all other matches that have in fact ever existed and, we can suppose, will in fact ever exist. Suppose, for example, he decorated the sticks in a certain elaborate way such that all the matches were similar with respect to those decorations, and suppose further that, as a matter of fact (but not of necessity) no other match so decorated has ever existed or ever will. Now if all those matches were rubbed in a similar way, it might be true that *every* match (in the history of the universe) having those properties ignites when rubbed. But this, though a true and perfectly general statement asserting how certain precisely described things invariably behave under certain conditions, admitting of not a single exception in the history of the universe, would be no law, simply because there is no necessary connection between a match's having those properties and behaving as it does when rubbed. If, contrary to fact, another match *were* to have those properties, but lacked, say, the property of dryness, it might not ignite. For a true general statement of this kind to count as a law, then, we must be able to use it to infer what would happen if something else, which does not happen, were to happen; for instance, that a certain match which lacks some property would ignite if only it had that property. This, however, expresses some necessary and not merely *de facto* connection between properties and events. There is some connection between a match's being dry and igniting when rubbed. There is not the same connection between its being decorated in a certain way and igniting when rubbed—even though it may be true that every match so decorated does ignite when rubbed. But this only means that the decoration on its stick does not have anything to do—has no necessary connection—with a match's igniting when rubbed, while its being dry does.

The Nature *vs.* the Knowledge of Causal Connections

Here one is apt to be reminded that we have no way of *knowing* what states, properties, and events are causally connected other than by noting which are invariably conjoined in our experience. If, for example, in terms of the foregoing example, we had no knowledge of matches other than that all the matches known to us did ignite when decorated in the manner assumed and then rubbed, we would have every reason to believe that there was a causal connection between such decorations and the igniting of the matches, it being, in fact, the same kind of inductive reason that we have for supposing a causal connection between the chemical composition of matches and their behavior when rubbed.

Whether this is true or not it has no relevance whatever to the point at issue. We are not inquiring how causal connections are known or inferred. We are asking, rather, what a causal connection is, and this is an entirely different question. We began by *assuming,* as is certainly true, that we sometimes know, by induction or otherwise, that certain events are causally connected—that the beheading of Anne Boleyn caused her death, for example. Our question is not, then, how we *know* this, but what we *mean* in asserting what we thus claim to know. It can be assumed, if one likes, that our knowledge of causal connections arises entirely from induction, from repeatedly observing what does in fact happen when certain other things happen; or it can be assumed, if one likes, that this is false. It is in either case irrelevant to the question at issue, which is a question concerned solely with the nature of the causal connection and not with the knowledge of it.

Causes as Necessary
and Sufficient Conditions

In the light of all the foregoing we can now set forth our problem more clearly in the following way.

Every event occurs under innummerable and infinitely complex conditions. Some of these are relevant to the occurrence of the event, others have nothing to do with it. This means that some of the conditions under which a given event occurs are *conditiones sine quibus non,* or conditions such that the event would not have occurred had those conditions been absent, while others are such that their presence or absence makes no difference.

Suppose, for instance, that a given match has ignited, and assume that this was caused by something. Now it would be impossible to set forth all the conditions under which this occurred, for they are numberless. A description of them would be incomplete if it were not a description of the entire universe at that moment. But among those conditions there were, let us suppose, those consisting of (a) the match's being dry, (b) its being rubbed in a certain way, (c) its being of such and such chemical composition, (d) the rubbing surface being of such and such roughness, (e) the presence of dust motes in the air nearby, (f) the sun shining, (g) the presence of an observer named Smith, and so on. Now some of these conditions—namely, (a) through (d), and others as well—had something to do with the match igniting, while others—(e), for instance—had no causal connection with it.

This we have learned from experience. Our problem, then, is not to state how we *know* which were the causal conditions of its igniting and which were not. The answer to this is obvious—we know by experience and induction. Our problem is, rather, to state just what relationship those *causal* conditions had to the match's igniting, but which the numberless irrelevant conditions had not; to state, for example, what connection the match's being rubbed had to its igniting, but which the presence of dust motes had not.

The most natural way of expressing this connection is to say that had the match not been rubbed then it would not have ignited given that all the other conditions were satisfied, whereas, given those other conditions that occurred, including the match's being rubbed as it was, it would still have ignited even had the dust motes been absent. This appears to be exactly what one has in mind in saying that the friction on the match head had something to do with its igniting, while the presence of the dust motes did not—the latter condition was not at all necessary for the igniting of the match, whereas the former was, given only those other conditions which in fact occurred. This, however, is simply a way of saying that the friction was a *necessary condition* of the match's igniting, given the other conditions that occurred but no others, whereas the presence of dust motes was not.

If this is correct then we can simply assert that the cause, A, of an event, B, is that totality of conditions, from among all those, but only those, that occurred, each of which was necessary for the occurrence of B. Now if this set of conditions, A, is thus understood, as it should be, to include *every* condition, out of that totality that occurred, that was necessary for the occurrence of B, then we can say that the set of conditions, A, is also *sufficient* for B, since no other condition was necessary. We can, accordingly, understand the relationship between any set of conditions A, and any set B, expressed in the statement that A was the cause of B, to be simply described in this fashion: That A was the set, from among all those conditions that occurred, each of which was necessary, and the totality of which was sufficient, for the occurrence of B. This appears to be exactly what distinguishes the causal conditions of any event from all those that occurred but which were not causally connected with the event in question.

It is now evident that this reintroduces the concept of necessity which Hume was once so widely believed to have eliminated. For to say of any condition that a certain event would not have occurred if that condition had been absent is exactly equivalent to saying that this condition was necessary for its occurrence, or, that it was such that the event in question would not have occurred without it, given only those other conditions that occurred. There seems, however, as we have seen, to be no other way to distinguish the causal conditions of any given event from those infinitely numerous and complex other conditions under which it occurs. We cannot distinguish them by introducing the concept of a law, unless we understand the law to be, not merely a statement of what does happen, but what must happen; for we can find true statements of what does happen, and happens without exception or invariably, which are not laws. The conjunction of properties and events can be as constant as we please, with no exception whatever, without there being any causal connections between them at all. It is not until we can say what would have happened, had something else happened which did not happen, that we leave the realm of mere constancy of conjunction and find ourselves speaking of a causal connection; and as soon as we speak in this fashion we are speaking of necessary connections.

Now to say of a given event that it would not have occurred without the occurrence of another is the same as saying that the occurrence of the one without the other was causally, though not logically, impossible; or, that in a non-logical sense, the one without the other could not have occurred. We can accordingly define the concepts of necessity and sufficiency in the following way.

To say of any condition or set of conditions, *x*, that it was *necessary* for the occurrence of some event E, means that within the totality of other conditions that occurred, but only those, the occurrence of E without *x* was impossible, or could not obtain. Similarly, to say of any condition or set of conditions, *x*, that it was *sufficient* for some event E, means that within the totality of other conditions that occurred, but only those, the occurrence of *x* without E was impossible, or could not obtain. The expression "was impossible" in these definitions has, of course, the same sense as "could not have occurred" in the discussion preceding and not the sense of *logical* impossibility. There are, we can grant at once, no logically necessary connections between causes and effects. In terms of our earlier example we can say that Anne Boleyn could not live long after being beheaded, or that it was impossible for her to do so, without maintaining that this was *logically* impossible, which it evidently was not.

The concepts of necessity and sufficiency, as thus defined, are of course the converse of each other, such that if any condition or set of conditions is necessary for another, that other is sufficient for it, and vice versa. The statement that x is necessary for E is logically equivalent to saying that E is sufficient for x, and similarly, the statement that x is sufficient for E is logically equivalent to saying that E is necessary for x. This fact enables us now to introduce a very convenient notation, as follows. If we let x and E represent any conditions, events, or sets of these, we can symbolize the expression, "x is sufficient for E," with an arrow in this way:

$$x \longrightarrow E.$$

Similarly, we can symbolize the expression "x is necessary for E" with a reverse arrow, in this way:

$$x \longleftarrow E.$$

Since, moreover, the expression "x is sufficient for E" is exactly equivalent to "E is necessary for x," we can regard as exactly equivalent the following representations of this relationship,

$$x \longrightarrow E$$
$$E \longleftarrow x$$

since the first of these means that the occurrence of x without E is impossible, and the second means exactly the same thing. It should be noted, however, that the arrows symbolize no *temporal* relations whatever.

With this clear and convenient way of symbolizing these relationships, we can now represent the conception of causation at which we have tentatively arrived in the following way.

Consider again a particular event that has occurred in just the way it has at a particular time and place, such as the igniting of a particular match, and call this E. Now E, we can be sure, occurred under a numerous set of conditions, which we can represent as $a, b, c, \ldots n$. Let a, for instance, be the condition consisting of the match's being dry, b its being rubbed, c its being of such and such chemical composition, d the rubbing surface being of such and such roughness, e the presence of dust motes in the air, f the sun shining, and so on, *ad infinitum*. Now some of these conditions—namely, $a, b, c,$ and d—were presumably necessary for E, in the sense that E would not have occurred in the absence of any of them, given only the other conditions that occurred, whereas others, such as e and f, had nothing to do with E. If, furthermore, as we can assume for illustration, $a, b, c,$ and d

were jointly sufficient for E, the relations thus described can be symbolized as follows:

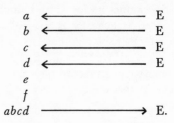

And since *a, b, c,* and *d* are each individually necessary for E, it follows that E is sufficient for each of these, and, being sufficient for each of them, it is sufficient for all of them, and we can accordingly symbolize this:

$$abcd \longleftarrow E.$$

And this permits us to express the causal relation, in this example, with the utmost simplicity as follows,

$$abcd \Longleftrightarrow E.$$

which means, simply, that the cause of E was that finite set of conditions, within the totality, only, of those that actually occurred, that was necessary and sufficient for E.

It is at this point that our metaphysical difficulties really begin, but before turning to those, two points of clarification must be made.

The first point is that this analysis does not exactly express the "ordinary use" of the word "cause," and does not purport to. The reason for this is not that the analysis itself is imprecise, but rather that ordinary usage, in most cases, is. Most persons, for example, are content to call "the cause" of any event some *one* condition that is conspicuous or, more commonly, some *part* of the causal conditions that is novel or within some agent's control. In the illustration we have been using, for example, the friction on the match would normally be regarded as "the cause" of its igniting, without regard to its dryness, its chemical composition, and so on. But the reason for this, quite obviously, is that these other conditions are taken for granted. They are not mentioned, not because they are thought to have nothing to do with the match's igniting, but rather because they are presupposed. Philosophically it makes no difference at all whether we say that given the other conditions necessary for the match's igniting, it was then caused to ignite by being rubbed, or whether we say that its being rubbed was, together with these other necessary conditions, the cause of its igniting. Its being rubbed has neither more nor less to do with its igniting than does, say, its being dry. The only difference is that it was, presumably, dry all the while and, in that state, was rubbed. It might just as well have been rubbed all the while and, in that state, suddenly rendered dry, in which case we could say that it was ignited by suddenly becoming dry.

The second point is that there is a perfectly natural point of view from which perhaps no condition is ever really necessary for the occurrence of any event, nor any set of conditions really sufficient for it, from which one could derive the absurd result that, on the analysis suggested, no events have any causes. We said, for instance, that the match's being rubbed was a necessary condition for its igniting. But, it might at first seem, that is not a necessary condition at all, since there are other ways of igniting matches—touching them to hot surfaces, for instance. Similarly, we said that rubbing the match was, together with certain other conditions, sufficient for its igniting. But this might seem false, since it would be possible to prevent it from igniting, even under these conditions—by applying a fire extinguisher, for instance.

This objection overlooks an essential qualification in the analysis, however. I said that the cause of an event E is that set of conditions that were, *within the totality of those other conditions, only, that in fact occurred,* individually necessary and jointly sufficient for E. If, in terms of our example, that totality of other conditions that actually occurred did not, in fact, include some such condition as the match's being in contact with a hot surface, nor the application of any fire extinguisher, and so on, then within the totality of conditions that *did* occur, its being rubbed *was* necessary for its igniting, and was also, together with certain other conditions that occurred, sufficient for its igniting.

Time and Efficacy

The analysis of the causal relationship, as it now stands, has one strange consequence that is immediately obvious; namely, that it does not enable us to draw any distinction between cause and effect. I have suggested that the cause of an event is that set of conditions, among all those that occur, which is necessary and sufficient for that event, from which it of course follows that if any condition or set of conditions, A, is the cause of another, B, then B is automatically also the cause of A. For concerning any A and B, if A is necessary and sufficient for B, and therefore, on this analysis, the cause of B, then it logically follows that B is necessary and sufficient for A, and therefore the cause of A. This is quite plainly absurd. One cannot possibly say that a match's igniting is any part of the cause of its being rubbed, that a stone's being warm is the cause of the sun's shining upon it, or that a man's feeling intoxicated is the cause of his having alcohol in his blood, despite the fact that the relationships of necessity and sufficiency between cause and effect are the same in both directions.

Earlier metaphysicians took for granted that the difference between cause and effect was one of power or efficacy or, what amounts to the same thing, that the cause of anything was always something active, and its effect some change in something that is passive. Thus, the sun has the power to warm a stone, but the stone has no power to make the sun shine; it is simply the passive recipient of a change wrought by the sun. Similarly, alcohol in the blood has the power to produce feelings of intoxication, but a man cannot, by having such feelings, produce alcohol in his blood.

Modern philosophers, on the contrary, have almost universally supposed that the difference between cause and effect is not to be found in anything so esoteric as power or efficacy, but is simply a temporal difference, nothing more. The cause of an event, it is now almost universally supposed, is some condition or set of conditions that *precedes* some other, its effect, in time. Thus, if our analysis of the causal relationship is otherwise correct then it should, according to this prevalent view, have some qualification added about time, such as to require that the cause should occur before its effect.

I believe this is one of the profoundest errors in modern philosophy and the source of more misconceptions than almost any other. By this simple expedient of introducing considerations of time, philosophers imagine that they no longer need to talk metaphysically of causal power or efficacy. In fact, of course, philosophers, like everyone else, do still speak freely of power and efficacy—of the power of various substances to corrode, to dissolve, to cause intoxication, to cause death, and so on. But in their philosophies they imagine that such terms express only ideas of *time,* and that they can be omitted from any exact description of causal connections just by the simple device of introducing temporal qualifications.

This whole problem is going to come up again in another context, when I consider the concept of preventive actions, or actions which are sufficient for the non-occurrence of certain events in the future, in contrast to "postventive" actions which are sufficient for the non-occurrence of certain events in the past. For now, however, I intend to show that what I have called an error—namely, that causes *must* precede their effects in time—is an error indeed simply by citing perfectly clear and typical instances of causation in which this is not so.

Before doing this, however, let us consider a related question. Let us suppose that there *is* a temporal interval between a cause and its effect, such that it is true to say that one occurs *before* the other. Now if the relationships between the two are otherwise identical—namely, are simply the relationships of necessity and sufficiency set forth above, or, for that matter, any other non-temporal relationships whatever—the question can be asked, *Why* should it be thought so important to regard only the prior condition or set of conditions as the cause of the subsequent one, and never the subsequent as the cause of the prior? There is, certainly, an absurdity in saying that a man's dying is the cause of his being shot, or that a man's being intoxicated is the cause of his having imbibed alcohol, rather than the other way around; but what *kind* of absurdity is it? Is it merely a verbal error, a wrong choice of vocabulary, or is it a metaphysical absurdity? If one were to point out that a woman cannot bear a child before being impregnated, he would probably not be *merely* calling attention to a point of vocabulary. He would be stating an obvious truth of biology. If, on the other hand, one were to say that one's brother's sons cannot be his nieces, but must be his nephews, he would obviously be making only a point about language, about the use of certain words. Now then, when one says that a cause cannot come after its effect, which kind of point is he making? Is he *merely* calling attention to a matter of vocabulary, or is he saying something metaphysically significant about causes and their effects?

It seems fairly clear that there is something metaphysically absurd, and not merely an inept choice of words, in supposing that efficient causes might work "backward." There is surely some reason why nothing can produce an effect in the past, and the reason cannot just be that if it did, we would not then *call* it a cause.

Consider the following illustration. There is a variety of ways in which one might ensure that a certain man—say, some political rival—is dead on a certain day. One way would be to shoot him through the head the day before. We can assume that this, together with all the other conditions prevailing, is sufficient for his being dead the next day and further, that in case conditions are such that he would not have died had he not been shot, then it is also necessary for his being dead then. But another, equally good way of ensuring that he is dead on that day would be to attend his funeral later on. This would surely be sufficient for his prior death and, in case conditions are such that his being dead is sufficient for someone's attending his funeral, then it is also a necessary condition of his prior death. Suppose, then, that one man shoots him, and another attends his funeral, and that both of these acts are related to that man's death in exactly the same way, except only for the difference in time; that is, that each act is, given only those other conditions that occur, both necessary and sufficient for his being dead on the day in question. Why should one man be blamed more than the other, or held any more responsible for the death? Each man, equally with the other, did something necessary and sufficient for that man's death. Either act guarantees the death as well as the other. The thing to note is that this question is *not* answered by merely observing that one of these acts occurred before the death, and the other after; that is already quite obvious and begs the question. Nor is it answered by noting that we do not, as it happens, *call* the subsequent event the cause. That is obvious and irrelevant; the word "cause" was not even used in the example. We do not hold a man responsible for causing an event unless something he does is a necessary and sufficient *prior* condition of it. That is granted. But merely *stating* that fact does not answer the question, Why not? It cannot be a mere question of *vocabulary* whether, for example, a certain man should be hanged for what he has done and another one not.

Part of the answer to this question, I believe, is that no cause exerts any power over the past, esoteric as that comment may be. The same idea is expressed, more metaphysically, by saying that all past things are actualized, and never at some later time potentially what they are not then actually, whereas a present thing can be actually one thing but potentially another. This would be expressed in terms of our example by saying that a man who shoots another *acts upon* him, or does something to him, or is an agent, whereas the man who is thus killed does not, in dying, act upon his assassin, but is the passive recipient, patient, or sufferer, of the other's causal activity. The man who merely attends the funeral, on the other hand, does not act upon him who is already dead. He is merely the passive observer of what has already been done.

This way of conceiving these relationships seems, moreover, to be the way all men do think of causes and effects, and it explains the enormous absurdity in the supposition that causes might act so as to alter things already past. For anything to be a cause it must act upon something and, as a matter of fact—indeed, of metaphysical necessity —nothing past can be acted upon by anything. The profound error of modern philosophy has been to suppose that, in making that point, one is making only a point about language.

Contemporaneous Causes and Effects

If we can now cite clear examples of causal connections wherein those conditions that constitute the cause and those that constitute the effect are entirely contemporaneous, neither occurring before the other, then it will have been proved that the difference between a cause and its effect cannot be a temporal one, but must consist of something else.

In fact such examples are not at all hard to find. Consider, for instance, a locomotive that is pulling a caboose, and to make it simple, suppose this is all it is pulling. Now here the motion of the locomotive is sufficient for the motion of the caboose, the two being connected in such a way that the former cannot move without the latter moving with it. But so also, the motion of the caboose is sufficient for the motion of the locomotive, for given that the two are connected as they are, it would be impossible for the caboose to be moving without the locomotive moving with it. From this it logically follows that, conditions being such as they are—both objects are in motion, there are no other moves present, no obstructions to motion, and so on—the motion of each object is also necessary for the motion of the other. But is there any temporal gap between the motion of one and the motion of the other? Clearly there is not. They move together, and in no sense is the motion of one temporally followed by the motion of the other.

Here it is tempting to say that the locomotive must *start* moving before the caboose can start moving, but this is both irrelevant and false. It is irrelevant, because the effect we are considering is not the caboose's *beginning* to move, but its moving. And it is false because we can suppose the two to be securely connected, such that as soon as either begins to move the other must move too. Even if we do not make this supposition, and suppose, instead, that the locomotive does begin moving first, and moves some short distance before overcoming the looseness and elasticity of its connection with the caboose, still it is no cause of the motion of the caboose until that looseness is overcome. When that happens, and not until then, the locomotive imparts its motion to the caboose. Cause and effect are, then, perfectly contemporaneous.

Again, consider the relationships between one's hand and a pencil he is holding while writing, We can ignore here the difficult question of what causes the *hand* to move. It is surely true, in any case, that the motion of the pencil is caused by the motion of the hand. This means, first, that conditions are such that the motion of the hand is sufficient for the motion of the pencil. Given precisely *those* conditions, however, the motion of the pencil is sufficient for the motion of the hand; neither can move, under the conditions assumed—that the fingers are grasping the pencil—without the other moving with it. It follows, then, that under these conditions the motion of either is also necessary for the motion of the other. And, manifestly, both motions are contemporaneous; the motion of neither is *followed* by the motion of the other.

Or again, consider a leaf that is being fluttered by the wind. Here it would be quite clearly erroneous to say that the wind currents impinge upon the leaf and then, some time later, the leaf flutters in response. There is no gap in time at all. One might want to say that the leaf, however light, does offer some resistance to the wind, and that the wind must overcome this slight resistance before any fluttering occurs. But then we need only add that the wind is no cause of the leaf's motion until that resistance is overcome. Cause and effect are again, then, contemporaneous.

What, then, distinguishes cause and effect in the foregoing examples? It is not the time of occurrence, for both occur together. It is not any difference in the relations of necessity and sufficiency, for these are identical both ways. But there is one thing which, in all these cases, appears to distinguish the cause from the effect; namely, that the cause acts upon something else to produce some change. The locomotive *pulls* the caboose, but the caboose does not *push* the locomotive; it just follows passively along. The hand pushes the pencil and imparts motion to it, while the pencil is just passively moved. The wind acts upon the leaf to move it; but it is no explanation of the wind's blowing to say that the leaf is moving. In all these cases, to be sure, what has been distinguished as the cause is itself moved by something else—the locomotive by steam in its cylinders, the hand by a man, the wind by things more complex and obscure; but that only calls attention to the fact that causes can themselves be the effects of other causes. Whether all causes must be such or whether, on the contrary, something—such as a man, for example—can be a "first cause" is something we shall consider later on.

Are All Causes Contemporaneous with Their Effects?

In order to show that it can be no part of the analysis of a causal connection that causes precede their effects in time, all that is needed is a *single* clear example of a cause or set of causal conditions which is entirely contemporaneous with its effect, and examples of this, we have just seen, are easy enough to point out. It should, in any case, be obvious just from philosophical considerations, for it is not difficult to imagine beginningless processes producing effects throughout all time past, even though it is doubtful whether any such processes exist. If it were discovered, for example, that the sun had always shone upon the moon, that this state of affairs had always existed, no one would be led by that alone to doubt that moonlight is caused by the sun, or to suppose that it would be arbitrary, in such a state of affairs, what one called the cause and what the effect.

It has, however, sometimes been argued most acutely that *all* causes are contemporaneous with their effects, that just in the nature of things neither a cause nor its effect *can* occur before or after the other. Thus it is sometimes maintained that a ball, for example, which is moved by the impact of another ball, is not caused to move by anything happening *prior* to such impact, but by the impact itself, and that this is simultaneous with the initial motion of the ball that is thus moved. Again, it can be argued that water is not caused to boil by *first* being heated to a certain point. Rather, it boils as soon as it is heated to that point, and not sometime later, such that cause and effect are again contemporaneous. And we get the same result, it is sometimes claimed, in the case of any causal connection described with sufficient exactness.

Now it is in no way essential, for the point of this chapter, either to affirm or to deny this. In order to show that a cause *need* not precede its effect in time, which has already been done, it is by no means necessary to show that *no* cause ever precedes its effect. Nor need we address ourselves to the arguments upon which this latter claim rests. They are, in my opinion, impossible to meet, for they involve enormous unresolved problems concerning the continuity of processes and the continuity of time itself. The reason we nevertheless need not address ourselves to them is that, however difficult they may be of refutation, their conclusion—that *all* causes are contemporaneous with their effects—is provably false. For if this were true, then there would be no such thing as a causal chain. Indeed, it would be impossible for any two events whatever to have any causal connection with each other in case there were any lapse of time at all between their occurrences. If some event A, for example, causes B, which in turn causes C, which in turn causes D, then in case every cause is simultaneous with its effect, it follows that when A occurs, then the others, and indeed every event in the universe that is in any way causally connected with A, must occur *at the same time*. This, however, is false. There *are* causal chains, and sometimes temporally separated events are causally related in one way or another. When a stone is dropped into the middle of a pond, for instance, this has at least *some* causal connection with the ripples that appear at the shore some moments later. There are, to be sure, many intervening causal connections, but this common state of affairs would be logically impossible if every cause were simultaneous with its effect—for all the intervening causal connections would then have to occur simultaneously with both the initial disturbance of the water and the subsequent appearance of ripples at the shore, which is absurd.

My conclusions, then, are compatible with the supposition that causes sometimes precede their effects in time. I only deny that they *must* precede them, and hence that this supposition plays any part in the nature or analysis of a causal connection. My conclusions are also compatible with saying that a given set of conditions, which is *antecedently* necessary for, or sufficient for, or both necessary and sufficient for another state of affairs, is the *cause* of that state of affairs. I only deny that its causal relationship to that state of affairs *consists* in that relationship, for a cause, as I have maintained, must *also* be something having the power to produce that state of affairs. My conclusions are *not* compatible with saying that a given set of conditions, which is subsequently necessary for, or sufficient for, or both necessary and sufficient for another state of affairs, is the cause of that state of affairs. This, however, is no consequence of "the way we use words." On the contrary, the reason we use words as we do here, and refuse to call such a set of conditions the cause of something happening earlier on, is that it would be absurd to do so. And the only basis for this, as far as I can see, is that causes have no power over the past—even though they may have precisely the same relationships of necessity and sufficiency with respect to things past as they have with respect to things future.

What Is a Cause?

A true interpreted statement of the form "A was the cause of B" means, in light of the foregoing, that both A and B are conditions or sets of conditions that occurred; that each was, given all the other conditions that occurred, but only those, both necessary and sufficient for the occurrence of the other; that B did not precede A in time; *and* that A made B happen by virtue of its power to do so. But this final qualification, *alas!* renders the whole analysis empty. For to say that A made B happen obviously only means that A *caused* B, and to say that it did this by virtue of its power to do so obviously means nothing more than that A produced B by virtue of its efficacy as a *cause*—or, in short, that A caused B. To say of anything, then, that it was the cause of something else, means simply and solely that it *was* the cause of the thing in question, and there is absolutely no other conceptually clearer way of putting the matter except by the introduction of mere synonyms for causation. Positively, what this means is that causation is a philosophical category, that while the concept of causation can perhaps be used to shed light upon other problems or used in the analysis of other relationships, no other concepts can be used to analyze it.

4

Causal Power and Human Agency

In the last chapter I tried to elicit the idea of power or efficacy that I believe is involved in the concept of causation, limiting myself mostly to causal relationships between inanimate things. We speak, however, not only of the powers of inanimate things such as acids, explosives, and engines, but also in various contexts of the powers of men. The various powers of inanimate things, sometimes also called "capacities," are not generally thought to be particularly problematical, and so it is quite natural for philosophers to suppose that essentially the same idea is operative in statements concerning the powers or capacities of men. Indeed, it is probably fair to say that the commonest thought underlying most philosophical theories of the causal determinism of human behavior is the supposition that the concept of a power or capacity of some object to do something is essentially the same, whether the object in question is an inanimate thing or a man. It is certainly not obvious, however, that one is saying the same sort of thing when he says that it is within his power, say, to wiggle his finger but not his ears, or when he says that a given acid has the power to dissolve a piece of zinc but not a piece of glass. In both cases there is a reference to a power, but perhaps not to powers of the same kind.

Yet there is one thing that powers of both kinds, if they are indeed different, have in common; namely, that in either case we can express the idea of power by the word "can." Thus, to say that it is within my power to move my finger, but not my ears, amounts to saying that I *can* do the one but *cannot* do the other. Similarly, to say that a given acid has the power to dissolve zinc but not glass amounts to saying that it can dissolve the one but not the other.

I shall in this chapter, then, elicit the idea expressed by "can" as it is used in contexts of human agency, but only in such very elementary contexts as imply neither special training, skill, strength, opportunity, position, nor office. I shall not, therefore, be concerned with such meanings as, "I can operate a typewriter" (which requires special training or skill), "I can run for the Senate" (which expresses the idea of opportunity), "I can do forty pushups" (which expresses the idea of strength or endurance), or "I can veto acts of the legislature" (which expresses the idea of a special position or office). Instead I shall restrict myself entirely to the idea expressed in such a simple assertion as "I can move my finger," wherein this is understood to mean that it is within my power to move my finger, and conveys nothing of the idea of special strength, opportunity, skill, training, or position. By thus limiting myself to the simplest possible case, which would otherwise be of no interest whatsoever, I hope to elucidate the simplest and most basic idea of the power of human agency, unencumbered by extraneous notions involved in more interesting and exciting examples. I therefore beg the reader to bear with this otherwise banal example, for while such an action as wiggling one's finger can hold no interest in itself, and is in fact chosen for its lack of significance, it will be used here repeatedly to shed light on one of the gravest and most persistent problems of philosophical thought.

I shall begin with a consideration of certain typical uses of "can" in contexts *not* involving human agency, as these ideas seem much easier to get at. It would, of course, be significant if the ideas of power, with respect both to men and to certain inanimate things, embodied in the notion of *can* turned out to be much the same, but it would be far more significant if the power of agency we ascribe to ourselves turned out to be utterly different from that of any inanimate thing.

The Idea of "Can"
in Contexts of Inanimate Things

Let us consider first statements of the form "X can E," wherein X designates some inanimate thing and E some state, event, activity, or property. For example:

1. A triangle can be acute (but not one-sided).
2. (Lucretius thought that) atoms can swerve from their paths.
3. This can be the restaurant we ate in last year.
4. This acid can dissolve a piece of zinc.

Now these four statements seem to express all of the philosophically significant senses of "can" as it is applied to inanimate things. These are, respectively, three senses of *contingency,* which I shall call *logical, causal,* and *epistemic* contingency and, in the case of the fourth statement, the sense of a causal capacity, or better, of *hypothetical possibility.*

What I want most conscientiously and carefully to determine, then, is whether a statement such as

5. I can move my finger,

which embodies the "can" of human agency or power, expresses an idea essentially like that of any of the foregoing. However undramatic such an inquiry might seem in itself, it is nonetheless crucial and laden with grave consequences, for in numberless philosophical discussions, particularly those involving the issue of free will, writers have ineptly fitted the "I can" of agency first to one and then another of these meanings, as best suited whatever doctrine they were endeavoring to uphold, seldom separating these distinctions very well and thus producing more confusion than wisdom.

Basic Modal Concepts

All five of the foregoing statements embody modal concepts; that is, in these cases, concepts of what is *possible,* as contrasted with statements of what does happen, what ought to happen, and so on. But the first four, quite obviously, do not express possibilities of the same kind. We must first of all disentangle these.

If we take the idea of impossibility as a generic and undefined one, we can then clearly define the ideas of *necessity, possibility,* and *contingency* in terms of it in this fashion:

E is necessary $= -$ E is impossible.
E is possible $= -$ (E is impossible).
E is contingent $= -$ ($-$ E is impossible) and $-$ (E is impossible).

Thus, more loosely, by these equivalences we can say that it is necessary that something should be such as it is, in case it is impossible that it should be otherwise; that it is possible, in case it is not impossible; and that it is contingent, in case it is neither necessary nor impossible. Now of course there is nothing sacrosanct about using the idea of *impossibility* as our basic and undefined term in defining the others. We could have begun with any of the other three and defined impossibility, together with the other two ideas, in terms of it. But somehow the idea of impossibility seems simpler and intuitively easier for most people to grasp, so we may as well have that as our undefined term.

It should perhaps be noted, however, that the idea of *contingency,* as it is here defined, is not the same as that of *possibility.* Anything which is, in any sense, necessary—such as, that a cube has twelve edges—is in that same sense also possible; but it is not therefore contingent. It is this idea of contingency, as applying to those things that are neither impossible nor necessary, that will be crucial in the development of the ideas which follow.

Since it is the idea of impossibility that is left undefined in the foregoing definitions we can next elicit, without trying to define, three quite distinct and familiar kinds of impossibility. By so doing we can then easily derive, by the foregoing equivalences, three distinct kinds of contingency, and these will correspond exactly with the first three senses of "can" that were illustrated in our first four statements above. The fourth sense of "can," which does not express the idea of contingency at all, will be treated separately.

Logical Contingency

In the first place, then, and most obviously, a proposition is logically impossible if it is self-contradictory—for example, "A one-sided triangle exists." This is not intended as a definition of logical impossibility, for it is my stated purpose to define logical contingency in terms of logical impossibility; thus the concept of logical impossibility, tolerably clear without definition, is assumed. Now some philosophers have spoken as though this is the only sense in which anything is ever *really* impossible, but we need not involve ourselves in that odd contention. The only thing to note is that something is *contingent* in this logical sense, according to our foregoing equivalences, when it is not logically impossible either that it should or should not exist. It is logically possible for a triangle to be acute, for instance, and just as logically possible for it to be obtuse, an idea that is well expressed by saying that it logically *can* be either, that neither property is logically impossible. This, then, is the first of our four senses of "can."

Causal Contingency

In the second place something is, in a perfectly familiar sense, *causally* impossible if there exist conditions sufficient, but not logically sufficient, for its non-existence, or for the existence of something causally incompatible with it. The kind of impossibility here referred to is, then, precisely the causal impossibility introduced in the foregoing chapter, which was not defined there, as it is not defined here. Thus, it is in fact impossible under normal circumstances for a man to live long after ingesting a certain quantity of cyanide, or for gasoline-soaked rags not to ignite when brought into contact with fire under certain conditions—though there are no *logical* impossibilities here involved. To say, then, that something is *contingent* in this causal sense is equivalent, by our definition, to saying that neither its occurrence nor its non-occurrence is in *this* sense impossible, or that existing conditions are causally sufficient neither for its occurrence nor its non-occurrence—in short, that it is *uncaused*. Now many philosophers deny that anything in nature *is* contingent, in this causal sense, but this is not to the point. No one would deny that some things are, in this sense, impossible; our purpose is merely to give content to the *idea* of contingency, defined in terms of this perfectly familiar sense of impossibility. Moreover, some theoretical physicists believe, as did Lucretius, that some things in nature *are* causally contingent. Again the correctness of their opinion is irrelevant, but there can at least be no doubt about what they mean.

This, of course, is the second sense of "can" that was illustrated above. If it were *true* of a given particle that its behavior was not causally determined, then we could say that it can, for instance, swerve, and also that it can fail to swerve, expressing exactly the idea of causal contingency.

Epistemic Contingency

In the third place, something is sometimes spoken of as impossible when it is only known to be false, though this is admittedly a philosophically odd, though nonetheless common, sense of "impossible." Someone might say, for example, "But that man *can't* be my father," meaning only that he knows he is not, or, "It is impossible for her to have been at the theater," again meaning that it is known that she was not. We can call this an epistemic sense of impossibility, and an epistemically contingent state or event is therefore one concerning which it is not *known* whether it occurred, or will occur, or not. This is the third sense of "can" that was illustrated and it is, in fact, exceedingly common. Thus, a man might say of a familiar-looking place that it *can* be the restaurant he ate in a year ago, at the same time realizing that it can be entirely new to him. Similarly I might say, after tossing a normal coin but before looking to see what came up, that it can be heads and it can be tails, even though knowing that in the *causal* sense one or the other of these speculations is impossible. Or one might even say of a column of figures that its sum can be 720, or it can be 721, meaning only that he does not yet know which, even though he knows that one or the other of these is *logically* impossible.

Capacities

Now the fourth sense of "can" illustrated above is perhaps the most common of all. Unlike the other three, however, it expresses no idea of contingency at all, but the very opposite. "Can" is, in other words, in this sense, an expression of a *capacity*, or of what *does* happen— indeed, what *must* happen—in case certain conditions are met. It thus conveys the idea of a *causal connection* between certain states or events. For example, the statement, "This acid can dissolve a piece of zinc," does not mean merely that it is logically contingent whether a piece of zinc would dissolve in it (though it is), nor, manifestly, that if some zinc were to dissolve in it, the dissolving would be *uncaused,* nor, equally obviously, that we do not *know* what would happen to a piece of zinc in that acid. It means that if some zinc *were* dropped in the acid, it would dissolve—that the chemical composition of the acid is sufficient, assuming certain other conditions to hold, for a lump of zinc's dissolving in it. And this, far from suggesting that the behavior of the zinc in those conditions is *contingent,* entails the very opposite; namely, that this behavior is causally necessitated by those conditions, or that any other behavior of the zinc under those conditions is causally impossible.

" Might and Might Not "

It should be noted next, then, that the first three senses of "can," but emphatically not the fourth, can be conveyed equally by the expression "might," so understood as to mean "might *and* might not." Thus, I could say of a red ball that it might be black, expressing the idea that its color is logically (though perhaps neither causally nor epistemically) contingent. Similarly, if I tossed a coin whose behavior was, let us suppose, causally undetermined, I could say that it might come heads and it might come tails, expressing the idea that the outcome is causally contingent. And finally, I could say of a familiar-looking restaurant that I might have eaten there before, and I might not have, only making the point that I do not know which.

But note that if I say of a jar of acid that is before me that it can dissolve a piece of zinc, I do *not* mean that a piece of zinc dropped into it might dissolve and might not. On the contrary, my whole point is that it *would* dissolve, or that, under those conditions, could not *but* dissolve, and I mean to *deny* that it might not.

The " Can " of Human Agency

Let us now turn to the idea expressed by "can" as it figures in certain contexts of human agency, such as our fifth statement, to see whether it is essentially the same as any one of the above, or whether it is, as I believe, an idea different from any of these.

The statement, "I can move my finger," as well as the statement, "I can hold my finger still," are *both* true (though their joint truth obviously does not entail that I can do both *at once*). This I take to be quite certain, and if anyone should doubt the truth of either, then I could show him in the most direct manner possible that he should not have doubted it. If, then, there is any philosophical theory which entails that one or the other of these statements must be false—and I believe there have been many such theories—then that theory is most doubtful.

What, then, do I mean by "can" in such statements? Obviously, I do not mean merely that it is *logically contingent* whether I move my finger, (although it is). If a physician were to ask me whether I can move it, he would not be inquiring whether it would be self-contradictory to suppose that I do, or that I do not. He already knows that it would not, without asking.

Nor do I mean merely that it is *epistemically contingent,* although perhaps it is. That is, when I say I can move my finger, the point I am making is plainly not that I do not happen to *know* whether I am going to move it, (though I may not). If a physician were to ask me whether I can move it, he would not be asking me to guess, speculate, or hazard a prediction concerning whether I am apt to move it.

It follows, therefore, that if "can," in this context, expresses an idea essentially like any I have elicited, then it expresses either the idea of *causal contingency,* the second sense of "can" illustrated, or of *hypothetical possibility* or *capacity,* the fourth sense. The remainder of this chapter will be devoted to showing that it embodies neither of these ideas, but has a totally different meaning; while this meaning entails that the event in question—a finger motion, in this case—is causally contingent (and hence, that one important version of the doctrine of free will is true), it is not equivalent to that.

Hypothetical Possibility

Let us consider first, then, the suggestion, very commonly found in philosophical literature, that statements like our fifth one, "I can move my finger," express the idea of a causal capacity or hypothetical possibility, and are thus like our fourth statement, "This acid can dissolve a piece of zinc." If this is so, then statements expressing the "can" of human agency must, like this latter one, embody the idea that *if* an event of a certain kind were to happen, then something quite different—a finger motion, in the case we are considering—would follow as a result.

Now the statement about the acid and zinc expresses, we noted, the idea of a capacity, or better, the idea of a *causal relationship* between different events or states—a piece of zinc being dropped into a certain volume of acid, on the one hand, and its dissolving, on the other. It is thus equivalent to a hypothetical in the subjunctive, or a statement about what would happen, in case something else happened. If, accordingly, the statement about my finger expresses essentially the same idea, then it too must be equivalent to some subjunctive hypothetical expressing the idea of a causal relationship between different events or states—some as yet unnamed event or state, presumably within me, on the one hand, and a finger motion, on the other. Or, to put the same point more vividly, if I am asked by the physician whether I can move my finger, and I reply that *I can,* then what I am telling him, if "can" here (as in the acid and zinc case) expresses a hypothetical possibility, is that *if* there should occur within me a certain (unnamed) event or state, then the finger motion would at once follow as a causal consequence.

Now that is certainly *not* what is expressed by "can" in this context. This can be seen very clearly from the fact that such hypotheticals as do undoubtedly express a genuine causal relationship between some antecedent occurrent state or event and some bodily change—such as a motion of my finger—regarded as its effect, do not even appear to convey the idea of "can" that we are seeking. There is the concomitant observation that such hypotheticals as do express this idea of "can" are mere grammatical equivalences, and far from conveying the idea of any discovered or discoverable causal relationships, state purely logical relationships between concepts; these are thereby ruled out *ab initio* as causal statements. We find, in short, that there is no hypothetical statement or set of such statements which, as in the acid and zinc case, *both* (a) expresses the idea of a causal relationship between events or states, *and* (b) expresses the idea of "can" that we are after. It has been one of the most persistent errors of philosophy to suppose that, since it is not hard to find hypotheticals that express the one idea or the other, and since both kinds *are* hypotheticals and thus grammatically and logically similar, then *some* one or more of them must somehow express both ideas at once.

Thus, it is very easy to supply subjunctive hypotheticals expressing a genuine causal relationship between some event or state within me, say, and the motion of my finger, which do not, however, convey anything like the idea of "can" that we are seeking, but which nevertheless express precisely the idea of "can" involved in the acid and zinc case. We can say, for instance, that if a certain muscle, well known to anatomists, were to contract, then my finger would move; but this might still be true, even if *I cannot* move my finger—for example, in case I cannot move the muscle in question. Again, if I happen to be subject to spasms of a certain kind, we can say that if a nerve impulse of such and such a kind were to occur, perhaps in my brain, then my finger would twitch. But this is not equivalent to saying that *I* can move my finger, for I might have no control over the occurrence of those impulses. Nor, let it be noted, does it approach any closer to saying that I can, if someone arbitrarily baptizes such an empirically discoverable nerve impulse, say, a "volition." A physician would not conclude that I can move my finger merely upon learning that I am subject to spasms of that sort. He might, in fact, reasonably regard it as evidence to the contrary.

We must, then, rule out these inappropriate hypotheticals—not because they do not express the idea of a causal relationship (for manifestly they do), and not because they do not express the idea of "can" as it is embodied in the acid and zinc case (for they do express that idea exactly), but because they do not express the idea of *I can.*

" Volitions "

It might be tempting at this point to suggest that "I can" expresses the idea of a genuine causal relationship in which a special kind of event fills the role of the cause—namely, a certain internal or *mental* occurrence, introspectively discoverable, and known to philosophers as an *act of will* or (synonymously) a *volition.* Thus, to be specific, the statement, "I can move my finger," must express the idea that if there were to occur somewhere within me or perhaps "within my mind" a particular one of these special events—namely, a motion-of-this-finger volitional event—I would find that event to be at once followed by a motion of the finger in question, which I might then reasonably conclude was its effect.

But if we refuse to be beguiled by the profundity of such a description, and just look at the picture it brings forth, how absurd it becomes! Surely when I say I can move my finger, and know that what I am saying is true, I am not expressing the idea of a causal connection between the behavior of my finger and some such internal hocus-pocus as this, the occurrence of which I can seriously doubt. Besides, even if this picture were not quite fantastic from the standpoint of ordinary experience, we can wonder whether I *can* bring about such an internal mental cause, and in particular, whether I can perform inwardly the elaborate and complicated set of such causes evidently needed in order to make my finger move in a similarly elaborate and complicated way, and if so, what "can" might mean in *this* case. If I *can,* then to what further internal events are *these* causally related? And if I *cannot,* how can we still say that I can move my finger after all?

Non-causal Hypotheticals

Not having found quite what we want in this direction, we turn more hopefully to those hypotheticals which in common usage do express just the idea of "can" that we are after, to see whether they might *also* be construed as expressing the idea of a causal relationship. But here we find that those usually proposed as substitutes are merely conventional equivalences of meaning rather than expressions of discovered causal connections. We also find that not only do we have no reason whatever for supposing that they express causal relationships between occurrent events or states, but that they simply cannot express such a connection; in fact, if so interpreted, they yield the same kind of absurdity as our previous example.

It is generally supposed, for example, that such a statement as, "I can move my finger," is equivalent to the hypothetical, "I will move my finger if I want to." And so it is—but this second statement surely does not express a causal relationship between occurrent events or states. If it did, we would have to understand it to mean that the occurrence within me of a certain state or event of a rather special kind, namely, of a certain wanting or craving for finger motions, would set my finger in motion, which is at best a doubtful picture, such "wantings" as this having every semblance of fiction. If we asked someone who had just moved his finger, *why* he had done so, and got the reply that he did so because he wanted to, we would be no wiser, recognizing that an explanation had been refused rather than given, only the fact itself being repeated that he had jolly well moved it. "I will move my finger if I want to" is essentially no different from "I'll have one more drink if I want to," uttered in a tone of defiance. Such a hypothetical can hardly, in justice to common sense, be construed as expressing any discoverable causal connections between events or states, whether these be "internal" or "external," "mental" or "physical."

For this and other reasons we must reject the other hypothetical renditions of "I can" that suggest themselves, such as "I will if I try," "if I intend," "if I wish," "if I choose," "if it suits my purpose," "if there's any point to it," and so on. Now all these hypotheticals can, let it be noted, be regarded as equivalent *in meaning* to the categorical, "I can." But being each of them equivalent in meaning to the same thing, they are equivalent in meaning to each other—which by itself sufficiently shows that they are not expressions of a causal relationship between occurrent events or states. For the events or states properly called "trying," "wishing," "intending," "having as one's purpose," and so on, if these be regarded as events or states that might actually occur within me, are *not* the same. Hypotheticals embodying these concepts, then, if they were interpreted as referring to such occurrent states or events, could not be equivalent in meaning. They are vastly more like such a pair of hypotheticals as, "You may have orange juice if you like" and "You may have orange juice if you choose," which are surely exactly equivalent, and neither of which means anything like "You may have orange juice if there is any." Both, in fact, mean no more than "You may have orange juice."

If, moreover, we ask, in the case of *any* such hypothetical that is seriously proposed as an expression of the relation between a cause and its effect, what might be the criterion for deciding whether it is *true,* we find this criterion to be the very occurrence of that event which is supposed to be regarded as the effect, rendering the relationship embodied in the hypothetical, not the empirically discoverable one of a cause to its effect, but the logical one of entailment between concepts. The fact, however, that a given event occurs, can never *entail* that another wholly different one will occur, or has occurred, if the relation between them is that of cause to effect. The fact, for example, that a piece of zinc is dropped into a volume of a certain acid cannot *entail* that it dissolves, nor vice versa, and if there were such entailment, the relation embodied in the hypothetical expressing that fact could not at the same time be regarded as one of causation. Suppose, then, that someone moves his finger, and we propose as a *causal* explanation for this, that he *wanted* to move it. How shall we, or the agent himself, decide whether this was in fact the cause? How do we, or how does he, know that this motion was not caused by, say, his wanting to move a different finger, or even his wanting to move his toe? Has anyone had numerous occasions to observe within himself this particular *want*, and then come to the realization that it is in fact always soon followed by that particular motion, until he has finally come to expect the one upon finding the occurrence of the other? Plainly not. Our entire *criterion* for saying what he *wanted* (or tried, or intended, or whatnot) to do, is what he in fact *did*; we do not infer the former from the latter, on the basis of what we have in fact found, but we regard the former as something *entailed* by what we now find, namely, just his moving that finger. This by itself shows that the relation expressed in the hypothetical, "I will move my finger if I want to," is, if the hypothetical is true at all, a logical relationship between concepts, resting only on an equivalence of meaning, and as such *cannot* be a causal relationship between states or events.

Simple Causal Capacities
and Simple Powers

One final consideration, though a fairly technical one, will serve to show further the dissimilarity between the "can" of agency and that of causal capacity; namely, that while in the case of the latter a certain type of subjunctive inference is not destroyed by the supposition that it is physically impossible for the capacity in question to be realized, such an inference is not always possible in the case of an agent.

Let us suppose, for example, that a given volume of acid has at a certain time the power to dissolve a given piece of zinc. Suppose further, however, that conditions are such as to render it physically impossible that it should then do so. We can suppose, for instance, that the piece of zinc in question is in a vault, heavily guarded, and so on, such that it is physically impossible for the acid then to dissolve it. We can nevertheless affirm that the acid still has the capacity to dissolve it, meaning by this, of course, that if (contrary to fact) that piece of zinc were then in the acid, under easily specifiable conditions, the acid would then be dissolving it.

But now suppose that conditions are such as to render it causally impossible for me to move my finger. We can suppose, for instance, that my hand is encased in a strong and tight cast, rendering any manual movement whatever impossible. Now here we *cannot* affirm that it is nevertheless within my power to move my finger. Unlike the capacity or power of the acid, my power is cancelled by the physical impossibility of exercising it. We cannot say that if (contrary to fact) the cast were not now on my hand, then I *would* move my finger. The most we can say is that, were it not for the cast, I *could* move it, that it would be within my power to move it. A looser way of expressing this difference is to say that when every impediment to the realization of an ordinary causal capacity of an inanimate thing is removed, then that capacity is forthwith realized, whereas when every impediment to the exercise of a simple human power is removed, then that power *can* be exercised. It is still up to the agent in question whether that power is in fact exercised or not.

Causal Contingency

We may conclude, then, that "can," in the context we are considering, does not, unlike the zinc and acid case, express the idea of causal capacity, or hypothetical possibility. The only thing left, therefore, if we are to suppose that it expresses a meaning similar to any of the first four I elicited, is to see if it expresses the idea of *causal contingency*.

In this case, the statement, "I can move my finger," means that my finger might move and it might not, where "might and might not" expresses the idea that the event in question is, not merely epistemically, but *causally* contingent, or that there are no conditions either causally sufficient for or causally incompatible with my finger's moving.

It is easy to show, however, that this is *not* the meaning of "can" in this case, for it is quite possible that the statement, "I can move my finger," is false, even in a situation in which "My finger might move and it might not," understood in the sense of causal contingency, is true. Suppose, for example, that I am paralyzed, so that I cannot, by hypothesis, move my finger. It is nevertheless imaginable that, despite this circumstance, my finger *does* move from time to time, and that its motions are uncaused. No doubt this never happens, but the point is that if it were to happen it would not warrant us to say that I can move my finger; it just moves, in this case, without my having anything to do with it.

One other possibility remains, and that is to insist that there is an essential difference between *my* moving my finger, and my finger merely *moving,* and hence, that "I can move my finger" expresses, not simply the idea that any motions of my finger are causally contingent, but, more significantly, that it is causally contingent whether *I* produce them.

That there is this essential difference seems beyond question, for my moving my finger is not even materially equivalent to my finger's moving, the first always entailing but never being entailed by the latter. To concede this, however, is already to abandon the possibility of understanding human agency according to the model of inanimate behavior, for in the case of the latter *no* such distinction ever need be made. The tree's waving its branches *is* equivalent to its branches waving, and the acid's dissolving the zinc *is* equivalent to the zinc's dissolving in the acid, assuming no other solvent to be present. Even in the case of robots and computing machines, we can describe completely what they *do* merely by describing what *happens* (in their wires, vacuum tubes, etc.), without any reference to their *doing* anything at all.

Quite apart from this, however, it can be shown that while the statement, "I can move my finger," together with the statement, "I can hold my finger still," *entails* that my moving my finger is causally contingent, and hence, that the motions of my finger are themselves causally contingent, it is not *equivalent* to that. If this is so, then the meaning of "can," in this context, evidently does not correspond to *any* familiar meaning it has in contexts involving only inanimate things.

The statements, "I can move my finger" and "I can hold my finger still," are, I said, normally both true, though their joint truth does not entail that I can do both at once. If, however, existing conditions are causally sufficient for my moving my finger, then it follows that it is causally impossible for me not to move it. If, on the other hand, existing conditions are causally sufficient for my holding is still, then it is causally impossible for me to move it. Since, however, it is true both that I can move it, and that I can hold it still, it follows that neither is causally impossible.

That the statement, "I can move my finger," does not express *just* this idea, however—that is, is not equivalent to saying that I might move it and I might not, understanding this in the sense of causal contingency—follows from the fact that this latter might be true in circumstances in which the former is not. That is, it might be true that it is causally contingent whether I move my finger (and not merely whether my finger moves), and yet false that I both can move it, and can hold it still. Suppose, for example, that I have a roulette wheel whose behavior is really causally contingent—for example, one whose end state is no exact function of the force with which it is spun. Suppose, further, that I resolve to move my finger if it stops on an odd number, and to hold it still if it stops on an even one, and that there are conditions (the certainty of death if I fail, for instance) sufficient for my not changing my resolve. Now in this situation it is certainly true that I might move my finger and I might not, understanding "might and might not" to express causal contingency. Until the wheel stops there are no conditions sufficient for my doing the one, and none sufficient for my doing the other. Yet it is not true that I *can* move it, and *also* that I *can* hold it still, assuming that my resolve *cannot* change. I know that I might move it, and that I might not, but not only do I not know whether I will move it—I do not even know, until the wheel stops, and assuming that I *cannot* change my resolve, whether I *can* move it. I just have to wait and see. What I do, in this situation, is no longer *up to me,* but entirely dependent on the behavior of a wheel over which I have no control.

"Power"

I conclude, then, that "can," in the statement, "I can move my finger," does not *ever* mean what it means when applied to inanimate things, although it *entails* what is meant by that word as it might be applied to some extraordinary inanimate thing, namely, one whose behavior is uncaused. What *else* is meant by "can," in this case, in addition to meaning that my moving my finger is causally contingent, is suggested by what was just said; namely, that whether or not I *do* move my finger is "up to me" or, to use a more archaic expression, is something "within my power." And this is certainly a philosophically baffling expression which I feel sure no one can ever analyze; yet it *is* something that is well understood. One can sometimes know perfectly, for example, that it is up to him, or in his power, to move his finger, and one can sometimes—as in the sort of example just considered— know that it is not up to him, but up to something else, even if it should nevertheless be contingent. We therefore understand what it *is* for something to be in our power, and the fact that no one can *say* what it is is no disconfirmation of this. This notion, however, is *never* embodied in the meaning of "can" as it is used with reference to physical things; for it never makes sense to say that it is up to a volume of acid whether it dissolves a lump of zinc, or up to a tree whether it waves its branches, or that it is within the power even of a causally undetermined roulette wheel whether it picks an odd number or an even one.

5

Simple
Action
and
Volition

In the last chapter I noted a difference in kind between mere motions and changes of my body, on the one hand, and such motions and changes of my body as represent actions of mine, on the other, even in those rather rare cases in which the two are behaviorally identical. I did not, however, consider the significance of that difference or the implications it has for a theory of human behavior, and that is my present concern.

Actions
and Mere Bodily Motions

Such things as the beating of my heart and the growth of my hair, for example, are motions and changes of my body, but in a familiar though somewhat baffling sense they are not things with which I have anything to do. So long as I am living at all these are just processes in the natural history of my body, or physiological processes which I am helpless either to make happen or to prevent from happening in any direct way. They are not, so far as I am concerned, much unlike the ticking of a clock or the growth of weeds around my window, except that I am apt to have a keener interest in them.

My arms and fingers sometimes move, on the other hand, or my body moves from place to place, carried hither and thither by my legs, and these motions seem clearly to be events of a wholly different kind. They are in some sense changes that are within my control, things that I am not helpless to make happen or to prevent from happening. Indeed, if they happen at all it is sometimes *because* I make them happen. And this seems manifestly different from my body, or my brain and nervous system, making them happen. The beating of my heart and innumerable other bodily processes are governed by my nervous system, though I nevertheless have nothing to do with them and they are no actions of mine. Some of these processes even occur without my being in the least aware of them, and some, such as certain of the processes involved in the homeostasis of my body, I am altogether ignorant of throughout my entire life. I am, moreover, occasionally surprised to find some part of my body, such as my finger or eyelid, moving or "twitching" in response, presumably, to some slight disorder in my nervous system, exactly to observation as though I had moved it myself. Sometimes, just as I am falling asleep, my body undergoes a convulsive jerk no different from what I could have done myself. I nevertheless somehow know that I had nothing to do with it, any more than with the motions of my hair in the wind.

There seems, further, to be a clear difference between the *thoughts* that merely occur within me and those which are within my control. For sometimes when I am daydreaming, or relaxing and waiting for sleep, thoughts and images just arise within me which I was not seeking, not trying to think, and for which I have no use, even thoughts that annoy me and which I try to dispel. But at other times thoughts come to me because I actively think them, or seek them, or bring them forth myself, as when I am trying to find my way out of some philosophical paradox, or solve a riddle, or complete a letter, or thinking through some projected course of action, or trying to recall a name. In the case of such thoughts, unlike the others, it seems to me that I am active or doing something, that I am bringing them forth, that what thoughts then occur to me are to some extent up to me, and that were it not for my actively thinking them they would be most unlikely to occur at all. Sometimes, moreover, the thoughts may be the same in either case; sometimes, for instance, someone's name, or a tune, runs through my mind, unsought, as when I am on the verge of sleep or otherwise not concentrating, whereas at other times the same name, or the same tune, may come to me because I call it forth.

We speak, however, not only of the actions or doings of men but of the actions or doings of inanimate things, like acids, explosives, and engines. Thus, it is perfectly intelligible to say of a given acid that it is dissolving zinc, or of a match that it started a forest fire, or of a tree that it shed its leaves, and so on. It looks like we might be expressing wholly different ideas of action in these cases, however, for it is certainly not obvious that I am saying the same sort of thing when I say of a match, for instance, that it started a forest fire, and when I say of a man that *he* started such a fire; or when I say that a tree is shedding its leaves, and that a man is shedding his clothes. In both cases I seem to be speaking of actions, and of men or things as doing these actions, but they are perhaps not actions in the same sense at all.

There is, nevertheless, one thing that actions of both kinds, if they are of different kinds, have in common; namely, that it is neither inappropriate nor misleading to use causal terminology in either case. Thus, we can say that I am moving my fingers, but not my heart, and the same idea would be suitably expressed by saying that I cause the motions of my fingers but not those of my heart. Similarly, we can say that a given acid is dissolving a piece of zinc, but not a piece of glass, and the same idea would be expressed by saying that the acid causes the zinc, but not the glass, to dissolve.

It is probably considerations of this sort that have, as noted earlier, led philosophers of other ages to attach great and fundamental importance to the concept of *action,* and the correlative notions of agency and active power, contrasting these with *passion* and such obvious correlates as *patient,* distinctions that have almost disappeared from philosophical literature, though they are still alive among the distinctions drawn by common sense and need only to be pointed out. When I am thinking or moving my limbs, I am acting—exhibiting agency or active power—according to this ancient conception, whereas when thoughts are merely occurring to me—as in dreams, or when someone is reading me a story—or when parts of my body are moving in a manner with which I have nothing to do—as in the case of my heart beating in response to internal impulses, or my hair being blown by the wind—I am passive, having something done *to* me. I suppose the common word *patience* has its origin here, as suggesting the idea of one who undergoes change not originated by himself, and without resistance. Certainly the clinical notion of a patient goes back to this distinction, as does the popular notion of a passion, and of suffering something as contrasted with doing something.

One way of putting the problems of the present chapter, then, is to ask whether such distinctions really apply to inanimate things; whether, that is, inanimate things are ever truly active beings in the sense in which men sometimes suppose themselves to be *agents,* or whether all the changes in such things can be regarded as passive, that is, as ordinary causal consequences of other changes. If, further, it should turn out that no concept of agency is needed for the description of the behavior of inanimate things, the question can be asked whether it is needed for the description of any human activity, or whether, on the contrary, human behavior cannot in every case be understood as passive—that is, as consisting of ordinary causal consequences of other changes, without the necessity of ever regarding men as agents in an irreducible sense.

Simple Actions

I shall be concerned here only with the simplest kinds of actions in order to bring into clear focus the concept of agency once deemed so elementary for the understanding of human nature. Consequently, I shall not consider such complex activities as piloting a ship, planning military strategy, writing a poem, and the like, but rather simple acts such as moving one's hand (as contrasted with having it moved) or recalling a name (as contrasted with being reminded of it). For surely if there is any act whose description is similar to that of ordinary changes in inanimate things, it would be such a simple act, perfectly familiar to everyone and requiring no special skill, training, strength, or wit. Everyone in a sense understands such simple actions perfectly well; yet, although they can be described, they remain unanalyzable. To derive such a conclusion philosophically, we must find, *first,* that an absolute distinction between acting and being acted upon can be drawn with precision, and, *second,* that the concept of an act cannot be analyzed in terms of the concepts sufficient for the description of inanimate behavior nor, in fact, in terms of any concepts either simpler or more clear. In this chapter I demonstrate the futility of certain more or less traditional kinds of analysis. In the chapter following I shall show why they were bound to be futile from the start and then outline what appears to be a more promising, though admittedly more metaphysical, approach to the basic understanding of human activity.

Voluntary and Involuntary Acts

The distinction between voluntary and involuntary behavior is sometimes crucial, particularly in certain contexts of ethics but is not of significance in this inquiry. By a voluntary act I mean only what is done "on purpose," that is, intentionally, deliberately, and so on, and when I speak simply of an act I mean exactly the same thing. When a man does something under threat or in compliance with a command that can be enforced, he does it on purpose or intentionally, his purpose being to avoid the consequences of disobedience; to that extent he does it "voluntarily," despite the fact that, in the ordinary sense, his behavior illustrates perfectly what is meant by acting involuntarily. I do not, therefore, by any means intend to deny the important distinction between voluntary and involuntary actions. It is only a distinction that has no relevance to what I want to consider. The contrast I want to draw is between behavior which constitutes acting, like raising one's hand, and behavior which does not, like the beating of one's heart or perspiring under the influence of fear. When I speak of "voluntary" activity I mean only to contrast it with bodily movements and changes of this latter kind, which are strictly not acts, rather than with activity performed under coercion.

The Elements
of a Simple Act

I shall restrict myself in this chapter to simple *observable* actions, that is, actions which involve or are expressed in *bodily movements,* leaving for later the consideration of mental activity.

Consider, then, a situation in which I make a mark with a pencil, a simple line for example. Now three facts can be discriminated in this perfectly commonplace situation, namely:

1. That I move my hand,
2. That my hand moves, and
3. That my hand moves a pencil.

Men often perform more complicated and interesting actions than these, to be sure, and sometimes actions extending over a considerable period of time, like running a race or directing a battle. They often perform simpler actions, too—one might simply move his hand without making any mark or moving any pencil, for instance. This, however, will serve as a paradigm of a fairly simple action, and it will be my purpose to elicit the complete difference in kind between these three simple facts contained in the action. To do this, I shall show first what a gulf separates the first fact, in which alone the notion of myself occurs as a subject, from the second, and then show what a similar gulf there is between the second and the third and, more significantly, between the first and the third. The first, as we shall see, involves the idea of an act of an active being, myself, while the second expresses only the idea of an event, change, or motion, without involving the notion of action or agency, and the third embodies only an ordinary causal relation, without agency, between two things.

Acts and Events

It might seem that there is no absolute distinction between the first two facts, the one consisting of my moving my hand and the other of my hand's moving, but only a slight and insignificant difference in the way one and the same idea is expressed. The first statement does, indeed, suggest the idea of *doing* something, but we often speak of inanimate objects as doing things without suggesting any special element of agency—as for example, of the moon waxing and waning, of a tree shedding its leaves, a river rushing into the sea, and so on. And just as in these cases we are plainly not expressing anything except the occurrence of processes or events, there might seem to be no need to suppose that the act of a man is any special case. To say that a tree sheds its leaves is only to say that, under certain presupposed conditions, the leaves of that tree drop off. Similarly, it might seem, to say that I move my hand is only to say that, under certain conditions that are presupposed, my hand moves, this event being regarded as an act of mine only by virtue of the fact that it is *my* hand that moves.

Now if this were true there would not, contrary to what has been suggested, be any gulf between our first and second facts, for they would be one and the same fact. That this is not true, however, and that an act of an agent is therefore essentially different from the behavior of any inanimate thing, in which no agency is involved, follows from the consideration that the first fact, that I move my hand, logically entails, but is never entailed by, the second fact, that my hand moves. When I say that *I* move my hand I am saying something *more* than that my hand moves, for this latter might be true even though the former were not. This difference is, indeed, the very difference between an act and an event; for while every act is an event, or entails an event, not every event is an act, it being very common for things to occur, even in one's own body, which neither he nor anyone else makes occur.

To illustrate what this logic proves, it is possible that I should have a nervous spasm or disorder, such that my hand moves from time to time, or perhaps shakes, or twitches, without my having anything to do with it. We could not then say that I had moved my hand, simply in virtue of the fact that the motion had occurred and was unquestionably the motion of *my* hand, for by hypothesis I had nothing to do with it. It just moved, in spite of me. Evidently, then, its moving is not equivalent to my moving it. In the case of the tree, however, the fact that its leaves drop off, and that it sheds its leaves, *are* one and the same fact. Given that trees are the kinds of things they are, namely, passive beings, there are no circumstances under which it could be true that a tree's leaves drop off, without it also being true that the tree sheds its leaves. From the fact that either occurs we can infer that the other does too, simply because they are identically the same thing. Similar remarks can, of course, be made concerning the behavior of any inanimate and hence non-active object whatever, such as the moon's waxing and waning, the river's rushing to the sea, and so on.

Transitive
and Intransitive Motions

The difference between the second and the third facts that I have discriminated is fairly obvious, and not at all crucial to our inquiry, since neither involves any special notion or agency. The significant difference is simply a difference in the sense of "moves" involved in each. The second fact, consisting simply of my hand moving, amounts to nothing more than my hand undergoing motion, or change of place. It does not entail that anything else moves. The third fact, however, consists of my hand's imparting its motion to another thing, a pencil in this case, such that here the word "moves" occurs transitively. The second fact, accordingly, does not entail the third, but the third seems to entail the second; for the second could be true without the third being true, but it is difficult to see how the third could be true without the second being true too.

Acts and Internal Events

Aristotle sometimes spoke as though a voluntary act were distinguishable from other things by the fact that its cause is within the agent whose action it is. Most philosophers since have assumed that this is true, even obviously so, though perhaps in need of refinement. It has seldom been sufficiently appreciated what overwhelming difficulties there are in the idea of something's being "within" an agent.

If this were true, however—that is, if an act, as distinguished from a bodily motion that is not an act, were simply a bodily motion caused by something within the agent whose act it is—then there would be no radical difference in kind between the first of the three facts discriminated above, which is an act, and the third, which is not. The third fact, that my hand moves a pencil, involves only the idea that my hand, in moving, causes the motion of a pencil, a simple, straightforward causal relationship. If the first fact, that I move my hand, could be adequately expressed by saying that something within me causes my hand to move, then this, too, would be a simple and straightforward description of a causal relationship, and our first and third facts would accordingly be much the same.

This, however, is most assuredly *not* the proper description of an act, for there are numberless examples of things which manifestly are not acts, but which nevertheless fit that description perfectly. The causes of my heart beats are assuredly within me, for instance, in the clearest sense imaginable, yet these are no acts of mine, voluntary or otherwise. The phenomena of growth, too, like the growth of my hair and fingernails, have their causes within me, but these are never things that I *do*. They are merely changes that my body undergoes. Fear sometimes causes a man to perspire, but this is no act of his. It is merely something that his body does. But when a man raises his hand we cannot say that this is merely something that his body does. When a man's death is brought about by an internal disorder it is not thereby inferred that he killed himself, though that would follow if the suggestion before us were true. The spasms and convulsions to which some people are banefully subject arise from internal causes, yet these are as good examples as one could find of passive motions that are in no sense acts of those who are so afflicted.

Spiritual Events
Within the Mind or Soul

In view of this obvious fact, that the mere *internal location* of its cause does not convert a bodily motion into an act, it has long been customary for philosophers to suppose that acts are distinguished from other events in having very special *kinds* of internal causes; namely, certain mental, or non-physical events, in the mind or soul, called "acts of will" or, what is exactly the same, "volitions." Thus, in case the causal antecedents of any bodily change are entirely physical in nature, then, whether those causes occur within or without the body, or both, that change is no act, but a mere bodily change, no different in kind from the changes found in inanimate things. But if, on the other hand, that bodily change includes among its causal antecedents some event that is mental and therefore non-physical in nature, and if in particular that non-physical event is an act of will or a volition, and is such that the bodily change would not have occurred in its absence, then, according to this view, it is an act of an agent in whose mind that non-physical event occurred. This theory, which I shall call "the volitional theory," simply describes acts as those bodily changes which have volitions as their remote or proximate causes.

I have already commented on this conception in the previous discussion of powers, and there is no need for repetition. Here it need only be noted that those who have embraced this opinion have not done so on the basis of any kind of experience whatever, whether "internal" or "external," "introspective" or "extrospective," nor has it been arrived at by psychological investigation, nor by the interpretation of any empirical data of psychology. The volitional theory is, in fact, nothing but the offspring of the marriage between a certain metaphysical presupposition, on the one hand, and the bewitchment of grammar, on the other. The metaphysical presupposition—which never has and never could be shown to be true—is that every event *must* have some other event as its cause, and hence, that there *must* be some internal event which is the cause of any bodily motion that is an act. If this internal cause of an act is not some bodily event—as it plainly cannot be, since it is just those bodily motions which have bodily causes that are *not* acts—then it must, of course, be some non-bodily event. Thus there arises the idea of "mental"—that is, non-bodily—causes. The grammatical trap with which this metaphysical presupposition has merged is the labeling in ordinary language of certain acts as "voluntary." The alleged internal causes thus receive a *name,* "volitions," suggested by the very word "voluntary"—and the illusion is thus complete that, there being this name, there *must* be some kind of event that it names.

I am not here suggesting that acts, or the bodily motions sometimes designated as acts, are uncaused. On the contrary, I shall later develop the idea that the cause of an act is, quite simply, the agent who performs it. This suggests, however, that the kind of causation involved in human behavior is the efficient causation of events by active beings, that is, by men, involving the exercise of active power. For the present, however, I mean to confine myself to showing—or, more accurately, to pointing out—that acts are not external effects of internal events, whether these are called "volitions," "acts of will," or whatnot.

The Non-empirical Character
of the Volitional Theory

No one has ever arrived at a belief in volitions by observing them. They find no place in the data of empirical psychology, nor does it appear that anyone has ever found volitions occurring within himself, or within his mind, by any introspective scrutiny of his mental life. It is doubtful, in fact, whether any such thing as a volition, as construed by this theory, has ever occurred under the sun, and this would seem at least to be a defect in the volitional theory, whatever might be its philosophical merits.

Suppose it were otherwise. Let us suppose, in other words, that the volitional theory were true. What then would one actually *find* whenever he performed any simple act? He would, obviously, find not merely that he was performing an act, but that he was performing *two* of them, one of these being a private or internal act of willing, in his mind or soul, and the other an observable bodily act, which would be the causal consequence of this. Even this, however, is highly misleading, for according to the volitional theory an observable act simply *is* a bodily motion caused by a certain kind of change in the mind called a "volition." What, accordingly, one would find, or should certainly be able to find, anytime he performs an observable act, is both *events*—the internal alteration in his mind or soul, followed by the observable change of his body. But in fact one finds nothing like this at all. When I speak voluntarily, I do not find occurring within myself a volition to speak, and then forthwith find my tongue and other vocal organs moving in response to this inner mental change. When I move my finger I do not, and cannot, discover the occurrence within me of a special mental event, and later observe the finger moving in response to this. What I am actually aware of when I speak is that I am speaking—not merely that my tongue and lips are moving and making words, and not that these are moving in response to something else that is happening inside me. What I am aware of when I move my hand, and all that I seem able to become ware of, is that I am moving my hand—not just that my hand is moving, *nor* that it is moving as a causal consequence of something *else* that I find happening. I will to speak in speaking, and will to move my hand in moving it. There are not two things I do in each such case, nor two things that I find happening, but just one; or at least, that is all I can *find*.

It is said that those who are subject to epileptic convulsions are forewarned of an impending convulsion by a certain feeling. They sooner or later learn, upon the advent of this peculiar feeling, to expect their bodies to begin behaving in certain ways. All of us, moreover, know what it is like to feel a sneeze coming on. There is a certain feeling which, we have learned, is always or often followed by that convulsive exhalation called "sneezing." Hardly anything could be less like a voluntary act than things of this sort; indeed, they are good paradigms of involuntary behavior or automatic responses. And yet if the theory of volitions were true, voluntary behavior would not differ in kind at all from this kind of behavior—only in its underlying subjective cause. Voluntary sneezes, on this view, would only be sneezes caused by certain inner changes called "volitions," while involuntary ones would be caused by certain other inner changes—certain nasal tickles, and so on. The only trouble is, that one can *feel* a nasal tickle, can say when it begins and when it stops, can try to get rid of it, and so on, whereas no one, apparently, can actually *feel* any sneeze volition, can say when it begins and when it stops, or try to get rid of it. Indeed, we seem unable to say anything at all about volitions, except that they cause our bodies to move in this way and that—sneeze volitions causing our bodies to sneeze, arm-raising volitions causing our arms to go up, and so on. And because we *can* say this sort of thing, there are philosophers who have persuaded themselves that such inner causes do actually exist in their souls, and even some who have spoken as though they could *feel* them occurring there, or introspectively *discover* them occurring there, with as little doubt as that we *feel* an irritation that leads to sneezing. Now others may say what they please; they may solemnly affirm, if they wish, that they are perpetually aware, or can easily become aware by some simple "inward" glance, of volitions occurring within them, volitions of the greatest diversity, and some of the most incredible complexity—like the volition of the sort needed to spell out a word, for instance, or to pronounce a complete sentence. For myself, to paraphrase a philosopher of an earlier day, I am quite certain that no such thing ever occurred within me. I do not believe that I have merely *failed to find* things that are in fact occurring within me daily, nor that, finding them, I have failed to *recognize* them. They appear to be pure fictions, for my behavior seems not one whit less voluntary in the apparent absence of such alleged inner causes.

The Characterlessness of Volitions

Quite apart from any introspective scrutiny of one's own mental life, one ought to suspect that volitions are fictional just from the way they are referred to in philosophical literature—and they are not, it is perhaps worth nothing, ever referred to elsewhere. They are always referred to and described in terms of their *effects*, never in terms of themselves, leading one to suspect that perhaps they have no inherent characteristics by which they even can be identified.

Now in any true causal relationship one can always, in case he knows what both events are, describe them independently of each other. If, for instance, I know that a window was broken by the impact of a brick, I can describe this cause quite informatively without any reference to the breaking of the window, which is its effect. I can say, that is, that this cause was the motion of a brick of such and such description, having such and such weight and moving at such and such speed, striking the window in a specific way, and so on. Similarly, a physiologist can give some sort of description of the causes of my heart beats, or the growth of my hair, without necessarily mentioning these effects at all. But it is quite *impossible* to describe any volition or act of will except in terms of its alleged effects. Can anyone, for instance, describe the volition to move one's index finger in the motion of a figure eight without reference to that finger and that motion?

Can anyone describe such a volition, adequately to distinguish it from, say, the volition to make a similar motion of the middle finger without reference to either finger? Can any particular volition be described at all? Seemingly not. If we ask just what *is* the volition to move one's finger, we only get as a reply that it is the internal or mental cause of just such a motion. The only thing that distinguishes it from the volition to move another finger is that it in fact caused the motion of *this* finger. Such an alleged cause is, evidently, pure fiction. When we ask for some sort of description of the cause, we get the one-word reply, "volition," and when we ask what on earth this might be, we are merely told that it is the cause of the voluntary motion of the finger—as if by this kind of discourse we should somehow feel wiser! It is exactly as though a physiologist were to announce that he had discovered the cause of the heartbeat and, upon being asked what that cause is, replied that it is the heartbeat impulse and then filled out the description of this by saying that by heartbeat impulse he is, of course, referring to those events which are the causes of heartbeats. No one would imagine that he had learned anything about the causes of heartbeats by such a disquisition.

Heartbeats

The heartbeat provides a good example of an involuntary motion. One can, to be sure, control its rate to some rather slight extent by doing something *else* voluntarily—by exercising, for instance, or by resting—or one can stop it altogether by, say, putting a bullet through it, but the motions of the heart cannot be controlled in the same direct way that, for example, certain motions of the fingers can. In this respect the heart's behavior is as far "removed from the will" as, say, the motions of a clock pendulum—which, incidentally, can also be controlled in an indirect way, by voluntarily making adjustments, or perhaps smashing it. Indeed, were it not for my knowledge, which was at some time learned, that my very existence from one moment to the next depends upon this pulse, I would probably consider it with the same relative indifference and idle curiosity that I do the ticking of a clock.

Why, then, should we not regard those inner impulses which control the heartbeat as acts of will or volitions? This question, so far as I know, has never been asked, because no one has ever seen the point of it. But surely we know that the regular contractions and relaxations of the heart are individually caused by impulses of some kind or other, whether they be mental, physical, or whatever. Why, then, shall we not properly call these impulses volitions?

The answer to this certainly *cannot* be that we are not consciously aware of those impulses, the way that we are of such things as headaches and tickles, for it has been abundantly stressed that no man is ever consciously aware of any volition, either. No man can ever truly say anything like, "Ah! there is an arm-raising volition—now it is subsiding, but now it is recurring with slightly greater intensity, and now I shall try to suppress it or ignore it," and so on. Indeed, as we have seen, no one can even begin to describe any volition at all—which he should certainly be able to do if he were ever conscious of one—except in terms of its alleged effect, of which he is plainly conscious. All that one is ever consciously aware of in performing a voluntary act is, besides the act itself, certain feelings of muscular effort and resistance, and one is not always even aware of these. When I am cleaning out my pipe, for instance, I am conscious only of cleaning my pipe, together with the certain slight muscular effort and resistance involved in doing so. The motions that I then make are not each and every one accompanied by additional events, of which I am ever conscious, which are the volitions to make those motions. They are accompanied only by the feeling of the pipe and its resistance, which is an effect, and certainly no cause, of the motions I then make.

Nor can the answer to this question be that the heartbeat impulses are of a physical nature, whereas volitions are ("by definition") mental. No one could ever show that heartbeat impulses and volitions, if there are such things, are not of exactly the same nature, whether this be called mental or physical. One can indeed define volitions as nonphysical events, but one can as easily define heartbeat impulses in the same way; the question will still remain whether there are volitions and heartbeat impulses, as thus defined, and if so, whether they are any different. This, of course, can only be decided by examination and experience, not by inventing definitions of words. If, as is very doubtful, there are such events as volitions within us, of which any man can become intimately aware every time he acts voluntarily, then there is no philosophical reason for denying that these events are of the same sort as those heartbeat impulses of which, however, we are not intimately aware. Since, however, it is seriously doubtful whether any one is ever aware of a volition, and quite certain that no one is ever aware of the impulses that control heartbeats, then the two are apparently similar in this negative respect, at least, and may be identical in others. We are, to be sure, sometimes aware of our intentions, purposes, motives, and the like, but that is not the awareness of any inner event of long or short duration which one finds to be the cause of a bodily motion, in any way comparable to that in which fear, for instance, is sometimes the cause of perspiration. To be "aware of one's intention" is only to have made up one's mind what he is going to do, now or later, to have settled upon a course of action, and to remember it. It would be quite unbelievable to suppose that bodily motions are literally caused by anything like this, and absurd to suppose that every voluntary motion must be.

It is, however, quite obvious why philosophers are never tempted to think of heartbeat impulses as volitions; namely, that the heartbeats are not voluntary. This does *not* mean that they are not "caused by volitions" since, for all we know, they may be. What it does mean is that they are not within one's immediate control. They individually occur in their own way and at their own pace, and quite in spite of the agent in whose body they occur, disregarding here the indirect ways that the pulse rate can be increased or decreased.

This good reason for excluding heartbeat impulses as examples of volitions is not, however, available to holders of the theory of volitions. For according to that theory, to say that something is "within one's immediate control" just *means* that it is caused by a volition. If, accordingly, there are such things as volitions, and it should turn out that heartbeat impulses are in fact the same sorts of things as these, then the holders of this theory would have to conclude that heartbeats are voluntary after all, which would be absurd. Nor can the holder of the volitional theory say that the heartbeat impulses themselves are involuntary and not within one's control, for again, all it means to say that something is voluntary, according to that theory, is that it is caused by a volition. Not knowing the cause of a heartbeat impulse, then, how can anyone say that it is not caused by a volition? If, to be sure, the heartbeat impulse should itself turn out to be a volition, then it might be meaningless either to affirm or to deny that it is caused by a volition, since the holders of the volitional theory often maintain that it is meaningless to speak of volitions as being either voluntary or involuntary. But it is certainly *not* meaningless to deny that the heartbeat impulses are voluntary or within our immediate control, for everyone knows perfectly well that they are not. Something's being voluntary or within one's immediate control cannot, therefore, be equivalent to its being caused by a volition.

Deciding, Desiring, and Choosing

Aware that there might be something vacuous in the theory of undergoing willings or having volitions, philosophers often try to save the view that actions are bodily motions having internal "mental" changes as their causes, by substituting for volitions certain alleged internal events that seem less esoteric; namely, decisions, desires, choices, and the like. I have already mentioned these, too, in the discussion of power, where it was noted that theories involving these concepts are only as good as the presupposition upon which they rest—namely, that actions *are* bodily changes having internal events as their causes—and that such theories cannot therefore be invoked to *substantiate* that dubious claim. Here it can be added, however, that decisions, choices, desires, tryings, intentions, and the like serve no better than volitions as the causes of actions, and for precisely the same reason—namely, that it is impossible, as it is not in the case of any known instance of a real causal connection, even to begin to say what these events are without describing them in terms of their alleged effects. What will be left, for instance, in one's description of the choice to move one's finger after we have eliminated all reference to the motion of the finger? And how shall we distinguish that choice from the choice to move one's toe without any reference to the motion of the toe? The only thing anyone can say, apparently, is that one is the choice to move the finger, and the other the choice to move the toe, adding, perhaps, that neither of these choices is a physical event but is, instead, a mental one—and we are absolutely right where we started, in total ignorance. The same remarks apply, evidently, to desiring, deciding, intending, trying, and so on—indeed, to anything one might suggest as the internal mental cause and accompaniment of an act. This is enough to suggest that, so far as anything that has been said is concerned, voluntary actions have no internal or mental events as their causes.

Nor is this the worst of it, for not only are we apparently unable to give any descriptive content to the notion of such internal causes, other than just saying that they *are* internal causes, but we cannot even describe them as causes without finally falling back upon the idea that they are somehow within the control of the agent who brings them about. If, then, such causes are postulated in an attempt to eliminate the notion of agency, they fail.

Thus, if I know that a window has been shattered by a flying brick and know quite thoroughly the details of this sequence, I can give some sort of explanation of the effect without mentioning any act of the brick and, indeed, without even mentioning the brick. I can say, for instance, that the glass was at such and such time subjected to a sudden pressure of such and such degree, exceeding the strength of the glass, and so on—and while there is more that *can* be said, what I have already said, without mentioning the brick, is informative. But suppose I explain an act of moving my hand by saying (perhaps in more philosophical language) that at such and such time the hand (or the relevant muscles or whatnot) was subjected to an internal or mental impulse or event, of such and such kind, sufficient to set it in motion, and that this impulse or event is what we call a "choice," "desire," "decision," or whatnot. Now even if we suppose this enormously dubious picture to be correct, which is hard enough, we still have not explained that motion *as an act* until the point is made that the internal event which caused it was something of *mine*. To say, however, that it was *my* internal event—that is, my choice, decision, desire, or whatnot—is not merely to say that it occurred within me, for that would be consistent with its not being mine at all, and its effect not my act. Suppose, for instance, that just as I may be subject to spasmodic bodily motions, such as twitchings of the eyelid and the like, with which I have nothing to do, so also might I be subject to spasmodic "choices"—occurrences of internal events which cause external motions—to occur from time to time, perhaps from known or unknown physiological causes, without my having anything to do with them and in spite of me. In that case I shall find the bodily motions in question taking place in response to those allegedly internal events called choices—but these sequences of things will occur in spite of me, without my control, even to my astonishment, embarrassment, and dismay. We can even suppose that the internal mental choosings are caused by some other person who has cleverly, and unbeknown to me, rigged me up to a device by means of which he can ("at will") produce the desired choosings within me, or within my mind, simply by pushing various buttons. On such suppositions as these I shall be in a position not unlike that of the epileptic or the victim of hiccoughs, not knowing what internal or mental event might happen next, or what bodily motion will ensue from it, or what might be its baneful consequences. In short, I shall not be *acting* at all, but will instead be the passive and helpless *victim* of internal or mental events and their behavioral consequences. The whole picture is admittedly ridiculous, but it is rendered no less so by our baptizing these internal or mental events under the name "choices," any more than by baptizing them under the name "volitions" or, for that matter, under any name at all ("decisions," "desires," "intentions," etc.).

To suppose, then, that certain of my bodily motions and changes are acts of mine it is not enough to suppose that they are merely motions and changes of my body, as we have long since seen, nor is it enough to suppose that they are motions and changes of my body resulting from events or states occurring within me, whether these be mental or physical or whatever. Many such motions and changes, like sweatings, tremblings, and twitches, are the straightforward effects of such inner changes but are not acts, whereas certain motions which are voluntary acts seem traceable to no such inner causes. What we must always say, in the case of events that are to count as physical acts and that are the effects of inner changes of any kind, is that these inner changes are themselves within my control, that they are things that I can make happen or decline to make happen, things which are up to me to perform or to decline to perform. We must, in short, in order to describe any event as an act, include in our description not only a reference to an agent, such as a man, but to an agent as active, or as doing something. With this result the whole attempt to avoid the concept of agency by interpreting acts as bodily motions resulting from the mere occurrence of internal events collapses.

6

Willing and Trying

To maintain, as I have, that an act of will is not an internal or mental cause of a bodily motion that is voluntary is not to say that there are no such things as acts of will. Similarly, to say that choices, desires, decisions, and the like are not the internal or mental causes of actions which are chosen, desired, or decided upon is not to deny that men sometimes act from choice, from desire, and from decision. All that I am rejecting is a certain quasi-psychological conception; namely, the conception of volitions, choices, and the like as inner, mental causes of outer, physical states or actions.

" An Act of Will "

In fact, of course, such expressions as "an act of will," "acting from desire," "an act of choice," "acting intentionally," and the like have perfectly good and familiar referents, just as do the kindred expressions, "acting from anger," "an act of malice," "an act of compassion," and so on, with which they can be very usefully compared. Acting from anger, for example, never consists simply of undergoing bodily motions and changes of which anger is the cause. Anger in a man can sometimes be the cause, in the most usual and straightforward sense, of such bodily changes as perspiration, trembling, dilation of the pupils, and so on, but no one wants to suggest that such changes as these are *acts* of anger, simply because they are plainly not acts to begin with. They are only bodily motions and changes caused by anger. Similarly, compassion in a man can sometimes cause the flow of tears, but no one would call this an act of compassion. It is only an involuntary change resulting from an emotional state, and no act at all, much less a compassionate one. To act in anger is to do something—to write a letter, for instance, or to strike some person or thing—while in an emotional state of anger, and perhaps from some such motive or principle as revenge or self-protection. To perform a compassionate act is similarly to do something—to help an injured animal or person, for instance—to alleviate suffering for which there is a felt concern. There is all the difference in the world between such an act, on the one hand, and the physiological changes that accompany it, such as tears, on the other. The former is an act or a deed, performed by a compassionate man, which may be guided by a motive or purpose but which is caused by nothing other than the man whose action it is, whereas the latter, the shedding of tears, is no act at all, whether of the man or of his eyes. It is caused by the feeling of compassion, and not by any agent, and it would be senseless to speak of its having any motive at all.

Acting from choice, similarly, is a perfectly common thing, and paradigm cases are easily supplied. Think of a man, for instance, walking through the cafeteria, who pauses before an array of a great variety of juices then reaches for a glass of orange juice. Here, certainly, is a perfect example of an act of choice; namely, the actual act, which consisted of taking one thing from among others that were offered, and doing so under circumstances in which those alternatives were, or were at least believed to be, equally available. No one should seriously suggest that this man's choosing was something accomplished entirely within his mind or his soul, and that the motions of his hands and fingers were simply the observable effects of that inner unobservable episode. There is no need for any such inner episode at all. Had any such thing occurred—had he said to himself, for instance,

"I guess I'll have orange juice this time," or something like that—and then, before taking it, tripped and fallen, or been otherwise prevented from taking the juice, no one would say that he had in fact *chosen* the orange juice and that his act of choice had then failed to produce its normal bodily effect. On the contrary, one would only properly say that he was *about* to choose the orange juice but was prevented.

And so it is, it seems quite clear, with an act of will. To perform an act of will is only to *act willfully,* that is to say, intentionally and deliberately. Humans being what they are, the idea of a "willful act" has also come to mean, in addition to this, acting badly or injuriously, but we need not concern ourselves with this; there is no reason, really, why one might not be willfully sweet, although this, of course, is not common. To act willfully is not, in any case, to perform or to undergo some inner, unobservable twitch or convulsion of the soul in the hope or expectation that this will somehow produce a desired twitch or jerk of the body, like the motion of a limb or the tongue. It is simply to act purposefully, with an end in view, with some more or less clear knowledge of what one is doing and why. One wills to speak, for instance, in speaking. To speak willfully or voluntarily or intentionally or deliberately is not first to will to speak, and then to find one's tongue and vocal apparatus carrying on from there, in response to what was thus inwardly initiated by the soul. To speak willfully or intentionally is just to speak with a knowledge of what one is saying and why. If our speech acts have inner mental causes, then the speech act of the man who asks his wife to throw out the supper and put the cat on the table doubtless has just as good an inner mental cause as any other. But no better example could be given of a man whose speaking was not deliberate and intentional, just because he did not know what he was saying or why he was saying just what he did. He did not say that "on purpose."

Trying

There is one candidate left, and certainly the best, to propose as the unique inner cause of those bodily motions we call voluntary, and that is *trying*. Thus, according to this idea, when one tries to move a limb, say, and that limb then moves in response, then the motion is voluntary or an act, whereas those changes and motions that occur without one's trying—heartbeats, sneezes, and the like—

are properly deemed involuntary or automatic. The difference, then, between a mere bodily motion and a motion that is an act is, according to this suggestion, that the latter is proximately caused by a trying whereas the former is caused by some other inner or outer events. It is as simple as that.

There are, however, certain difficulties in this view which are suggested by things I have already said. We should note at once, for instance, that such an inner trying can be described only in terms of its alleged effect, rendering it a dubious candidate as the cause of anything. If one's arm were to move as a consequence of his trying to move his foot, then no one would consider that motion voluntary, in spite of the fact that it would be the effect of a trying. The only kind of trying that can count as the cause of a voluntary motion of one's arm is his trying to move that arm. Having noted this, however, we can ask what can be said about such a trying, other than that it just is a trying to move an arm, and of course we find that nothing more can be said about it at all. The only thing that distinguishes trying to move one's foot from trying to move his arm is that the effect of the first is the motion of a foot and the effect of the second is the motion of an arm. If we eliminate any reference to such an alleged effect we find that there is nothing whatever that we can say about any particular trying, that these tryings are, like volitions, perfectly characterless. Tryings of the sort postulated by this theory seem, then, like volitions, to be the fictional creations of philosophy and not empirically discoverable things at all. One can certainly wonder whether such things have ever occurred under the sun, for surely, if anyone had ever found such a thing, we could expect that he would at least be able to say something about what he had found, rather than contenting himself with saying whatever is simply implied by a philosophical theory.

This suggests something that is obvious as soon as it is noted; namely, that the concept of trying is, as such, entirely empty, having no meaning whatever apart from the *act* with which a particular trying is logically related. We cannot attach any meaning at all to an assertion that someone is "trying" until we are told what it is that he is trying *to do*. We need to remember, though, that the whole point of introducing the idea of trying was to give a clear meaning to the concept of acting, so as analytically to distinguish actions from such bodily motions and changes as are not acts. If, in order to understand what is meant by trying, we need already to have a clear idea of what is meant by an act, then plainly we are going to get nowhere in attempting to analyze acting in terms of trying to act.

Just like acts of will, acts of choice, acts of anger, and the like, however, there plainly are certain things that are properly called tryings or, better, acts of trying. These are not inner causes of bodily acts, however, but those very bodily acts themselves. One can be truly said to be trying, or performing an act of trying, whenever he is actually doing something with the view, purpose, or goal of accomplishing something, whether that goal is in fact achieved or not. Thus, one can be said to be *trying* to open a door when he is in fact pushing or pulling it, having as his purpose to make it come open; one can be said to be trying to swim across a lake when he is in fact swimming in the direction of the opposite shore, having as his purpose to reach that shore; and so on. If, however, trying to do something is always, as it seems to be, actually doing something with a view to accomplishing a certain result, then no one is going to get very far in attempting to shed light on the concept of actually doing something by introducing the concept of trying. We shall always have to fall back upon our prior understanding of doing something before we can have any understanding of trying.

The Paralyzed Leg

There is, nevertheless, one kind of experience which does seem to some philosophers to indicate the existence of some inner, mental, or psychological kind of trying, and that is one wherein one tries to perform some simple bodily motion and *nothing happens*. Suppose, for example, that a man's leg has become paralyzed—has "gone to sleep," as some people put it—and that he does not yet realize this. He then, it is claimed, at a certain time tries to move it, and suddenly discovers that it does not move. *Something* evidently has happened, and since it is by hypothesis no bodily change that has occurred, we must suppose that it was an inner, mental change which can properly be called trying. Indeed, how else could that man have learned that his leg was paralyzed, if not as the result of trying to move it, and failing? Between this man, who tries and fails, and another who, we can suppose, tries to move his leg and succeeds, there is evidently only one significant difference; namely, that the one leg does and the other does not move. There is, however, evidently one significant thing in common between the two men; namely, that both *try*. And we must, it seems, believe that there is this common factor of trying, because the difference in question—namely, the occurrence in the one case and the non-occurrence in the other of a certain bodily motion—would have existed even had the man with the paralyzed leg *not* tried to move it. A paralyzed leg is not merely one that does not move, for no one supposes that his legs are paralyzed during all those times when they are not moving. One *discovers* that his leg is paralyzed, not just by noting its motionlessness, for it may be motionless long before he realizes that it is paralyzed, but rather, it seems, by trying *in vain* to make it move.

This argument, properly seen and appreciated, is obviously very strong and convincing, one of those arguments that seems pretty much to settle things. Yet it cannot be correct, and not merely because it would overthrow the main thesis of this chapter, but because the picture it conveys is a false one, a picture of a situation that simply does not, and never can, occur.

To get ourselves out of this picture of the situation and into what I believe will be a clearer and more realistic conception, let us first get very clear about the notion of *trying* that is involved in it. Trying is here supposed to designate a certain species of mental occurrence, a purely mental effort that is supposed to precede or accompany a certain bodily motion or, when that motion is rendered impossible, to occur *quite by itself*. The man whose leg is paralyzed is supposed to *discover* that fact by inference, that is, by exerting a certain psychological effort and then noting that this is not followed by its accustomed bodily effect.

We have already noted, however, that in typical circumstances in which one can speak of trying to do something, trying to do one thing consists of *actually* doing something else, and having some object or goal in view in the doing of it. In case what one is trying to do is something requiring physical effort, as it usually is, then the trying itself involves the exertion of actual physical effort. It does not consist in just having something called "trying" occurring in one's mind; it is not just a spiritual effort of the soul. Thus, one tries to jump over a fence by actually jumping, and if the jump does not carry him over, then he has tried and failed. One could not possibly be telling the truth if he said he was trying to jump over a fence, at the same time just sitting there and doing nothing in the way of jumping, but just mentally trying. Similarly, one tries—in vain, let us suppose—to open a door by actually and successfully doing something else—

by grasping the knob, pushing or pulling and, in fact, exerting physical effort. If one insisted that he was trying to open a door, and it was apparent that he was performing no bodily action at all—grasping nothing, exerting no effort, and so on—then he could not be telling the truth. If he said that *all* he was doing was "just trying," that is, trying without actually doing anything except just mentally trying, then at best his "trying" would consist only of *concentrating* on the door, perhaps *wishing* it might open, or vividly *imagining* it opening, perhaps reciting magical formulae to himself, and so on. But no mental doings of this sort can count as trying to do anything. The man with the paralyzed leg who tried to move it did not just wish that it might move, or imagine it as moving, or concentrate on its moving, or recite formulae. If he did in fact try to move it, it was not just this sort of thing that he did. Again, one cannot try to wiggle his ears without actually succeeding in doing something else—clenching his teeth, perhaps, or tensing various facial muscles. If one supposes that he is "just trying" in his mind alone to wiggle his ears, and makes sure that he is not actually doing any of these other things— tensing no muscles or anything of that sort—then he finds that his mental trying consists, again, of nothing but wishing or concentrating, which is plainly not the sort of trying we are after. It is for this reason, evidently, that no man can even *try* to wiggle his hair, or a particular hair, in the same direct way that he can try to wiggle a finger. There is simply nothing for him to *do* in the way of wiggling a hair—no muscle to tense, no physical effort to make, nothing, so to speak, to get hold of. If trying were a mental affair, however, it is hard to see why one should not try to wiggle a hair, for the absence of any suitable muscles to tense can be no impediment to making the appropriate effort of the mind. The mind neither has nor needs any muscles of its own. It should be added, incidentally, that no one ever *learned* that he could not wiggle his hair by *trying* and *failing;* yet we do certainly know this. It cannot be maintained, then, that no one *could* know this, *unless* he had tried and failed— for no one has ever tried it, and no one even knows how to try it, and yet everyone *does* know that he cannot do it.

If, then, trying to do one thing consists of actually doing something else, what does the man whose leg is paralyzed actually *do,* if he does not move his leg? I suggest that what he does is something very much like what one does when he tries to open a door that is jammed; namely, he exerts a physical effort, which involves a clearly felt and even observable bodily tension. This is, certainly, what one actually finds—he finds that the felt physical effort to move the leg is futile, and this felt effort is an actual effort exerted by the body, not an effortful straining of the mind. The fundamental supposition of the original argument is therefore false. That is, it is not true that no bodily change occurred when he tried to move his leg, and that therefore the change in question was purely mental. There was a bodily change, not *caused* by his trying but in fact identical with it, a change that consisted in his actually doing something, namely, exerting a physical effort. His failure did not consist in his failing to do anything but in his failing to do all that he was trying to do; namely, to move his leg. He could not have failed had he not succeeded in doing something—in this case, in making the effort or putting forth a certain physical exertion.

The Paralyzed Man

The next move in the argument is, obviously, to postulate a man who cannot move anything, that is to say, one who is quite paralyzed throughout, and hence one who can make no bodily effort whatever. Indeed it has been claimed—truly, I shall suppose—that there are drugs which, when administered in massive doses, have precisely this effect; namely, the total paralysis of all of a man's muscles, such that he can move nothing at all and must even rely upon an oxygen tent for respiration.

Now such a man, surely, can discover that his leg is paralyzed, can he not? And how else can he discover this than by trying to move it, and failing? And such trying, since it can by hypothesis involve no bodily effort and no motion of any bodily part, must be a purely psychological effort or mental trying, must it not?

The only allowable thing to say here, really, is that no one knows. We are supposing a man who can exert no physical effort at all in the attempt to move his leg, for if there were anything at all that he could do, this would have to count as trying. If we supposed that in trying to move his leg he managed nothing more than a slight and futile abdominal tension, then we could suppose that just that futile tension constituted his trying, for it would be something that he had done in the attempt to move his leg. We have to suppose, then, a man so paralyzed that he cannot even do that—a man who is totally paralyzed. Can such a man try to move his leg?

No one knows, for no empirical data on this question can prove a thing. It is not the data, but the interpretation of the data, that is at issue. There is, nevertheless, no absurdity in saying that such a man cannot even try. If there is nothing whatever that a man can do, in the way of trying to move his leg—if he is as helpless with respect to this as the rest of us are with respect, say, to suddenly reducing our bulk to that of an acorn—then it would be idle to insist that he might nevertheless at least try. That man might in good faith insist, if he had any way of insisting, that he was helpless even to try, that he was not only powerless to move his leg, but powerless even to try, as powerless as the rest of us are to try wiggling our hair or reducing our size to that of an acorn. He might, indeed, do *something* just "in his mind." He might mentally urge his leg to move, or wish that his flaccid muscles would contract, or concentrate for long periods on the image of moving legs. Mental exercises of this sort, however, are not remotely like anything a healthy man does when he tries to move a stiff leg.

Suppose, then, such a man is told to move his leg and then subsequently, when the paralysis has worn off and he has regained the normal control of his body and speech, he insists in good faith that he *tried* to comply but found he could not. Are we to understand this as meaning that, while he has not moved his leg, he has nevertheless done *something*? Are we to suppose that, while he has failed to comply with the order given, he has done something that would have counted as complying with *another* order, in case it had been given; namely, the order to *try* moving his leg? There is no reason to suppose this, for there is not all that much difference between the two orders. If a physician asks such a man to move his leg or, alternatively, to try moving his leg, these are not *different* or *alternative* actions that the physician wants to elicit. They are only two ways of expressing one and the same request, namely, the request to move the leg. The latter way of putting the request, the request to *try*, only carries with it the suggestion that compliance is not entirely expected. A physician who asked such a man to try moving his leg and got no response would not describe the situation misleadingly, much less falsely, if he said, "I asked him to move his leg, but he couldn't," or equivalently, "I told him to try moving his leg, but he couldn't." The physician is not by such a request trying to elicit some sort of urging in the patient's mind or soul and has no interest in such a thing even if he could somehow determine its occurrence. He only wants to see whether the patient can move his leg yet, and *that* is what he tries to get him to do by asking him to try. A man who *can* move his leg does not do one thing in complying with the request to move it, and do a quite different, easier thing in complying with the request to try moving it; he does exactly the same thing in either case, provided he complies. This paralyzed man's subsequent sincere avowal, then, that he tried to move his leg, but failed, evidently does not mean that he did do something called "trying." It means only that, upon being told to move his leg, he found that he could not. "I tried," then, does not in this context mean "I did something, though not quite all that I meant to do." It means, rather, "I didn't move my leg, but that is only because I couldn't," and *that* is surely consistent with one's having done nothing at all.

How, then, could such a man ever come to *discover* his state of paralysis and, in particular, the paralysis of his leg? Here it is natural to suppose that something must have *apprised* him of his baneful condition, and what else could this have been, other than his futile effort to move? But since he was totally paralyzed, what could this (futile) effort have been, other than a purely subjective or mental episode, unaccompanied by its accustomed effect?

There is, however, not the least reason to put the thing this way. Men are sometimes quite capable of knowing something, without being apprised of it by something else that they know. Not all knowledge is gained through knowledge of something else, and this is particularly true of one's knowledge of certain of his own states and abilities. Not all knowledge is arrived at through clues, else it would be impossible to know such clues. An unparalyzed man, for example, knows that he cannot wiggle his hair the way he wiggles his fingers, or retract his nails like a cat. Nor does he know this as a result of having tried and failed; for in fact, one cannot even try to do such things as these, except in some highly extenuated sense of trying which includes saying prayers and reciting magical formulae. How a man knows something like this is beside the point, for the fact is that he does know it, and he does *not* discover it as a result of trying and failing, for he also knows that he cannot try. Similarly, the paralyzed man we are considering knows in the same way that he cannot move his leg, simply because he finds that he cannot. How he finds this is again beside the point; we need not, in any case, suppose that he *finds it out* from something *else* that he finds, namely, from the failure of his (purely mental) effort of trying. Somewhere this chain of cognitions, from things inferred to those things from which they are inferred, has to stop. I suggest that it should stop with the man's discovery that he cannot move his leg, and that there is no reason whatever, outside of a common but misleading mode of speech, for supposing that it stops only with his discovery that he tries to move his leg and, failing, *infers* that he cannot. There is no reason to suppose that he succeeds in some purely mental action of trying but fails only in what he is trying to do. He fails completely.

7

Conclusion

So far I have sought, vainly, the differentia between those bodily motions which are acts and those which are not in terms of their causal antecedents. This has always seemed to philosophers to be the most promising approach. Indeed, it has for most of them seemed quite obviously to be the only possible way of making the distinction at all.

There is, as I have emphasized, sometimes no sure criterion, just in the observation of a bodily motion, for saying whether it was an act that was done by an agent or just an involuntary response. Nearly everyone has experienced certain bodily twitches which he knows are involuntary, though they seem behaviorally identical with things he could do voluntarily. A trivial example is a recurring twitch of the eyelid. A more familiar example is sneezing. We sometimes sneeze involuntarily, and yet one can make a perfectly good imitation of such a sneeze, good enough to fool everyone except himself. A normal sneeze, caused by a nasal irritation, is usually no act. It is simply something that one is seized with. But a pretended sneeze is an act, and the pretense seems to consist not in a behavioral difference but in a difference in how the sneeze is brought about. Again, most persons have experienced that spasmodic jerk that sometimes comes upon one just as he is falling asleep, a motion which is in no sense a voluntary act. Yet one can make just such a motion voluntarily. If we consider pathological disorders, which there is really no need to do, the distinction is similarly clear. Some persons, from a nervous or other disorder, undergo motions—tremblings, twitches, and jerks— which another person can sometimes perfectly imitate. Such motions are not acts of any agent, though the imitations of them certainly are. Now all this indicates, or certainly seems to suggest, that the difference between a bodily motion which is an act and one which is not must consist in a difference in the causes of those motions, for the effects are, or at least sometimes can be, identical.

Beyond such special considerations, moreover, every man seems sometimes to know, within himself—independently of any observations of his own behavior—which motions and changes in his body are within his immediate control and which are not. The distinction seems, therefore, to be a clear and obvious one, and yet it is not a distinction in behavior, but rather in the sources of behavior. Or at least, so it certainly seems.

The search for some kind or class of inner events which are always and exclusively the causes of acts has been futile, however, and we have found ample reason for suspecting it is hopeless. Most such alleged inner causes, such as volitions, tryings, and the like, turn out to be pure fictions, and in the cases of those which are not, such as felt desires, anger, and the like, we can easily find examples of bodily changes which are the effects of these but which are not acts.

The result of this inquiry has therefore been almost entirely negative but nonetheless, if what I have said is true, quite invaluable. My observations have, I think, not only fairly demolished an old and still well entrenched philosophical tradition, in which most of the philosophical conceptions of human nature developed over the past several generations find a place, but have also, I hope, unsettled what seems to be a natural and habitual way of trying to understand human nature, on the part of philosophers and others as well. As soon as people begin speculating about themselves as human beings, they seem to have an irresistible tendency to suppose that they are just objects whose behavior can only be understood on the model of the behavior of other things. When difficulties arise in this they tend to get resolved, or rather pushed out of sight, by inventing minds and special mental operations which are supposed to push and pull these objects, men's bodies, hither and thither; a whole vocabulary, containing such words as "volition," "motive," and the like, comes into use to fortify this tendency. If my observations have, as I believe, really made that whole approach to an understanding of human behavior quite hopeless, then perhaps the way has been made clear for understanding human behavior better in terms of the ideas of agency and purpose.

The Source of Certain Philosophical Theories

Most conceptions of human activity, I have suggested, seem to arise from a double source. There is first of all a certain metaphysical presupposition, reminiscent of the Parmenidean dogma that "from nothing, nothing can come"; the presupposition, namely, that every change must have some other change as at least part of its cause. From this it of course logically follows that nothing, and in particular no man, can initiate a change without first undergoing a change himself, this change being, in turn, the effect of still another, and so on *ad infinitum*. That this never has been and obviously never could be proved seems hardly to diminish its force, which is a good reason for calling it a metaphysical presupposition. The other source, as I have noted, is a certain convention of speech, wherein actions are sometimes distinguished from motions which are not actions by calling the former "voluntary." This word suggests another, namely, "volition," and the temptation is almost irresistible to conclude, without any attempt at verification, that this latter word and others like it name precisely the sort of change the metaphysical principle seems to require as the cause of a voluntary act. This is a trap, and it is doubtful whether there has been a philosopher who has considered the problem of action, or the related problem of free will, who has not fallen into it, though some have preferred words in more common use than "volition." Indeed, it seems to me that rather few have to this day extricated themselves from it.

The "problem of action," I have said, is essentially that of supplying the difference between mere bodily motions and those that represent acts. There are other problems of action, surely, especially since some acts, interestingly enough called "mental," seem to involve no bodily motions at all. But, at any rate, this is the first that demands our attention. That there is a difference is perfectly obvious, for the fact that a man makes a motion certainly entails that such a motion occurs, whereas the fact that such a motion occurs never entails that he makes it, or that it is his act.

Obviously, the difference is that something more is contained in an act than in an otherwise similar motion that is not an act. We can say, moreover, that acts are "caused" by the agents who perform them. These elementary observations are enough to set the trap.

One would not ordinarily be willing to say that a man had done something unless he were also willing to say that he had in some sense done it voluntarily, intentionally, deliberately, or whatnot. It thus seems obvious that the difference sought consists in an element of volition. Note, however, that all that is accomplished by this observation is to *baptize* the difference. That is, given that there is a difference between the two kinds of change, one has by this observation only given a name to that difference, calling it the element of volition. Nothing has been brought forth to indicate that there is such an element.

Now, however, the metaphysical presupposition that every change *must* have another change among its causal conditions takes over, and it is simply assumed, in virtue of the verbal achievement just reached, that there really *are*—indeed, *that there must be*—changes which are the causes of our acts and that these changes are, of course, volitions. Some may prefer other names for them, but it is hard for many persons to doubt, in any case, that there are changes which are thus named. The metaphysical postulate seems to guarantee that there *must* be, so it is of small account that they are not, apparently, very easily found. Indeed, there are philosophers who even profess to *find* these changes within themselves every time they make bodily motions. When pressed, however, it appears that all they have found is the difference with which we began and, in deference to a metaphysical assumption, given it a name.

The theory is philosophically appealing. In one form or another it has seemed to ever so many philosophers to leave nothing more to be said, and has constituted the very foundation of many theories of ethics. It is at best a stop-gap theory, however, for the very questions it at first seems to answer appear all over again as soon as we push on a bit further. This can be shown in the following way.

Let us suppose the theory is correct, and that bodily motions which are acts are really always the effects of other changes. So as not to get involved in a dispute about what these other changes should properly be called, let us just call them x's allowing anyone to substitute for "x" whatever name he pleases, such as "a choosing," "a volition," "a wanting," or whatever. All that we need insist upon is that these x's are *changes,* within an agent, that they are literally the causes of bodily motions which are his acts, and that they therefore occur at certain *times,* namely, just before those bodily motions which are their effects. Ordinarily one would suppose that they must occur at certain *places* as well, that is, within some bodily organ, such as the brain, but since they are in fact never found there or anywhere else, the difficulty of locating them is avoided by saying that they occur "in the mind." This, I believe, means nothing more than that they occur, but cannot be observed to occur, and is a useful device for giving them a "place" of sorts, at the same time rendering it idle to seek out that place. We can overlook all this, however, for all we need for the present is the admission that they are datable events which actually do occur. Now, if this is the case, there is clearly no reason why they might not arise from a variety of causes, the more so since few, even among those who are firmly convinced of their reality, have any clear theory of what causes them. In any case, there is no absurdity in supposing that they can be artificially induced, perhaps by the injection of some drug into the spinal column, with the result that, this drug having been introduced, these changes then occur in a regular way—every thirty seconds, let us suppose, over a period of perhaps fifteen minutes. During this fifteen-minute period the patient so treated will *find* certain bodily motions occurring every half minute or so, in response to these inner changes of which, incidentally, he may or may not be aware. But just from this description it is obvious that those bodily motions will be things with which he has nothing to do, things that occur in spite of him, motions which he is entirely helpless to prevent— and all this *despite* the fact that they are, on the theory before us, his own acts. Nor will it do to say that these motions are indeed his acts, but not his free or voluntary acts, on the ground that the causes of them are themselves caused; for on the theory before us, *all* causes of changes are caused, and the point in calling an action "voluntary" in the first place was not to imply that either it or its cause was uncaused.

Now anyone really devoted to this theory of action can, indeed, insist that in the situation just described the agent is in fact acting. But this is only to refuse to see that the very problem this theory was intended to solve has simply recurred in a new form. In fact, no better example could be given of a man who is not acting, but is simply the helpless victim of events within himself and whose behavior is entirely governed by a drug. We cannot make such a man an "active being" simply by prescribing a set of conditions to be fulfilled, and then noting that they are indeed fulfilled. What we find here is a man who is not acting at all, who is no more acting than one who is seized with epilepsy. We can thus only conclude that the conditions set forth— that the bodily motions must be caused by certain kinds of inner changes, whether these be called "volitions" or whatever—are not sufficient after all. All this theory accomplishes is to analyze the concept of an act by postulating certain extraordinary changes and giving these names. The names having been duly bestowed, it is easy not to notice that we can ask, concerning those changes, the very questions that troubled us about acts. We might as well have saved ourselves this detour into the mind and its internal physics by just declaring, at the outset, that *all* bodily motions are acts of an agent, simply by virtue of their being motions of his body, and just refusing to ask any difficult questions about the causes of those changes.

Why Acts
Are Not Analyzable

I have said that the concept of an act cannot be analyzed in an informative way, and we have seen how discouraging any such attempt is. We are now, however, in a position to see just why this must be so, or why those attempts were futile to begin with.

To give an *analysis* of an act would be, presumably, to take some statement embodying that concept and then supply another statement or set of statements in some sense equivalent to it. Suppose, then, that we begin with the simple statement of an act,

1. I move my hand,

bearing in mind the distinction between this and the passive statement that my hand moves. Now there are, so far as I can see, just three ways in which any proposed statement or sets of statements might be equivalent to (1); namely, (i) it might be *logically* equivalent, such that the conditions expressed in it would be logically both necessary and sufficient for the assertion of (1), with which we began, or such that the assertion of (1) and the denial of the analysis, or vice versa, would be a contradiction. Or (ii), the proposed statement or set of statements might be *materially* equivalent to (1), such as to be true if and only if (1) were true. Or finally, (iii) the analysis might be what we can call *nomically* equivalent to (1), such as to warrant counterfactual inferences either way. That is, the analysis might be such that if (1) *were* false, whether in fact it is false or not, then the proposed equivalent statement or set of statements would be false too, and vice versa, though no formal *contradiction* would result from the assertion of either and the denial of the other.

Now it is fairly easy to see that while equivalences of the first and second kind can easily be supplied, they are utterly uninformative and philosophically worthless, while an equivalence of the third kind, while it would be informative and valuable if given, cannot in fact be given without begging the whole question at issue, namely, whether statements like (1) express the idea of an ordinary causal relationship between different events.

Logical Equivalence

Thus, we can supply a *logical* equivalent to (1) simply by producing *any* statement that is synonymous with it, or by concocting such a statement and declaring it to be synonymous. Here the logical equivalent would be guaranteed, in the only way it can be guaranteed, by the synonymity. We might say, for instance, that (1) has the same meaning as "my hand moved, and this motion was my act," or "my hand moved, and this was something I did," or "my hand moved, and I caused this motion," and so on. It is obvious that any of these statements is synonymous with (1), that it would be a contradiction to affirm any of these and deny (1) or vice versa. It is also obvious that they are all worthless as analyses. Or again, we might say that (1) has the same meaning as "my hand moved, and this motion was caused by my willing it to move." Now obviously, this latter statement can be *regarded* as synonymous with (1), though here we have to beware of supposing that anything more has been achieved. If we assume this to have the same *meaning* as (1), then it really has no philosophical interest because, resting wholly on an equivalence of meanings, it is perfectly compatible with there being no such thing as a willing which functions as the cause of the motion of a hand, and hence, no such thing as an act, as so analyzed. If it should happen to be the case—and no equivalence of meanings can provide any reason for supposing it is not—that there never has been such a thing as a motion of a hand caused by someone's willing that motion, then the logical equivalence embodied in this analysis, being nothing more than an equivalence of meanings, would not be affected in the least. In order for the analysis to have any value, we need somehow to find out whether the concept of an act, as so analyzed, is *also* the concept that we apply to certain familiar events, such as the motions I make with my hands, that we do in fact regard as acts. If it is not then we shall not have learned anything about acts—that is, about those things we do in fact regard as acts—but will have learned only that a certain pair of expressions has, or is to be regarded as having, the same meaning in some language. This is, of course, a difficulty with any logical analysis; namely, that it rests upon certain beliefs which can be false.

In fact, of course, those who are tempted to give such a logical analysis of an act simply *assume* that the concept so analyzed is in fact the one that applies to what we ordinarily consider to be the act of moving one's hand, or that these events that we consider to be acts *are* acts, *as thus analyzed.* They thus imagine that they have gained some insight into human activity. But this is precisely what has to be shown before anyone can suppose himself to have learned anything about acts by such a procedure.

Material Equivalences

Similarly, we can supply a material but non-logical equivalence to (1) simply by setting forth *any* statement that is true, given only that (1) is true, or any statement that is false provided (1) is false. For instance, assuming that (1) is true, we can cite as materially equivalent the statement that the moon is round, since this is also true. It is obvious, however, that no such material equivalence is of any use to us whatsoever as an analysis of anything.

Nomical Equivalences

Finally, we can attempt to supply what I have called a "nomical" equivalence to (1) by giving some condition or set of conditions the truth of which is necessary and sufficient for the truth of (1) but which are nevertheless logically independent of (1) and such as to allow counter-factual inferences. An analysis of this kind would be such that we could, as in the case of material equivalences, affirm (1) and deny the analysis, or vice versa, without contradiction but not without error. Unlike material equivalences, however, but like logical equivalences, we could infer that if (1) *were* false, the nomically equivalent statements would be false too, and vice versa.

Such an analysis or proposed equivalence to (1) would be a statement of the form, "My hand moved, and this motion was caused by an event of the kind x," wherein x stands for some mental or physical event, but wherein there would be no logical contradiction in asserting (1) and denying this statement, or vice versa. This is, of course, the only kind of analysis that can be of any interest in shedding light on the concept of an act, but it seems apparent that such an analysis simply cannot ever be given, for either of the following two reasons.

In the first place, x must be either a mental or a physical event, (assuming this distinction to be clear, as of course it is not). If it is a physical event—which we might define as something discernible in principle to observation, for example, a nerve impulse—then the analysis is worthless because it will always be perfectly possible that the statement proposed as an analysis is true while (1) is false. It will always be perfectly possible, in other words, that my hand moves as a result of the occurrence of that physical event x within me, which we can suppose to have been brought about by an electrical impulse, drug, or whatnot, but that I did not move it, or have anything to do with its moving. If, on the other hand, we suppose x to be a mental event, such as the event consisting of the occurrence within me at a certain time of a certain volition, desire, or whatnot, then again the analysis will be worthless for the same as well as an additional reason. For again, it will always be possible that my hand moves as a result of the occurrence of that mental event x within me, but that x was itself brought about by an electrical impulse, drug, or whatnot, such that the movement of the hand was in no way anything that I performed or was in any way responsible for. The stipulation that x must be something "mental" does not, obviously, preclude this possibility at all, for mental events, if they are events at all, can have extraneous causes no less than can physical ones. If, furthermore, x is allowed to stand only for mental events, then it will always be possible that (1) is true while the statement proposed as an analysis of it is false; or in other words, that I move my hand, even though x does *not* occur.

This seems to be the case no matter what mental event, class of these, or disjunction of these *x* is allowed to stand for. It cannot, of course, be *proved* that not all acts are caused by mental events of one kind or another, but there is in any case no evidence whatever that they are. Philosophers who are *convinced* that they are, rest this conviction on their assent to such logical equivalences of meanings as we have considered, scarcely noting that no such logical equivalences can lend the slightest support to an empirical claim for the existence of anything at all.

The second reason that no such nomical analysis is possible is that the event for which we allow *x* to stand, whether this be mental or physical, will always have to be understood as something that I *do* if the analysis is to have any plausibility at all. That is, we shall have to say that in moving my hand I contracted a certain muscle, or that I performed a certain hand-moving volition, or that I choose to move my hand, and so on. So long as we can imagine that some such event occurred, perhaps as a result of being artificially induced in me by electrical impulses or drugs, and that it thus occurred in spite of me and that I had nothing to do with bringing it about, there is hardly any temptation to regard its occurrence, together with the occurrence of the bodily motion in question, as sufficient for the truth of (1). Since, however, it is the very concept of doing something or of performing an act that the analysis is intended to make clear, we get absolutely nowhere by reintroducing that very concept into our analysis.

How an Important
Question Is Begged

Here the important point emerges that no analysis of this third kind, and hence no informative analysis at all, can even be sought without presupposing the truth of a certain metaphysical thesis; namely, that all events, including those that are the acts of men, are causally determined by other events—a presupposition that would obviously beg the very question likely to be at issue in any discussion of the nature of human activity. That anyone who happens to defend a thesis of indeterminism should be unable to give an informative analysis of an act is therefore no difficulty or source of embarrassment for him. It is only a logical consequence of his position. We are thus entitled to conclude that one can hope to give an informative analysis of an act, as opposed to inventing or supplying synonymous expressions, only if he is willing to assume that all human conduct is causally determined by certain events within the agent. The reasonableness of such an assumption can never be shown by *giving* such an analysis, however, for the analysis itself will of necessity carry with it any implausibility in that assumption, nor can any doubt ever be thrown on the denial of that assumption by the mere failure to give such an analysis, this being entailed by that very denial.

I have cited plenty of reasons for doubting that any mental events causally sufficient for the occurrence of other events which are regarded as acts exist. It hardly follows, of course, that the thesis of determinism is false, for it is always possible that someone might someday actually find such events, as contrasted with merely defining them or giving them names, which has been amply done. The foregoing reflections should, however, sweep away what has seemed to many thinkers a good reason for thinking the thesis of determinism true; namely, the belief, arising from the plausibility of certain definitions and analyses, that certain mental events which are the invariable causes of acts have been found in men's experiences, that they have been described and are well known. All that is well known in this area is the meanings of certain words, while the alleged things those words are supposed to name remain as elusive as ever.

Part Two

Action

and

Purpose

8

The Description of Human Action

While there seems to be no informative way to analyze the concept of a human action which is not at least question-begging, this does not preclude describing actions and thus trying to discover what it is that distinguishes actions from everything else, and this seems to me the more promising approach. Such descriptions can be philosophically useful if we can derive certain things from them which are significant in themselves and such that anyone who believes himself to be active, in the sense suggested by these descriptions, will also be likely to accept what is derived from them.

Description and Imputation

We must first, however, consider the possibility that the concept of human action is not a descriptive concept to begin with, and hence that there is nothing uniquely describable about actions. The presupposed distinction between those items of human behavior which are actions and those which are not may not, in other words, be a real or natural distinction. It may, on the contrary, be a merely relative distinction men draw for practical purposes—like the distinction between things which are and are not tools, for instance, or things which are and are not food, and so on. In asserting that a given object is a tool, one is not strictly *describing* the object, but rather *imputing* something to it—namely, utility as an instrument for fabrication and the like. Similarly, in asserting of a given specimen of human behavior that it is someone's act, it may be that one is not describing anything at all, but is rather imputing something to that person, namely, responsibility for the behavior in question.

This is an immensely appealing theory, for it offers hope of explaining a perfectly common and familiar distinction, which has always been easily drawn by common sense, without any excursus into metaphysics at all. In saying of some specimens of behavior that they are acts and of others that they are not acts, we are not, according to this conception, calling attention to any inherent differences in the respective behaviors at all, and it is hard, in fact, to see how we could be doing that, since the specimens of behavior may be identical so far as anyone can see. Nor are we calling attention to any differences in the sources of such behavior, since those sources, too, may be identical, so far as anyone can see. Instead we are, on this view, drawing a distinction which is relative to certain purposes, such as the purpose of fixing blame and so on. In calling certain of a man's motions, along with their resultant states, his acts, then, and thus distinguishing them from events that are not acts, such as reflex and spasmodic motions and things resulting from these, we are only, on this view, asserting that such behavior and its consequences did occur and that a certain man is responsible for that behavior and its consequences. To say that he is responsible, however, does not describe him, but rather ascribes or imputes something to him, namely, responsibility. We do not *find* something in him which we then label his responsibility for his behavior, but rather, *impute* that responsibility to him, and thereby *invest* his behavior with the status of an act.

Apart from its promise of making short shrift of metaphysical difficulties, it cannot be denied that this view does fit quite nicely the actual distinctions of responsibility that men make. In the atmosphere of enlightened morality we do in fact hold men responsible only for such things as represent or are the causal consequences of their own activity, and this is obviously nothing more than an analytical consequence of the theory before us.

Yet such a view cannot be right. It may well be, as I believe it is, that responsibility is something that is imputed to men for certain practical purposes of morality and law, not something discovered, and hence to say that a man is responsible for something is not to describe him. And while it is doubtless also true that behavior for which a man is responsible and that for which he is not accords, more or less, with behavior which does and behavior which does not represent his acts, this latter distinction simply cannot be drawn in terms of the former one without getting things backward.

In the first place, it is not true that responsibility is always imputed to a man for his acts. There are certain acts which men undoubtedly perform for which nevertheless no imputation of responsibility can sensibly be made, simply because those acts have no practical or moral significance. Between two twitches of my eyelid, for instance, one of which I voluntarily make and the other of which is spasmodic, it makes no sense to say that I am responsible for the one but not the other, assuming neither of them to have any practical consequences either for myself or others. Or, if someone were to insist that I am responsible for the one but not the other, he clearly would have to know which motion was voluntary and which spasmodic, thus rendering any distinction in terms of an imputation impossible.

Moreover, it is quite possible and even quite common to be *mistaken* in holding a man responsible for some act, whether morally, legally, or otherwise, whereas this would be logically impossible if his being responsible consisted merely in his having this imputed to him. The ascription of responsibility is in this respect like the ascription of any common predicate—not like the ascription of those predicates sometimes embodied in so-called "performatory utterances." Some things, in other words, are made true simply by virtue of being declared true under certain specifiable conditions. When a preacher, for example, under certain conditions declares a certain man and woman to be man and wife, his pronouncement automatically renders them such. He could not, assuming certain formal conditions to have been fulfilled, be mistaken, for he is not *discovering* that they are married, but declaring them to be such. Most statements are not, however, in any similar way a guarantee of their own truth. A judge, for example, might under certain formally satisfactory conditions pronounce a man guilty, and still be mistaken, despite the fact that the man in question does thereby acquire a certain social and legal status of guilt. This ascription of guilt is consistent with his being, and subsequently being discovered to be, quite innocent. Now the imputation of responsibility is plainly like the imputation of guilt in this respect. The latter, in fact, presupposes the former, since no man can be deemed guilty of anything without thereby being deemed responsible for it. And the imputation of responsibility is to that extent unlike the preacher's ascription of matrimonial status; as in the ascription of guilt it can be misapplied in the same way, even when all formal conditions have been met. It is quite possible to hold a man responsible for some item of his behavior for which he is in fact not responsible. Some further condition is needed, then, beyond the mere imputation of responsibility to him, however solemnly and formally this might be done. And, it seems obvious, the further necessary condition is that he must actually have done that for which he is deemed responsible, that the behavior in question must be his act and not mere bodily behavior of his with which he had nothing to do. This the mere imputation of responsibility does not take into account, however, for the proposition that the act was his follows immediately from his being held responsible for it.

And finally, this view would render any statement to the effect that some man was not responsible for some act of his a self-contradiction, which it nevertheless plainly is not. A child, for instance, does many things for which he is in no sense responsible, and so do many adults, there being innumerable excusing conditions under which the imputation of responsibility for a given act is withheld, but which nevertheless have no tendency to cancel the judgment that the behavior in question was an act. Now one can, of course, simply refuse to regard any behavior as an act except under those indefinitely numerous conditions in which he is willing to impute some sort of responsibility to its author, but this would simply obliterate the distinction with which we began, and which it was the purpose of this theory to make clear. There is an absolute difference, of which one can sometimes be quite certain within himself, between those bodily motions which are one's acts and those which are not, and it is a distinction that each of us can often draw quite independently of incurring responsibility of any kind. That I should move my eyelid, on the one hand, and that it should similarly move as the result of a nervous twitch over which I have no control, on the other, is a distinction of which I can sometimes be perfectly aware. It would be absurd, though, to suppose that such a distinction arises as the result of some non-descriptive imputation, for neither motion is apt to have the least significance which would call for the imputation of anything.

The Description
of Human Activity

I shall for the remainder of this chapter, then, first set forth some simple examples of fairly typical but exceedingly simple actions, and then make some fairly obvious observations upon them which will eventually turn out to have considerable significance. In describing these activities I shall not resort to recondite data, allegedly gleaned from some special method of observation, such as introspection. I shall instead describe them in the simplest, most straightforward manner possible, trying to be influenced by no philosophical preconceptions. My examples of actions will be as simple and unexciting as possible in order not to be diverted by extraneous factors, and at the same time as diverse as I can make them. With such examples before us we can then declare activity to be precisely what we *find* it to be in such examples, rather than what any customary uses of words, definitions of terms, or metaphysical presuppositions might suggest it ought to be.

Four Examples

Suppose, first, that I am asked to hold up one finger and, having done so, to move it to the right or the left, either way. I comply by moving it (say) to the right. Now there is no doubt but that I have done something, that I have performed a simple act, there being probably nothing in the world of which I could be more certain. It is equally obvious, however, that I do not know how I know this or what makes me so certain, other than my awareness of the fact itself.

Secondly, we suppose that I am in a physician's office and am told to hold my breath for about a half minute, which I do. Again, there is no doubt that in complying with this instruction I have done something, and something that required some effort.

Thirdly, let us suppose that I am approached by a police officer and asked to relate whatever I remember having seen and heard in the vicinity of my neighbor's house the day before. Suppose that, after a bit of groping about, I am able to recall and reproduce the tune I heard my neighbor whistling all afternoon. Here again I have done something, and something that required a certain effort of recall.

And finally, suppose that I am being carried up a ski lift, and as the height becomes frightening my hands perspire and I grasp the seat tightly. Now it is obvious that in perspiring I am not acting, that this bodily change is simply an automatic reaction with which I have nothing to do and cannot control. My grasping the seat, on the other hand, does seem to be something I do, or an act of mine. Had I been convinced that I would receive an electric shock by so doing, I perhaps would have refrained. I do not, however, refrain from perspiring, even though convinced that the lift is quite safe. Even though I should be convinced that by perspiring I shall receive a strong shock, I perspire anyway, and cannot help it.

From such examples which are diverse in content but are examples of human activity we can derive certain suggestions about the nature of activity itself. We probably cannot concoct any significant definition or analysis of an act from them, but we can make some instructive statements about them.

Acts and Commands

The first and most obvious thing to note is that acts, such as those I have described, are things which can without any incongruity be commanded, requested, or forbidden. Indeed, all but the last were performed in response to a specific request. This last act, too—that of grasping my seat on the ski lift—might without any absurdity have been commanded or forbidden. There is, on the other hand, a fundamental absurdity in requesting, commanding, or forbidding anything which is not an act. Thus, while it is not absurd that riders should be requested to grasp their seats, it would be absurd to request them to perspire or to refrain from perspiring. And this, it should be noted, is *not* because they cannot help doing it, but because it is something with which they have nothing to do in the first place and is accordingly no act. Grasping the seat is not just something my hands do, but something that I do with my hands. Perspiring, in contradistinction, was something my hands did, not something I did with my hands. Yet it would be absurd to command my hands to perspire—and not just because they have no eyes or ears or minds with which to perceive the command, but just because hands are not agents. They are not things that act, but things with which an agent acts. Perspiring, like the motions of one's heart but unlike certain of the motions of one's hands, is something that either does or does not occur, depending upon the circumstances. Except by altering those circumstances one is powerless either to make it happen or to prevent it. This is not true, however, of the acts I have described. Thus, it is not true that the motion of my finger, or my recalling events of the past, are things that either occur or do not occur, depending upon the circumstances, and such that, except by altering those circumstances, I am powerless either to make them occur or prevent them from occurring. My moving my finger does not consist in removing obstacles to its motion, nor does my holding it still ordinarily involve counteracting such forces as are already tending to move it. Its motion, or motionlessness, are sometimes things that are in my own power to control, rather than things that are, like my perspiring, simply up to the circumstances in which I find myself and over which, given those circumstances, I have no power.

This does not mean, of course, that nothing is an act unless done in obedience to a request or command or omitted in response to a prohibition, for obviously many things are done that were never commanded. Nor does it mean that, having been requested or commanded, an act is thereupon done, for many things are done in violation of commands. In fact an act need not even be something which *could* be done, if commanded, or avoided, if forbidden. In my last example, for instance, we can suppose that my timidity was such that, try as I might, I could not refrain from grasping the seat; yet there can be no doubt that in doing so I, and not merely my hands, did something. There is a certain absurdity in commanding one to perspire, unless this is a command to do something *else,* such as to exercise vigorously, in order to induce perspiration. There is no similar absurdity in commanding one to move his finger, or to grasp one's seat, and so on, and such commands are not commands to do something *else* in order that more remote events should follow. The contrast here is between things one does and things that just happen to him—not between things which he can and things which he cannot help doing. If I cannot help doing something then it follows that I do it, whereas if something merely happens to me it follows that I do not do it, even if we suppose I could have avoided it. Hence the absurdity in commanding or forbidding me to perspire does not result simply from the fact that I cannot refrain from perspiring, but rather, that my perspiring was no act of mine and not strictly anything that I did, but just something that my hands "did," or rather, underwent. Only acts of an agent can be requested, commanded, or forbidden, and even though a given act should be such that, given the circumstances in which one finds himself, it is impossible for him to do it, or impossible to leave it undone, it is still not absurd, though it may be unreasonable, to command or forbid it, for it is nonetheless an act. What cannot without absurdity be commanded or forbidden is simply that which is not an act, and such a command or prohibition would be absurd, not because it would be "expecting too much" and would on that account be unreasonable, but simply because it would be nonsensical.

Here it must not be suggested, as it so often is by those who have given little thought to the matter, that an act is a bodily motion that can be caused by a command or request, or that it is something that an agent can be caused to do by a command or request. In my first example I moved my finger to the right in response to a request that I move it one way or the other. I would have complied with the same request no less by moving it to the left, though this assuredly would have been a different act. Had my moving it as I did been caused by that request then it would follow that, the request having been made, I could not have failed to move it, nor moved it otherwise than I did. There is absolutely no reason whatever for supposing this true. There was nothing at all about the request or in the situation itself that posed the slightest difficulty to my moving it other than I did, or to my not moving it at all. If I am startled by a noise behind me, and jump in response, then we can say that my bodily motion was in the clearest sense caused by that sudden noise. Given precisely those circumstances, I could not help jumping as I did. It was nothing that I could decline to do, or do otherwise. A request or command, however, does not act upon me in any way comparable to this. I do not hear a request and then find my body moving in response, nor do I just find myself moving some part of my body in response. Having been requested to do something, it is then at least sometimes up to me whether or not to comply and if so, just how.

Acts That Are Not Bodily Motions

The second thing to note in my examples is that an act, and even an act involving overt behavior, need not be a change, but can be the absence or cessation of change. Thus, in the second example my act consisted of my *not* breathing over an interval of time. Nor would it do to say that this act consisted of my stopping my breathing, and that it was therefore a simple change of state, for it does not take a half minute to stop breathing and yet my act was something that persisted throughout that half minute. During all and any part of that time I can truly be said to have been doing something other than merely ceasing to breathe; namely, to be holding my breath. Nor, obviously, does one express the fact that I held my breath by just saying that during that interval my breathing ceased, for this would be true even if I were not then holding my breath—in case, for instance, I had been made breathless by a momentary paralysis or a blow. Nor, of course, would it be true to say that during that half minute I was really doing nothing, or simply refraining from doing something, regardless of the fact that what I was doing involved no overt bodily change through that interval. In holding my breath for a half minute I did something that required a considerable effort before I was finished. This can be expressed only by saying, not merely that I or my body ceased to be breathing for awhile, which expresses only part of the fact, but by saying that I *held* my breath for awhile.

Unobservable Acts

We should note, in the third place, that an act, even though it is something that occurs at a definite time and does not involve merely the cessation of change, need not be anything that is overt or observable. Thus in my third example I recalled a certain tune, and such recalling is not a change that anyone ever observes in any ordinary way. Another example would be attending to something, which is sometimes accomplished only with difficulty but which need not involve observable behavior. Nor can it be claimed that such changes do not represent acts, for we have the same reason for saying they do that we have for saying that certain of my bodily motions represent acts; namely, that more is involved in them than their mere occurrence. Thus, in saying that I recalled a certain tune it is not enough to say merely that the tune occurred to me. It would have occurred to me had I simply been reminded of it, by overhearing it, for example. There is no difficulty in drawing the distinction within oneself between the two cases. In recalling it I did not simply remind myself of it in any ordinary sense—I did not produce it, in order that I might thus hear it and thereby be reminded of it, for instance, the way someone else might have produced it in order to remind me of it. Moreover, a certain effort of recall was required, but it was no muscular or physical effort. This element of effort is expressed metaphorically by my "groping about," but what a metaphor this is! It does not involve the straining or tensing of any muscles, or of my brain or nerves, or of any part of my body at all. In my example I perform an overt act as well, to be sure, for I reproduce audibly the tune I have recalled, but the act of recalling is quite separable from this. I might, from the desire to protect my neighbor, have declined to reproduce what I had recalled.

We get the same result, it should be noted, if we apply here the observation made above; namely, that acts, and only acts, are things concerning which it makes sense to speak of their being commanded, requested, or forbidden. Thus, there is no absurdity in asking someone to recall something, or to attend to something, and one can comply with such a request without saying what he has recalled or attended to. Similarly, there is no absurdity in asking someone just to think about something, such as the probable consequences of a proposed policy, or to make up his mind about something or come to a decision. One's failure to report his reflections or his decision, or even to act upon a decision once made, would be no proof that the request had not been fulfilled. Overt actions are only guides to a man's thoughts and intentions and are never identical with them, particularly since one sometimes conceals or dissimulates.

The general significance of all this, of course, is that the concept of an act cannot, as is so often supposed, be understood in terms of overt behavior together with such covert "behavior" as intending, deciding, and the like, for two obvious reasons. The first is that not all acts involve any overt behavior, and the second is that such concepts as intending and deciding are themselves sometimes used as concepts of activity. Any analysis of an act in terms of overt behavior together with certain "subjective" or "inner" changes must, therefore, be at least sometimes circular when applied to observable actions, and false when applied to those that are not observable.

The Essential Reference
to an Agent

The fourth and most important thing to note is that there must always be an essential reference to an agent in the description of any act. Thus, in my first example we cannot say merely that my finger moved, but rather, that *I* moved it. In the second, we cannot say merely that my breathing ceased, but that I held my breath. In the third we cannot say merely that a certain tune occurred to me, but that I recalled it. In the last example, to be sure, we need not say that I perspired, for we can express the whole fact here by saying, instead, that my hands perspired, or equivalently, that perspiration developed on my hands. But this is precisely because my perspiring is *not* an act, and is nothing that I do. It is but a physical change of my body, as are my heartbeats and the growth of my hair.

It is of the utmost importance to note that this essential reference to some agent as the performer of an act is required, not just to make clear that the act is peculiarly his, but precisely to convey that it is an act. Concerning anything whatever one must in some way or another refer to me in order to make the point that the thing in question is mine rather than another person's, but that is not the point that is being made here. The point is rather that in describing anything as an act there must be an essential reference to an agent as the performer or author of that act, not merely in order to know whose act it is, but in order even to know that it is an act.

Another way of making this important point is this. If we consider the perspiration of my hands or the beating of my heart we can adequately describe what these consist in, given that we know enough about physiology, without mentioning me at all. We can say, for instance, that at a certain time perspiration develops on a certain hand that is located at a certain place, that this is the result of the contraction of certain sweat glands which are activated by adrenaline, and so on, with whatever further detail we please. We shall not, to be sure, convey the fact that it is *my* hand that perspired until we find some way of referring to me, but we shall nevertheless convey completely the fact that it was the perspiration of a hand. If we compare this with some act, such as the act of moving my hand, then however detailed we make the description, we shall not describe it as an act until we state that some agent has caused it. It need not have been me, even though it was my hand that moved, since another person can grasp my hand and move it for me. If we wish to say whose act it was we must refer to the agent who caused it, but even prior to that we must in one way or another say that it was caused by some agent, merely to convey the idea that it was an act. Nothing of this sort is called for in the description of those events which are not acts. Another person can move my hand for me, in which case it is his act and not mine despite the fact that it was my hand that moved, but no other person can perspire for me, or perspire my hand for me, nor is this even anything I can do myself, it being no act in the first place.

It is tempting at this point to suppose that this reference to an agent in the description of any act is not essential, that it is perhaps elliptical or even misleading, but in any case no more necessary than a reference to an agent as the cause, say, of perspiration. Thus, instead of speaking of this or that agent doing something, we might convey the fact more accurately by saying that something within him, or something intimately connected with him, or perhaps even some part of him, was the cause of the change in question. We shall see shortly that, far from being a more accurate and less misleading way of describing an act, such a description would entail that the alleged act was in reality not an act, and could hardly, therefore, provide an accurate and non-misleading description of an act. For now, however, we need only note how immensely implausible such a suggestion would be if applied to such an act as is described in my third example. When after some groping I am finally able to recall a certain tune, it is quite impossible to believe that *all* that has happened here is that this memory was caused in me by the occurrence of something else—such as, for instance, my willing to remember that tune—and that it is only because it was *that* sort of thing that caused my memory that we can say that it was *my* act of recalling something, whereas if anything *else* has caused the memory then we would have to say that it was just a case of being reminded. If I am not the cause of my own act of recalling something, then it is no act of mine in the first place, but only another instance of being reminded of something, and it matters not in the least whether the "real cause" is something outside me or something within me. If, to be sure, I recall the tune only by doing something else with the view to reminding myself of it—by playing a phonograph record, for instance—then the immediate cause of my recollection is, indeed, something other than myself; namely, the sounds of the record. But in such a case I am not simply recalling a tune. I am, on the contrary, doing something else in order to be reminded of the tune, and my act is no simple act of recalling, but one of making arrangements adequate for reminding me.

There is, then, an inherent implausibility in the suggestion that, whenever I can truly say that I am doing something, this ought to be understood to mean that something not identical with myself is the cause of whatever is then being done. The implausibility of this leaps up when the act in question is some such inward act as recalling, attending, or making up one's mind about something, for here it is quite impossible to see what this other "real" cause could ever be. Besides this implausibility, we have no basis whatever in experience for saying that any such real causes, other than an agent himself, even exist. When, for instance, in response to a request I am able to recall a certain tune without making any simple or elaborate arrangements, like playing records, for reminding myself of it, all that I am *aware* of is that I am groping for the tune and that as a result of this groping I finally get it. This sort of experience is nothing like idly waiting for something to remind me of it, or for something to occur that will evoke it within me. Even to speak of my "groping" is somewhat misleading, being clearly no more than a metaphor. There is really nothing that I am actually doing that could be properly described as groping. We can, indeed, say that I *intentionally* recall it; but all this means is that I do recall it, knowing what I am doing or aiming to do, and having some purpose in doing it.

Agents as Causes

There must, moreover, not only be this reference to myself in distinguishing my acts from all those things that are not acts, but it must be a reference to myself as an active being. Another perfectly natural way of expressing this notion of my activity is to say that, in acting, I make something happen, I cause it, or bring it about. Now it does seem odd that philosophers should construe this natural way of expressing the matter as really meaning, not that I, but rather some event, process, or state not identical with myself should be the cause of that which is represented as my act. It is plain that, whatever I am, I am never identical with any such event, process, or state as is usually proposed as the "real cause" of my act, such as some intention or state of willing. Hence, if it is really and unmetaphorically true, as I believe it to be, that I sometimes cause something to happen, this would seem to entail that it is *false* that any event, process, or state not identical with myself should be the real cause of it. But it is not, in fact, hard to see why philosophers should want to insist that these natural ways of expressing the matter really mean something quite different from what they seem to mean; namely, that it has been the firm conviction of most philosophers for generations that in the case of any event that occurs, another *event* must be at least part of its cause. If, accordingly, it is true that I am the cause of my acts, as it evidently is, then in view of this principle we must suppose that the real cause is some event intimately associated with me—and then, of course, the chase is on to find it or, failing that, at least to give it a name and create a semblance of having found it. The alternative I urge is that I am sometimes the cause of my own actions, that such an assertion is neither incomplete nor metaphorical and hence has no "real" meaning different from, much less inconsistent with, itself as it stands. In that case, however, we must conclude that the word "cause" in such contexts has not the ordinary meaning of a certain relationship between events, but has rather the older meaning of the efficacy or power of an agent to produce certain results. This idea can be otherwise expressed by saying that an agent is something that originates things, produces them, or brings them about. It might be wished that some clear definition or analysis of this idea of agency could be given, in place of merely synonymous expressions, but we have already seen that this cannot be done, and we have also seen why. To give an analysis of agency or of the sense in which an agent is the cause of his actions would amount to giving an analysis of an act, an analysis which would of necessity presuppose the truth of a metaphysical presupposition that is not only dubious, but probably false.

The Initiation of Change

The final point to be made concerning simple acts of the sort I have illustrated, and the one presenting the greatest possibility of misunderstanding, is that nothing can be represented as a simple act of mine unless I am the initiator or originator of it. This means that if there are conditions causally sufficient for the occurrence of any given change, which are nevertheless not sufficient for my causing it to occur, then that change cannot be my act. If, on the other hand, there are conditions causally sufficient for my doing something, and hence conditions which are such that, given those conditions, I cannot refrain from doing it, then, since the fact that I do something or cause some change to occur logically entails that the change occurs, there are in that sense conditions sufficient for its occurrence. Thus, in terms of the simplest example, if there are antecedent conditions sufficient for, say, my hand and certain of its muscles moving but not causally sufficient for my moving it, then it cannot be true that I move it. If, on the other hand, conditions are causally sufficient for my moving it, then those same conditions are sufficient for its moving, but it is nevertheless true that I do move it. The points involved here can be elicited in terms of some of my previous examples.

Suppose, for example, that just as I am about to move my finger in response to a request that I do so someone grasps it and moves it for me, either in just the way that I would have moved it had I been left alone or perhaps in some other way. No one would suggest that I had moved my finger, for that motion was not initiated by me but by someone else. Nor is the situation altered if we suppose that this motion is brought about, not by external coercion of another agent, but by some internal cause. Had my finger moved in response to a nervous spasm, for instance, and even had it thus moved in precisely the way I would have moved it had the spasm not occurred, then its motion would still be no doing of mine, in spite of the fact that it might look as though it were. Nor, again, is the situation altered if we baptize such an internal cause with a special name, like "a volition." If such an event is, simply by virtue of its occurrence, causally sufficient for my finger's moving, then that motion cannot be represented as any act of mine. It is nothing but the causal consequence of something happening inside me. Here one is apt to pause, and suppose that the situation *is* altered by introducing such special, perhaps "mental" internal events, but this, I believe, is only because one is apt to think of these internal events—volitions or whatnot—as things of my own doing. That is, one is apt to suppose, not merely that such internal events occur, but that I cause them to occur, or initiate them. This would amount to saying, however, that I am the cause of my finger's motion by virtue of the fact that I am the initiator of some cause of its motion—and it is obvious that this amounts to no denial of what I am maintaining. It only renders it more complicated. If I can initiate those covert, internal changes upon which the motion of my finger is alleged to depend, then there is no reason why I might not initiate the motion of my finger itself, and we can therefore get on without introducing any such internal causes at all.

To cite another of my examples, suppose that just as I am on the verge of recalling a certain tune, after considerable groping for it, I am suddenly reminded of it by overhearing someone whistling it. We can easily suppose that I am thus reminded of it in exactly the way I would have been had I not been trying to recall it at all. Now we cannot, I think, say that my recalling was pointless and wasted. Nor, again, is this situation altered if we supposed that I was reminded of it, not by another person, but from something arising within me with which I had nothing to do. This kind of example, while a bit odd in some respects, is quite useful in throwing light on the things at issue, for probably no one would even be tempted to suppose that my recalling something, as contrasted with being reminded of it, consists simply of being reminded of it by something within me, whether this be called an intention or a volition or whatever—unless, of course, this is only another way of saying, quite innocuously, that I do intentionally or voluntarily recall it.

Agency and Determinism

The foregoing observations do not entail, as they might at first seem to, that I cannot be the initiator of my own acts unless those acts are causally undetermined. There is at least one kind of circumstance in which this is not true; namely, in case there are conditions causally sufficient, not only for the occurrence of the event in question, but for my initiating it. Suppose, for example, that I am the cause of some change, such as a motion of my finger. Suppose further, however, that there are conditions causally sufficient for my doing just that—such as, among other things, my conviction that only by so doing can I save my life. Now since the fact that I move my finger logically entails that it moves, it follows that, there being conditions causally sufficient for my moving my finger, these same conditions are causally sufficient for its moving. We cannot in such a case conclude, though, that this motion is no act of mine—for by hypothesis, it is. In fact we have in the last of my previous four examples an act of just this sort, for the description of that act suggests that my timidity and fright were sufficient to cause me to grasp my seat tightly. Yet it can hardly be doubted that this was something I did, and not, like the perspiration of my hands, simply a change in the state of my hands with which I had nothing to do. Of course, one *might* suppose that it was not an act but only an involuntary reflex or reaction of my nerves and muscles, but it is certainly not obvious that we must suppose this, even though we should assume that it was an act that I could not avoid performing.

The point of these reflections is that there is nothing in the concept of agency, as such, to entail that any events must be causally undetermined, and in that sense "free," in order for some of them to be the acts of agents. Indeed, it might well be that everything that ever happens, happens under conditions which are such that nothing else could happen, and hence that in the case of every act that any agent ever performs there are conditions causally sufficient for his doing just what he does. This is the claim of determinism, but it does not by itself require us to deny that there are agents who sometimes initiate their own acts. What is entailed by this concept of agency, according to which men are the initiators of their own acts, is that for anything to count as an act there must be an essential reference to an agent as the cause of that act, whether he is, in the usual sense, caused to perform it or not. The concept of agency is, therefore, perfectly compatible with the thesis of universal causal determinism to which one might at first want to oppose it. It would not, however, be consistent with any claim to the effect that every event can be fully understood and explained in terms of certain conditions sufficient for its occurrence and without any reference to an agent, or with a claim to the effect that, there being conditions sufficient for everything that ever happens, agents therefore have nothing to do with their acts and are never the causes of them. There is, however, nothing in human experience to render such claims as these plausible in the first place.

It should be added, however, that while the concept of agency as it has been thus far elicited is logically compatible with the thesis of universal determinism, that is, with the thesis that there are antecedent conditions sufficient for everything that ever happens, including everything that an agent ever does, it hardly entails such a thesis. The claim that an agent is sometimes the initiator of his acts and that there is always some essential reference to an agent in the conception of any event as an act is obviously compatible with the supposition that there may *not* be antecedent conditions sufficient for an agent's doing everything he ever does. The concept of agency, or the initiation of actions by agents, is compatible both with the assertion of determinism and with its denial, leaving entirely open the question whether every agent is caused to do everything that he does. If something causes me to do everything that I do, then my acts are all causally determined, but this can hardly entail that I do not do them. This would be entailed only by the claim that everything that happens to me can be explained in terms of antecedent causal conditions without any reference to me as an agent. While the concept of an act as something that is initiated by an agent is thus compatible with the assertion of determinism, it is nevertheless worth noting that it renders doubtful most of traditional grounds for belief in determinism—such as, for instance, the claim that an act is a change that is caused by a volition or an act of will, or some other internal event.

Action
and Necessary Conditions

A corollary of the foregoing is that, while there doubtless are always necessary conditions for any event that is an act, no set of such conditions can be sufficient for its occurrence except in the secondary sense that they may be sufficient for an agent's performing it. Thus, I cannot move my finger unless the finger is unobstructed, unless it is connected in the normal way to certain muscles, unless it is unparalyzed, and so on; but the satisfaction of all these necessary conditions does not guarantee that my finger moves, nor does the combination of them guarantee that I move it. Something more is required, and that is, simply, that I cause it to move. The temptation here is to say that the further thing required is an act of volition, but this, as we have abundantly seen, is either just false or misleading. If by a volition is meant just the occurrence of a certain event within me which is, together with certain other conditions such as those mentioned, sufficient for my finger's moving, then far from entailing that I move my finger, the assertion that these conditions occur and are together sufficient for my finger's moving entails that, although it moves, I do not move it. It is simply caused to move without my having anything to do with it. But if by a volition is meant an act of will, then the assertion that I perform this act of will in the presence of other conditions that are necessary for its motion does indeed entail that I move my finger, but only by entailing that I do something else—namely, that I perform that act of will. And surely, it cannot *always* be a necessary condition for doing something, that I first do something else—for in that case no action could ever get started, and nothing could ever be done.

Or consider my act of recalling a certain tune. There are, of course, certain necessary antecedent conditions—for instance, I cannot recall a tune that I have never heard, I cannot recall it if I am not awake, or if I have amnesia, and so on. But again, the totality of all such necessary conditions are not sufficient for my recalling it—I can have heard the tune, be awake, have no amnesia, and so on, and still not bother to recall the tune. Something more is needed, and this is, simply, my bringing it before my mind, as contrasted with having it brought to mind—that is, with being reminded of it by a further condition. But all this means, obviously, is that I recall the tune, and this can hardly, except in a trivial and analytic sense, be any necessary condition of my doing so. Here, of course, there is less temptation to say that the further condition needed is that I should will to recall the tune, and that this willing is, together with such other conditions as are necessary for recalling it, sufficient for my recalling it. My willing to recall a certain tune, as contrasted, for example, with my merely wishing that it might somehow come to me, consists of nothing but my recalling it, as contrasted with my being reminded of it. It is not some separable thing that I do, with a view to bringing the tune to my mind, for again, it cannot possibly be true that, in order to do anything, I must always do something else first. If that were true then I could never get started doing anything at all, not even anything so simple as recalling a tune. And if anyone were to suggest that one cannot recall a tune without first willing to recall it, but that he can will to recall it without doing anything else first, then he would be granting that there are *some* things that one can do without doing anything else first. If there are such things, why can we not say that simply recalling a certain tune might be one of them—that this is an act of such simplicity and, sometimes, of such ease of performance that there is, in fact, sometimes nothing whatever that one must do first with a view to doing this?

Simple Acts

This suggests that some acts are complex, such that it makes sense to describe how they are done, while others are simple, such that it makes no sense to describe how they are done. In the case of these one can perhaps be shown, but not told. For instance, tying a square knot is fairly complicated, and someone who does not know how to do it can sensibly ask for directions. Now the directions will consist of a set of simpler acts to be done, the completion of all of which will amount to the completion of the act in question. Note, however, that in rendering such a set of instructions no one would ever include, among the things to be performed, certain acts of will. The directions, if very elaborate, would include instructions to move various fingers in various ways, but they would never include instructions to will that that fingers should move in those ways. That would be ridiculous and could only be understood as a roundabout way of instructing one to move the fingers in the ways indicated. It would never be understood as instructing one to perform certain mental acts with the view to getting the fingers to move in those ways. Nor is the reason for this that an act of will is so simple that no one needs to be told how to do it. Nothing can be simpler than moving one's fingers, and yet no one needs to be told how to do this. If one did not know, he could not possibly be told; he could only be shown.

Tying a square knot, in short, is a complicated act that can be analyzed into simpler acts, such as various prior graspings and turnings, and these can be analyzed into still simpler acts, such as moving one's fingers this way and that. Some of these simpler acts are absolutely simple, however, in the sense that they cannot be broken down or analyzed into any simpler acts at all, even though they may not be simple events. Moving one's finger, for instance, involves moving one's finger muscles, moving one's fingernail, and so on, but these, though distinguishable motions or events, are not distinguishable acts. Now the simplicity of certain acts has to be admitted by everyone, since the only alternative would be to say that *every* act one performs is infinitely complex or consists of infinitely many distinguishable acts, which would be absurd.

The only question is, then, whether such an act as moving one's finger is a simple act, involving no other act, or whether it is complex, like tying a knot. It seems to me that such an act is utterly simple. It is not an act concerning which one would sensibly ask for directions on how to perform it, for no act can be simpler, and direction on how to perform any act can only consist of instructions to perform certain others. To deny this is to affirm that there are acts which are simpler than this, and which are always involved in the performance of it, such as, for instance, acts of willing. Since, however, such simpler acts are in fact never mentioned in any directions on how to do something complex, and since one cannot, in fact, be instructed on how to do something as simple as moving one's finger but can only be shown, it does look like these allegedly simpler acts are unreal, are nothing but the inventions of philosophers who cannot see how one could move a finger without willing it to move, but who somehow see no similar difficulty in supposing that one might will it to move without first doing something similar to that, *ad infinitum*. Having reduced a complex act like tying a knot into actions as simple as moving one's fingers in certain ways, why is there any reason to suppose that there must be acts that are more simple still, such as willing to move one's fingers in those ways? The answer to this cannot be that no act can be performed without doing something else first, for that would entail that no act is simple. And if one were to say that willing to move one's finger is always involved in moving one's finger, but that no further act is involved in such willing, why should we not stop one step before that and say that moving one's finger is a simple act, such that no further act, not even an act of willing, is involved in it? Since we have to stop somewhere, at some act that is simple, why not stop here? There is no philosophical reason why we should not, since it must be granted by anyone that some acts are simple, and the only question is that of which acts these are. Nor does there appear to be any empirical reason why we should not, since no acts simpler than these are ever discovered, or ever even referred to outside of philosophical discussions. We never learn what acts of will are like the way we learn what acts of moving one's fingers are like, namely, by performing such acts. We only learn how to use the locution, "an act of willing," in philosophical arguments, and we learn this through reading philosophical books.

9

Causation by Agents and Causation by Things

In the light of all the foregoing we are now in a much better position to see the great difference between the kind of causation that is involved in the relations between inanimate things and the kind that is attributed to agents.

The difference can be illustrated quite nicely in two such ostensibly similar statements as:

1. This man started that forest fire,

and

2. This match started that forest fire.

Now these two statements are grammatically identical. Indeed, they are in every way identical except for the difference in their grammatical subjects. Yet how utterly different are the ideas they express! The first conveys the idea of an act of an agent and can be construed as quite literally true, though incomplete, as it stands. The second conveys the idea of the ordinary causation of one event by another and is neither complete nor literally true. A match does not *start* a fire, in the sense in which a man might do so. Again, the first statement might, though it need not, constitute an ultimate though incomplete explanation of something, for that chain of events that leads to the forest fire might literally *start* with the man in question. The second statement, however, cannot constitute an ultimate explanation of anything, for the very reason that this chain of events cannot literally *start* with the match. Another way of expressing this would be to say that a match cannot, even with the help of other things such as dry leaves and the like, really start a fire; it can only be *used* to start a fire. A man on the other hand can, with the help of dry leaves, matches, and the like, start a fire, and could not in any similar way be used to start a fire. He could only be exhorted, threatened or otherwise induced to start a fire.

To say that a certain match started a forest fire means something like this: that a certain set of conditions occurred and were causally sufficient for the beginning of that fire that spread to the magnitude of a forest fire, and that some change in this particular match, namely its igniting, was among those conditions—in short, that certain changes in the match figured causally in the occurrence of the fire, such that had they not occurred, the fire would not have occurred either, given only those other conditions that obtained. Now even if these conditions were all spelled out in detail this would not provide any ultimate explanation for the fire, for we would still need to know who ignited the match or, in case no one did, how it came to ignite. It could never be true that the match just ignited all by itself, that it wrought this change in itself, without anyone or anything causing it to ignite.

No similar meaning can be given to the statement that a certain man started a forest fire, for something would thus inevitably be left out. We cannot just say, for example, that a certain set of conditions occurred and were causally sufficient for the beginning of that fire, and that some change in this particular man—such as, for instance, his hand's moving in a certain way while holding a match—was among those conditions. Here, unlike the match case, it is not enough to say that certain changes in the man figured causally in the occurrence of the fire, such that had they not occurred, the fire would not have occurred either, given only the other conditions that obtained. This, though it might be true, would not be enough, for it would be consistent with the *falsity* of the statement that this man started the fire. We can easily suppose, for instance, that it was indeed his hand that so moved, and that the fire would not have occurred had this not happened, and then add to this that his hand was moved, not by him, but by some other person who forcibly moved it. This would entail that it was really this other man who started the fire, that the first man, or rather his hand, was only *used* to help start it. In order to convey the idea that the first man was the one who *started* the fire we have somehow to express the idea that that change in himself, which figured causally in the beginning of the fire, was somehow wrought by him, or that the series of causes and effects that led to the fire was originated by him, and these are conceptions that would make no sense if applied to the match. Unlike the match, the man *can* bring about such a change as a motion of his arm quite by himself. Unlike the match, the man can, using a match, start a fire—he is not himself merely an object that is used to start a fire. A man can literally grasp a match and move his hand to start a fire, but in no similarly literal sense can a match ignite its own head to start a fire. In short, a man is sometimes an agent who originates a change, and is not, like a match, merely a passive object which undergoes change in response to other changes. This is why our first statement, that a certain man started the fire, might constitute an ultimate causal explanation for the fire, though of course not a complete one. We may not know *why* he started all this, but at least we know he started it. In the case of the match, however, it not only is senseless to ask *why* it started all this, we in fact know that it did not. It only, unlike the man, underwent a change, induced by something other than itself, which was causally significant in that series of changes culminating in the forest fire.

Some Significant Entailments

In describing and illustrating acts, and contrasting them with those changes that are not acts, we are continuously hampered by the fact that there is really no better, clearer, or more precise way of saying that an agent does something than just saying, simply, that he does it. In the case of complex acts, like tying a knot or assembling a machine, one can state precisely how an agent performs them by listing in detail the simpler acts he performs. But when one gets to those simpler acts themselves, to acts that are not simply composed of others, there just is no way of stating *how* they are performed, or what they consist of, just because they are simple acts. One can, to be sure, analyze them into numerous constitutent events. One can note, for example, what muscles are involved in moving one's finger and that sort of thing. But there is no clearer or more exact way of saying that a man moves his finger in a certain way, other than just saying that he does. A simple act can be demonstrated or illustrated, but it cannot be described or analyzed. It cannot logically be analyzed in terms of simpler acts, and it cannot be analyzed in terms of changes which are not acts, for such an analysis would be inconsistent with its being an act.

There are, however, certain entailments between statements of acts and those which are descriptive of changes that are not acts, and there is probably no more precise way of eliciting the differences between these than by eliciting these different entailments.

Consider, then, any four statements of the following forms, wherein A designates some agent and *e* some change or bodily motion, each statement thus describing a relatively simple change or an utterly simple act:

1. *e* occurs.
2. Something makes *e* occur.
3. A does *e*.
4. Something makes A do *e*.

Four such statements would be, for example, the following:

1. My finger moves.
2. Something makes my finger move.
3. I move my finger.
4. Something makes me move my finger.

Now no one of these statements is, on any interpretation of A or *e*, equivalent to any of the other three; that is, there are no two which logically entail each other. Some of them are such that, if they are true, then at least one other of the four statements is true too, and some are such that, if they are false, then at least one other of the four statements is false; but not one of them is such that, if it is true, then some other of the four is true too, and if it is false, then that same other statement is false. From this it follows that any four statements of this pattern express four entirely different ideas, and that none of these four ideas is reducible to any of the others or to any combination of the others.

Thus, every statement in such a group entails *every* statement above it, but none of the statements entails *any* of the statements beneath it. From this it follows that no two such statements are equivalent. Any two are such that their truth values can be different.

This can be illustrated as follows. Suppose I move my finger. Then it certainly follows that something makes my finger move, namely, that I do, since this is logically equivalent to saying that I move it. It also of course follows that it moves, since it would be a contradiction to say that I move it but that it nevertheless does not move. But it does *not* follow from this that anything makes me move it. If anyone holds a special philosophical theory according to which no one ever does anything unless there is some cause for his doing it then he can, in the light of that theory, infer that if I move my finger then something makes me move it; but no such inference can be made without such a theory. Again, suppose we know only that my finger moves. Now from this knowledge by itself it cannot be inferred that I moved it, since it might have been moved by something else or even by another person, and hence we cannot infer that anything made me move it. Indeed, we cannot even infer that anything made it move at all. If anyone holds a theory to the effect that in the case of anything that happens there must be something that causes it, then of course he can, in the light of that theory, infer that if my finger moves then there must be something that makes it move. But no such inference follows from the mere fact that my finger moves; the theory is needed in order to get it. Or again, if we suppose that something makes me move my finger, then all the other three statements follow at once, but from the truth of all these other three statements together it does not at all follow that anything makes me move my finger. And finally, from the fact that something makes my finger move we cannot at all infer that I move it, since it might be moved by some other person who grasps it and moves it, or even by some impersonal force, such as a falling stone or whatnot.

These entailments are obviously of enormous significance. They illustrate in the briefest way, but probably better than anything else could, the absolute difference between bodily motions which are and those which are not acts. It is one and the same bodily motion that is involved in all four statements, namely, in our present illustration, a certain finger motion. Yet the four statements are demonstrably different in meaning. If they were not, then their entailments would be different. The third and fourth statements refer, necessarily, to acts, while the first two statements need not; for from the bare facts expressed in these one cannot infer that any act has been performed at all. It is quite possible for one's finger to move, for example, and even for something, such as a nervous spasm or a falling object, to cause it to move, without any agent having anything to do with its moving.

Moreover, it should be noted, it is in the third and fourth of these statements—namely, in those describing acts—that there is an essential reference to an agent as the cause of the motion—no such reference is needed in the other two. It was this reference to an agent, whether explicit or merely understood, that was singled out earlier as essential in any statement descriptive of an act. It is of crucial importance to note again, however, that this reference to an agent is not needed merely in order to make clear *whose* act is being referred to. Its purpose is not merely that of making clear the identity of some person. *That* kind of reference is required in the other two statements as well, and those are not descriptions of acts. For in the first two statements it is explicitly stated that it is *my* finger that moves, and without this reference it might not be clear whether it was my finger or that of another person that is referred to. In those statements descriptive of acts, like the third and fourth, the essential reference to an agent is required, not just to clarify what person the statement refers to, but to express the fact that the change mentioned is an act, or that the agent referred to is the cause of that change. Nothing of that sort is implied by the other two statements which leave the cause unmentioned. We can speculate that the cause of the change was the possessor referred to by *my,* or that perhaps it was some other agent, or possibly an impersonal force. Indeed, the first statement (that my finger moves) is logically consistent with the supposition that there is no cause of this motion at all.

Here there will not, it is hoped, be any temptation to assimilate acts to bodily changes which are not acts by suggesting that the third statement, for example, means nothing more than that something within me, namely, some volitional event, is the cause of my finger's moving. This would make the third statement merely a case of the second, which asserts only that *something* makes my finger move, and would thus eliminate any fundamental and significant difference between those changes which are and those which are not the acts of an agent. To show again the vanity and foolishness of such a suggestion would, however, require the recapitulation of a considerable part of what has already been said.

Caused and Uncaused Events

I have already noted that the first statement is logically compatible with the supposition that there is no cause of my finger's motion. This is not, of course, to suggest that such events ever *are* in fact uncaused. The point is only that *if* there are ever events that have no causes, and if, in particular, the finger motion referred to in the first statement were uncaused, that would not in the least affect the truth of that statement. It is doubtless true that my finger never moves from no cause whatever. Nevertheless, if it were to do so then the first of our four statements would be true, though the second, to the effect that something makes it move, would not, which shows well enough that the first two statements are not logically equivalent.

Another way of making this same point is this. Let us suppose it to be true, as it doubtless is, that if my finger moves, then something causes it to move, that such a change as this cannot occur all by itself, from no cause whatever. Now in case that is true then that supposition, conjoined with our first statement, entails and is entailed by our second statement. The fact nevertheless remains that, however indubitable this supposition may be, the first statement does not entail the second without it.

If, accordingly, we were (somewhat arbitrarily) to define the expression "a free and spontaneous event" as any event that is uncaused, then we could say that the motion of my finger, referred to in the first statement, is a free and spontaneous event in case the first statement is true and the second one false. Of course there may be no such thing as a free and spontaneous event, in this sense, or if there are such events probably finger motions are never among them. If so, then we can be sure that if the first statement is true then the second is true too. Obviously, however, we cannot *decide* whether or not there are free and spontaneous events, or whether finger motions are ever such, by simply *affirming* that if the first statement is true then the second must be true too, because in order to affirm this we would need *first* to know whether or not there are free and spontaneous events, and whether or not the event mentioned in the first statement is such.

Free and Unfree Acts

I have already noted that while the fourth of the statements we are considering, to the effect that something makes me move my finger, certainly entails the third, namely, that I do move it, the reverse of this does not hold. That is, from the fact that I move my finger it clearly does not *follow* that anything makes me move it. Some might indeed want to maintain that the two statements are materially equivalent, such that if either is true the other is true too and if either is false the other is false, but nothing like this is at all implied by the statements themselves. It could, in fact, only be derived from the theory that no one ever does anything unless something makes him do it—a theory that has been quite widely believed by philosophers, but is nevertheless not at all implied by any of our four statements or any combination of them.

If, accordingly, there ever do happen to be any instances of a man doing something without anything causing him to do it, and if, in particular, the act described in the third of our four statements is an instance of such, then this does not at all affect the truth of that third statement. It may be true, as some determinists have maintained, that I cannot move my finger unless something causes me to move it. Nevertheless, if I were to move it, and if it were the case that nothing caused me to move it, the third statement would still be true, though not, of course, the fourth, which indicates that the two statements are by no means equivalent.

Suppose, then, we were to define the expression "a free act," not as an uncaused bodily motion, which would be no act at all, but as an uncaused act. A free act would thus be conceived, not as something that just happens from no cause, but rather, as something that is in fact caused to happen by some agent, but under circumstances which are such that nothing causes him to do it. There are doubtless other and indeed more adequate meanings for the expression "a free act," but that is not to the point, since I am not here inquiring into the true and proper meaning of this or any other expression.

Now if we do so define "a free act," then we can say that the idea expressed in the third of our four statements is that of a free act just in case that statement is true and the fourth statement false. It is as simple as that. There might, to be sure, be no such thing as a free act, as thus defined, in which case we can be sure that the third statement cannot be true unless the fourth is true also. The point remains that we cannot *decide* whether or not there are free acts simply by *affirming*, as ever so many philosophers have in effect done, that if statements of the form of our third are true then corresponding statements of the form of our fourth must be true too. In order to affirm that, we would first need to know whether agents ever perform free acts, and in particular whether the act here referred to might be an instance of one—precisely the thing at issue. And that question— whether agents ever do perform free acts—cannot be decided by any philosophical analysis, or by any examination of such statements as those before us. *All* of these statements differ in meaning. Whether they also differ in what they refer to cannot be discovered by any comparison of these meanings, which are different to begin with. There is plainly no reason under the sun why these four statements, demonstrably different in meaning, might not also differ in their references, that is, might in fact sometimes refer to four different things. In case they do, and if, in particular, the third of them should happen sometimes to be true and the fourth false, then it would follow from this that there are free acts as I have defined them. Whether any act is in fact free, or whether a statement of the third form is ever true under conditions such that the corresponding statement of the fourth form is false, is something that no one knows. It is also something that no one can ever find out by an examination of such statements themselves, even given that they are all true. The question whether there can be such a thing as a free act is nothing but the question whether circumstances could ever be such that a statement in the third form might be true and a corresponding interpretation in the fourth form false. Both such statements would be descriptions of acts, and acts which would, to observation, be identical. The fourth would describe an unfree act. The third would describe a free act, just in case it were true and the fourth not true.

The Libertarian Thesis

Do men ever act freely, in the sense of performing free acts as they are here conceived? The answer to this question, I have suggested, must be the same as the answer to the question whether the third of our four statements might be true and the fourth false, for it can surely be assumed that, if it is possible to act freely at all, then it is possible for me to move my finger freely, that is, without anything causing me to move it. Removing the issue from the context of finger motions, however, the question whether men ever act freely can be expressed by asking whether *any* statements of the form "A performed act *e*" are ever true and the corresponding statements "Something caused A to perform *e*" false, where "A" designates some agent and "*e*" designates an act of that agent. Another way of expressing the same question is to ask whether a man ever does anything such that it is true both that he does it and that nothing causes him to do it.

It is fairly clear that this question cannot be answered one way or the other on the basis of anything so far discussed. It can, I think, be answered or at least well understood in the light of certain considerations as yet to be adduced, particularly considerations having to do with the ideas of deliberation and purposeful behavior, to which I shall turn later. Here it is important only to note that there is nothing in the concept of an act, or of behavior that is caused or initiated by an agent, from which it can be derived that all acts are caused or that they are not. It is entirely consistent with the truth of any statement to the effect that an agent performs a given act to affirm that something caused him to perform it. It is likewise consistent with the truth of such a statement to deny that something caused him to perform it. Such an assertion, or such a denial, may be inconsistent with something *else* which is true, but neither is inconsistent with the simple statement that this agent did perform this act. This is, of course, nothing but a consequence of the fact that statements like the third of our four do not entail any statements like the fourth; that is, that no statement to the effect that an agent performs some act ever, by itself, entails that anything caused him to perform it.

Some Familiar
Deterministic Arguments

It is, nevertheless, exceedingly common to find in philosophical literature certain arguments purporting to show that the very concept of a free or causally undetermined act implies certain absurdities. One also finds arguments purporting to demonstrate the exact opposite, that no human behavior that is causally determined can even be represented as an act in the first place. Now neither argument can really be correct, for it is a consequence of the diverse entailments I have elicited that no conclusion whatever concerning the truth or falsity of determinism can be derived from the mere concept of an act. Such arguments are, nevertheless, so common that their very popularity gives them a certain significance, despite their lack of worth. I shall, then, consider three, and show where each of them goes wrong.

The First Argument. It is often alleged that, if the libertarian thesis were true, and if, in particular, some of men's acts were free in the sense of being uncaused, then free human behavior would be chaotic, random and unintelligible.

Suppose, for example, that certain of the motions of my limbs are free, in this sense; namely, that these motions are uncaused. In that case, it is claimed, these limbs will from time to time move this way and that, with nothing whatever causing those motions. They will perhaps sometimes move forth vigorously, up and down or from one side to another, and sometimes just drift aimlessly about, being entirely free and uncaused and, therefore, uncontrolled. Indeed, if the motions of one's legs were free, in this sense, then he should not be astonished to find them, quite unexpectedly, suddenly moving back and forth and transporting his body hither and thither, without his having anything to do with these motions at all. Now clearly, this is hardly a description of free behavior as we ordinarily think of it. Motions which are entirely uncaused and random are not motions that are within the control of an agent or motions with which he has anything to do. Far from being a description of free, voluntary and responsible actions, such motions as these could not be described as the actions of any agent at all. They are just motions that occur, quite by themselves.

This is an old and familiar argument, and it quite misses the point. It confuses a free *act* with what I have called a free and spontaneous *event*. Now a free and spontaneous event—that is to say, an event that occurs but has no cause, in case there is such a thing—cannot even be an act in the first place, much less a free one. To say that any change, such as the motion of one's limb, is the act of some agent implies at least that it is caused, for to say that an agent performs an act is exactly synonymous with saying that he makes something happen or is the cause of it. To assert, accordingly, that a certain agent performs a certain act, such as moving his legs, does not imply that the motions of his legs are uncaused, but that they are caused. To further assert that he performs this act *freely* also implies that these motions are caused, since this is already implied by calling those motions his act. To say that he thus acts freely further implies, however, that nothing causes *him* to so act.

The confusion here can be neatly untangled in terms of the various entailments elicited before. Given that those entailments are correct, as they clearly seem to be, it can be seen that the strange and fallacious argument we are considering rests upon the supposition that if the third of our four statements is true and the fourth false, and if, accordingly, the act referred to in these statements is a free act, then the second statement must be false too. Far from being so, however, we have already noted that the third statement, quite by itself, entails that the second one is true.

The Second Argument.   Another familiar kind of argument, resting on a similar confusion but drawing a very different conclusion, is to the effect that if the thesis of determinism were true, then not only would there be no such a thing as a free act, there would not even be any way of distinguishing anything as an act in the first place, and all human behavior would be reduced to the status of mechanical reflexes.

Suppose, that is, that all events, including all the changes and motions of a man's body, are caused. In that case, it sometimes seems to some people, there can be no such thing as an act, for any bodily motion or change whatever must then be considered to be nothing but the causal consequence of some previous change, either within or without the agent, and therefore something which the agent himself cannot control, and with which he has nothing to do. Now this is indeed true of some bodily motions, such as the pulsations of the heart. These are the causal consequences of other changes within one's body, which are in turn the effects of other changes, and so on, and this is precisely why such changes as these are not considered acts of any agent, free or otherwise. They are just changes resulting from other changes, and the agent, whose heartbeats they are, has no direct or immediate control over them. But if all bodily changes were like this, and if, for instance, those motions of one's limbs which he supposes are within his control were nothing but the causal consequences of other changes occurring within or without him, and these other changes were, in turn, the causal consequences of still others, and so on, then they could be entirely explained without any reference to the activity of any agent at all. All those bodily movements which we are accustomed to thinking of as acts would instead have to be thought of as the effects of changes with which, ultimately, the agent himself has nothing to do. There would therefore be no difference in kind between what we consider our voluntary acts, on the one hand, and those automatic changes and adjustments of our bodies which we deem involuntary, on the other. The difference between these two would be no more than a difference in their causal antecedents, but no agent would need to be mentioned among the causal antecedents of either. Men would, then, on this conception be nothing more than automata, or beings whose bodies reacted in various ways to various internal and external influences, but which, like automata, never really acted or caused anything to happen at all.

This argument, too, is fairly familiar, but it likewise rests upon a confusion between an act and a bodily change. No bodily change which was simply uncaused, in case there were such a thing, could be the act of any agent, as we have seen. The supposition that a given bodily change is caused cannot, therefore, possibly entail that it is not an act. Indeed, if it happens to be caused by some agent, then this entails that it is the act of that agent. To say of some bodily motion that it is the act of some agent, and to say that this agent is the cause of that motion, are simply two ways of saying exactly the same thing, and since this latter statement asserts that the motion in question is caused, the former statement, which is equivalent to it, can hardly imply that it is not. The question whether the libertarian or the determinist thesis is true is not, in fact, a question about the motions and changes of men's bodies at all, but rather, a question about their acts. It is a question whether these are all causally determined; whether, that is, all men are always caused to do everything they do. The affirmation of neither theory can, therefore, possibly entail that men never do anything. The affirmation of libertarianism cannot entail that men's free actions are simply bodily motions with which they have nothing to do and of which they are therefore not the causes. To say of anything that it represents the act of some agent entails at least that it is caused by that agent, whether freely or not. To affirm the thesis of determinism is to affirm that men never act freely. It is not to affirm that they never act. And to affirm the thesis of libertarianism is to affirm that they do sometimes act freely, and this, too, is not to deny that they act.

The confusion in this second argument can, then, like the confusion in the first, be neatly exhibited in terms of the various entailments previously elicited. This argument assumes that if the fourth statement is true, then this entails that the second statement is true too, as indeed it does. But then the truth of the second statement is assumed to entail the falsity of the third. This cannot possibly be so, however, for it is perfectly obvious that the fourth statement by itself entails the third. It cannot be true, therefore, that the second statement, which is entailed by the fourth, can possibly entail that the third statement is false.

The Third Argument. A third very familiar argument—one that has cropped up in one form or another throughout this discussion—is that the thesis of determinism can be derived from the fact that men are sometimes the causes of certain changes, as they must be if they ever act at all. Far from implying a thesis of libertarianism, then, the notion of activity, or the causation of changes by agents, by itself implies the thesis of determinism.

Thus, it is often suggested that whenever a man acts by moving some part of his body, such as his arm or his finger, then he is the cause of that motion, it being, in fact, one and the same thing to say that such a motion is his act and that he is the cause of it. A motion or change, however, can be caused only by some other motion or change. When, accordingly, one speaks of a man as the cause of certain motions and changes in his own body, this can only mean that some change within him is the cause. And it must be some change within him, for otherwise the effect of it could not be properly thought of as *his* act. At the same time, the cause of a voluntary motion cannot be just *any* change within the agent, for involuntary motions, or motions which the agent does not cause, such as heartbeats, are caused by certain changes within him. The cause of a voluntary motion, then, or of any change which the agent can correctly be said to have caused, must be some special kind of change within him, namely, his own desires, motives, choices, and the like. And these, in turn, being changes, must be the effects of still others, and so on.

So much has been said about this conception of activity already, and about the numerous varieties it may assume, that further general comments are not called for. Here I need only note whence the confusion arises in terms of the entailment relations between our four statements. The argument assumes that the third of our four statements implies the second, as of course it does. The second statement is then simply assumed to be equivalent to the fourth, which is obviously not so, since the fourth might be false even though the second is true. And then, strangely, the truth of the second statement is considered to imply that the third is not strictly true, for the third asserts that some agent is the cause of a bodily motion, whereas the second is interpreted as meaning that something other than an agent is the cause of that motion. There is, of course, no justification whatever for any such transformations of meaning, nor can they possibly be reconciled with the relationships of entailment I have elicited.

The " Self "

Throughout this entire argument I have spoken quite unabashedly of agents as sometimes being the causes of their own behavior. I have in fact claimed that unless an agent is the ultimate cause of a given item of his behavior, then that behavior is no action of his, it being one and the same thing to say that a given man does something and that he causes it to happen. If the ultimate cause of any change is anything not identical with a given agent, or if the sequence of changes, involving muscular motions, changes within the nervous system, and so on, cannot be traced to some agent as its ultimate cause, then, I have contended, no matter how intimately connected with him these changes might be, none of them represents any act of his. They are instead only the causal consequences of things that happen to him or within him, and things, accordingly, with which he has nothing to do. If some change of my body, such as a heartbeat or the motion of a finger, is the effect of some spasm or other change within my nervous system, or of some volition or other change "within my mind," then, unless I am the cause of that spasm or other change within me and thus the ultimate cause of the change in question, it cannot be truly thought of as my act. It must instead be thought of as something that happens *to* me, something that I *undergo,* rather than something that I do, or produce, or cause to happen.

Now this conception of agents as causes has given rise to the most dreadful and bizarre conceptions in the minds of some thinkers, leading them to speak of "the self" or sometimes even "the substantial self," which is forthwith thought of as something non-observable, perhaps ghostly or at least non-material or "mental" in its nature, something that is intimately associated with the animal body of a man but nonetheless somehow distinct from it, and which nevertheless acts upon that body to produce those changes and motions which are deemed his acts. There have even been learned and extensive philosophical discussions of "the self" or "the mind" and its nature and powers, wherein it is implied that this being, the "self," is terribly important, yielding to explanation all sorts of things that are otherwise wrapped in the darkest mystery. Some suspicion of all this should be aroused by the fact that no such thing is ever mentioned outside philosophical literature.

Nothing of this sort is implied in anything that I have said. In saying that my acts are caused by myself, I mean *only* that I cause them or make them occur, and this is in fact inconsistent with saying that something else, to be referred to as my *self,* is the real cause of them. One can indeed say that his acts are caused by his self, but this is at best a strange and ungrammatical way of saying that they are caused by himself or, better, that it is he who performs them. Now if this is all that this strange locution means in the first place, then nothing but darkness can result from substituting it for a common, straightforward expression which everyone understands well. If I say that I am the cause of some change, that I bring something about or make it occur—that I, for instance, make my finger move or cause a forest to burn or something of that sort—then there is not the slightest difficulty in understanding what is being said. It cannot, therefore, be any *improvement* on this way of speaking, it cannot be any more *precise* or *accurate,* to say that my *self* causes these things to happen. At best, this can only mean that I cause them, which is what we started out by saying. At worst, it can suggest that something else, some "self" which is not identical with me but is instead something that I "possess" and which is a veritable agent in its own right, is the cause of them. And this, plainly, would be *inconsistent* with saying that I caused them. If, however, all we begin with is the supposition that I am the cause of some change, it should be quite obvious that we cannot deduce from this a conclusion which is inconsistent with it. All that is in fact deduced is another statement that is exactly synonymous with it. If we begin with the idea that a man is the cause of his own voluntary activity, thus distinguishing his actions from those automatic changes of his body with which he has nothing to do, we can then say that his voluntary activity is caused by himself. But this is no deduction; it is merely another way of saying exactly the same thing. If we then allow ourselves to speak of his activity as being caused (not by himself but) by his *self,* then either we are still saying exactly the same thing, though ungrammatically, or else we are saying something which, though grammatical, is inconsistent with that from which we profess to deduce it.

What are selves but persons? And what are persons but living men?

The three notions are absolutely coextensive, there being no living man who is not a person or a "self" and vice versa. No philosophical consideration has ever been brought forth to suggest that this is not true. Indeed, the concept of a *self* could never have entered philosophy by any other route than an odd transformation of grammar. Thus, when any man uses the expression "me" or "myself," he is plainly referring to exactly what any other person is referring to when that other person refers to *him*. But when this other person refers to him, he is referring to a certain man. He is not referring to some *self* which is something other than a man and perhaps inside of him. To suppose otherwise is only to suppose that when anyone refers to himself he is referring, not to the very man who is making that reference, but to his self— a supposition that seems fostered by the temptation to regard such an expression as "myself" as having the same reference as "my self."

Whenever, accordingly, one is tempted to speak oddly of selves, as though these were beings to which one must be introduced through metaphysics, he can instead speak simply of men, which are perfectly familiar things known to all. There is, in fact, no such thing as "the self," any more than there is such a thing as "the person" or "the man." There are only men, sometimes referred to as persons, and sometimes oddly referred to in philosophy as selves. To enter into discourse about the powers of the self, accordingly, and into the question whether this acts, thinks, has free will, and so on, is only to discourse mysteriously upon the powers of men, and to ask whether men act, think, have free will, and so on. And in fact we do know that men, for example, think and act, and we can understand perfectly the question whether they ever act freely. These answers have implications which are interesting to philosophy, to be sure, but at least the answers themselves are not entirely unknown. They only appear to be unknown when they are formulated in the context of "the self," whereby one is led to feel that the discovery of those answers must depend upon the profoundest metaphysical inquiry.

A man can sometimes assert with certainty "I am thinking." He can also sometimes assert with as much certainty "I am acting." A metaphysical philosopher, confronted with such indubitable data, is then likely to be most anxious to know what this *I* might be which is said to think and act. Then, as if this question were *answered* by supplying uncommon synonyms, he is apt to insist that it is really a self or ego that thinks and acts. One can then gravely assert that the ultimate source of a man's actions is a self or an ego, that it is this which wills, moves the body and its parts this way and that, and so on, thereby suggesting, by the very terminology, that it is something quite unfamiliar and strange that does these things, that it is not a man himself but something within him or perhaps even within his brain, something that is properly denominated *his self*. The model at work here is, I think, fairly captured and the absurdity of it expressed in Roderick Chisholm's cartoon:

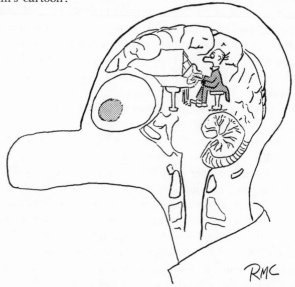

Clearly, however, all that one is entitled to assert, and all that we begin with, is that I am a man, and that this man, which I refer to as myself (and not, really, as my *self*) is the cause of those acts that are mine. Generalizing, we can say, not that selves, but that men are the causes of their acts—which means no more than that men act or, equivalently, that they do various things. We thus can avoid any reference to selves or egos just by speaking instead of men. The claim that selves or egos act in such a way as to produce voluntary bodily motions appears to be a profound metaphysical thesis, whereas the claim that men act, which expresses precisely the same idea, is at least not wholly unclear and is at least known by everyone to be true, quite apart from philosophical inquiry. One may, if he wishes, insist that men are really selves, or egos, but by the same token we can insist that these selves or egos are, after all, nothing but men. And whereas some persons are apt to be puzzled as to what a self or an ego might be, and even think it doubtful whether there are such things, no one has any doubt as to what a man is, or doubts that there are such things as men. Let us, then, not speak mysteriously of selves or egos as things that act, but simply say, quite unmysteriously, that men act.

But what is a man, really? Must we not say that a man is really a self or mind or something of that sort, somehow intimately associated with a physical object which this mind or self calls its body? Clearly, we need not say that at all. We can instead say that a man is a living, thinking being, having limbs, heart, muscles, nervous system, and so on—and there is no doubt whatever that such a description is true as far as it goes, that is, that there are men, as so described. When, accordingly, we assert that a man is sometimes the cause of his own bodily behavior, or that men sometimes act, we are saying simply that these living, thinking beings, possessed of limbs, hearts, muscles, nerves, and so on, act. And there is, again, no doubt but that such a statement is true. Certainly much more *could* be said, and of course there are many things about men that are not known at all, but the point is that we do not succeed in saying anything *more* when we say that men are "really" selves, egos, or minds. We only succeed in saying what was already said, though mysteriously. One can, surely, say that men "have minds," but what is this but another way of saying that men sometimes think? And if it is known by everyone that men sometimes think, what but confusion is gained by expressing just this fact in a way that might lead someone to think it is not true, and that it is not men, as we ordinarily think of them, who think, but rather their minds? Similarly one can, if he likes, say that the ultimate cause of a voluntary bodily motion is a self, but what is this but another way of saying that men sometimes act, or that they are active beings? If that is known by everyone to be true, as it surely is, what but confusion is gained by expressing this same fact in a mystifying way that might suggest that it is not true?

Of course, none of this is meant to imply that there is nothing about human nature that is unknown to common sense, science, or philosophy. It is meant only to suggest that whenever we feel tempted to introduce such terms as "mind," "self," "ego," and so on, we should ask whether what we are saying with such terms cannot be said in a simple way, such that we can then know, simply in terms of what all men do know, whether what we have said is true.

10

Reasons and Causes

It does little good to say, as I did in the last chapter, that men, and not their minds, souls or "selves," are the causes of their own voluntary behavior, and just let it go at that. This, though true, hardly affords any explanation of this or that man's behavior—though it should not be overlooked that it amounts to *some* explanation, at least in ruling other possibilities out. If a man has been killed, for example, and it is discovered that this event was a voluntary and intentional act of an identified man—that it was the result of his shooting him, for example—then it would be fatuous to insist that *no* explanation had been given for it. It would at least rule out alternative possible explanations, such as accident.·It would still be idle, however, to say that such a discovery amounted to a complete explanation, leaving nothing more to be said.

What we must now do is to consider what more needs to be added, once we have traced something to some agent as its ultimate cause, in order to have explained it. Here, it seems to me, philosophers have long been cramped by a felt need to fit explanations of this sort into a certain framework, borrowed mostly from the sciences, which has never in fact been used to explain men's actions in areas where such explanations have been sought and found.

Agency and Explanation

If some events were ascribable to agents as ultimate causes of them, then, it is often suggested, those events would really be inexplicable, or matters of the purest fortuity. This, it is rightly believed, is a good reason for doubting that men can be agents, or that they can be ultimate causes of their voluntary behavior, since a man's voluntary acts are not in fact always inexplicable.

There are a number of confusions to untangle in this familiar line of objection. It should be noted at once, for example, that the theory of agency as such implies nothing whatsoever with respect to the question whether human behavior is explicable. To say that a man does something is perfectly consistent with supposing that there are, sometimes or always, conditions which are causally sufficient for whatever he does. No theory of agency implies anything to the contrary. To assert that no man can ever help doing whatever he does is to deny that men ever act freely, but it is not to deny that they act. On the contrary, it is to imply that they do, for it would be a contradiction to affirm that a man could not help doing what he did and then infer that he did not really do anything. To say that a man does something is equivalent to saying that he causes something to happen, and it is to deny that any other thing or agent causes it to happen. Having said that, there is no inconsistency whatever in adding that something caused him to do what he did. Indeed, all men know that they are sometimes caused to do certain things, that they are sometimes even forced by circumstances which make it causally impossible for them to do otherwise. The assertion that men have "free will" is only the denial that this is always so. It is not the denial that they ever act at all.

Suppose, however, that men do act freely on occasion. We need not affirm that this is so, but let us for now just suppose that it is. Would it follow from that supposition that human behavior is sometimes inexplicable, or that any instance of a free act would also be an instance of a random, causeless, fortuitous, and therefore inexplicable, change?

Hardly, for as I have already indicated, such a notion rests upon a confusion between a free act and a free and spontaneous event. The supposition that a man acts, and that nothing causes him to act as he does on a given occasion, is not the same as supposing that his body behaves in a certain way and that nothing causes his body to behave in the way it does. It is in fact, as we have already seen, to imply the opposite, for to say that a man does something is certainly to imply that there is a cause for whatever it is that is done. This remains true whether whatever he does is done freely or not, for to say that a man's act is free entails, not that there is no cause for what he does, but rather that there is no cause for his doing it.

Causes and Purposes

What, then, about one's act itself? In case there is such a thing as a free act, in the sense of one's doing something but not being caused to do what he does, must we suppose that any such act would be inexplicable or fortuitous, in some sense in which free human behavior is generally supposed not to be inexplicable and fortuitous? Several comments are in order here.

In the first place, if one means by saying that something is inexplicable nothing more than that it is uncaused, then it is an immediate consequence of any act's being free that it is inexplicable; indeed, it is only to say the same thing over. The question then arises, however, whether a man's free action might be explicable in some manner other than just giving the causes of it. It seems quite plain that it might. Men's actions are often explained, indeed sensibly and intelligibly, by reference to the aims, purposes, or goals of the agents who perform them, without any reference, hidden or other, to any causes of them. This is in fact the way they are normally understood. The question, "Why did you do that?", which is clearly a request for a reason, is almost never a request for a recital of causes. It is rather a request for a statement of purpose or aim. If someone raises his hand and I ask him why he did so, he might point out certain circumstances which left him no alternative, circumstances sufficient for his doing just that, such as that he was commanded to do so under threat of death, or that he had been hypnotized, and so on. This would be a causal explanation which would surely indicate that he had not acted freely.

On the other hand, he might explain his act, not in terms of what caused him to do it, but in terms of some purpose or goal. For instance, he might say that he raised his hand in order to get someone's attention. Now that would be an explanation not in terms of what made him do it but in terms of his goal or purpose or aim. It can hardly be doubted that it would be an explanation—in fact a typical one men ordinarily use. Since, moreover, it is an explanation which in no way refers to causes, it is consistent with the absence of such causes, or in other words, with the supposition that the act in question, as distinguished from the bodily motion it accomplishes, is not caused at all, or is performed freely. It can hardly be claimed, then, that a free or uncaused act is by its very nature an inexplicable event. It is only, at worst, inexplicable in terms of what causes it. It is not inexplicable in terms of the purpose or aim of the agent who performs it.

Here, of course, it will be suggested that explanations of acts in terms of the purposes of agents are but a variety of causal explanation, and that any such explanation can, accordingly, be "reduced" to an explanation in terms of causes. But this is dead wrong. If one says he did something, *because* such and such factors caused him to do it and were such as to leave him no alternative, he is giving an explanation in terms of causes, and his statements are false in case those factors did not exist. If, on the other hand, he says that he did something *in order* that a certain end might be achieved, he is giving an explanation in terms of his purposes, and his statement is not in the least rendered false in case that end is not achieved. One might raise his hand in order to get someone's attention and yet fail to get that person's attention. An explanation of this second kind, in terms of one's purpose, aim, or goal, is of an entirely different type than an explanation in terms of causes and can in no way be reduced to it. Nor is it true, as is often suggested, that when one explains his behavior in terms of his purposes he is really only saying that these purposes exist, "in his mind," perhaps, and that these purposes, together with certain other things, *cause* him to act as he does. Purposes do not *cause* one to do anything; they only render intelligible whatever it is that he does, and are often perfectly compatible with his doing something quite different, as causes are not.

This line of thought raises a host of new questions, however, which had best be left for separate discussion in a later chapter. Here I mean only to show that a free act would be "inexplicable" only on the supposition that explanations in terms of causes are the only explanations allowable, a highly dubitable thesis. Human behavior is in fact usually explained, not in terms of causes, but in terms of purposes, and in case purposeful explanations are not simply a variety of causal explanations, as I am certain they are not, then even the free acts of men, in case there are such things, are at least sometimes perfectly explicable in terms of the purposes of the agents who perform them. That much is not even arguable, the only thing now in question being whether there can be such a thing as an explanation in terms of one's purpose which is not at the same time an explanation in terms of causes.

Let us suppose for now that there can be. This by itself does not, of course, rule out an explanation in terms of causes, and it should, then, be possible to imagine some act which is explicable in terms of the purpose of the agent, and *also* explicable in terms of causes. Now if we can imagine such an action—and it is, in fact, not very hard to do —then we can further suppose the same action to occur as a result of those same causes but *without* any purpose. We can also suppose the same action to occur for the same purpose but *without* any causes, showing well enough that either kind of explanation is capable of standing by itself, neither depending upon the other.

Imagine, then, the following case. I am host to a social gathering and at some point I ask one of my guests to leave. Asked why, I reply that he was becoming rude and I did not want him to spoil the whole party. Now that would be an explanation of my action in terms of my purpose, and it would be a satisfactory one quite by itself. It would render my action intelligible to others; they would, if they believed me, understand why I had acted as I did. And it would not be an explanation in terms of the causes of my act, or at least it would not need to be so understood, for it would be consistent with the truth of my explanation to suppose that I had acted freely, as I have defined this, and that I could have refrained from acting as I did. One *might* suppose that my desire for a pleasant evening had *caused* me to act as I did, such that, given that desire in those circumstances, I could not have acted otherwise, but one *need* not suppose this at all. My explanation is adequate as a statement of my purpose even if we suppose that nothing made me act as I did, and that I could, even in those circumstances and having that purpose, have done otherwise.

Suppose further, however, that there were causes for my acting as

I did, even causes that were wholly unknown to me and unconnected with my purposes. To fill this out somehow, we can suppose that the guest in question bore a strong resemblance to some hated relative of my childhood and that the associations subconsciously evoked by this were sufficient for my banishing him, quite apart from any good reason or purpose. This is doubtless a bit far-fetched, but it is not absurd and it will do for my argument.

Now it is perfectly clear that, even if I had not had a purpose for acting as I did, and had not concocted one, and supposing I had not known any explanation for my action, it would nevertheless have had an explanation in terms of its causes. Someone having sufficient knowledge of my childhood might perhaps have known it. I was caused to do what I did, there were circumstances which made me act in that fashion, whether these were known or not. The causal explanation, then, provided there were causes, is in this case entirely independent of any explanation in terms of purpose and stands quite by itself.

It is just as clear, however, that even if there had been no such causes, known or unknown, my action would have had an explanation in terms of my purpose, for the recital of this would, or at least could, entirely explain my behavior. I could say why I had acted as I had simply by stating what I meant to accomplish, and such an explanation would obviously have no connection whatsoever with what we are assuming to have been the real causes of my action. It stands just as well even if we suppose those causes to have been non-existent. This sort of consideration sufficiently shows that an action can be explained in terms of the purpose of the agent without any reference to any causes, even when we suppose such causes to exist, and such an explanation is no less adequate if we suppose the action to be have been without any causes at all.

Inexplicable Acts

The foregoing comments apply to those actions which are explicable, either in terms of their causes, in case they are unfree actions, or in terms of the agent's purpose, whether the action is free or not. Suppose, however, that an agent does something, and his action is such that nothing causes him to do it—that is, there are no circumstances causally sufficient for his doing it—and at the same time he has no purpose. Such an action would really be inexplicable. Would it therefore be one that could not occur?

There seems to be no reason whatsoever for thinking so. We often do things which are such that we at least do not know of anything that makes us do them—which of course does not entail that nothing does. These are actions which at any rate seem to be free. Most men in fact believe that, sometimes at least, nothing makes them do what they do. This may be an erroneous belief, for it may be that whatever a man does there are factors which render it impossible for him to do otherwise; but it is not an absurd belief. There is no sign of a contradiction in it, nor is it even implausible except in the light of certain speculative theories of philosophy. Now suppose a man were to perform such a simple act as, say, moving his finger to the right. Suppose he is aware that he caused his finger to move to the right, that this was an action of his, but is not aware of anything that caused him to do so. Suppose further that there was in fact nothing that caused him to do so; that is, that there were no circumstances which rendered it causally impossible for him to have acted otherwise. And finally, suppose he can give no reason for moving it as he did, can cite no purpose, aim, or goal, or anything that he intended to achieve by his act. It would then follow that there was no explanation for his action: He could explain the motion of his finger by simply saying that he had moved it, but there would be no explanation of his moving it. Does any of this suggest that no such action is possible? There is plainly not the slightest suggestion of this. Anyone can perform a simple action like this which at least appears both to the agent and to any observer as both causeless and pointless. One can, for example, simply move his finger in a random pattern, such that it certainly *seems* to him that, while he is making his finger move in that way, nothing is causing him to move it in just that way, and he has no purpose or aim in so moving it—not even the purpose of showing that he can. We do sometimes find ourselves acting in this way, or at least, so it *seems*. We might be mistaken in supposing that there are, in such cases, no causes for our doing what we are doing, and no purposes either, but the point is that no philosophical consideration whatever can *show* that we are wrong. Any action of this sort, in case it is what it seems to be, is strictly inexplicable, but from this it hardly follows that it cannot occur. All that follows is that there is no explanation for it. Some persons may want to believe that nothing can ever happen for which there is not some known or unknown explanation, but surely the grounds for such a philosophical opinion can be no better, and hardly as good, as the grounds we have for believing that we are quite capable, on occasion, of performing simple actions of just this sort.

An Example

Most of the points just made can be illustrated with a single example, simple and uninteresting in itself, but all the better for that. Suppose, then, that I am playing cards with a friend when the table suddenly moves, and I want an explanation for that. My question is, What made the table move? Several answers are possible. For instance, (i) it might be said that nothing made it move—it just moved all by itself. That reply would be rejected by me, simply because I believe that free and spontaneous events of this sort never occur. Or (ii) my partner might say that *he* moved it, perhaps by bumping it with his foot. This would explain why the table had moved, though it would not explain why he had moved it, which was not, however, what was asked. Or (iii) he might say, simply, that his foot had bumped it. This too would explain why the table had moved, though it would leave unanswered the question what had caused his foot to bump it, which was not a question that was asked. Or (iv) he might say that something—a rolling object, for instance—had pushed his foot against it. This would be consistent with the third answer, but not with either of the first two.

Suppose, then, that the second answer is the one actually given— namely, my partner's answer that he moved the table by bumping it with his foot. I could now ask, not just what had made the table move, but why he had thus moved it, and I would then be asking for an explanation for an act, which is something quite different from what I had originally asked (an explanation of an event). If he replied either (v) that something, such as a rolling object, had bumped his foot against the table, or (vi) that the motion of his foot was spasmodic, perhaps the result of a disorder of his nervous system, then he would not be giving me an explanation for his action at all, for these statements imply that no action was done. He would instead be giving me a causal explanation for the occurrence of a certain event, namely, the motion of his foot. But if he replied (vii) that he moved his foot in that fashion because he had been previously hypnotized to do so, he would be explaining his act in terms of the cause of it, pointing out, not merely what had made his foot move, but what had made him move it.

This explanation would not contradict the claim that he had moved his foot, but would confirm it. It would, however, imply that he had not done it "on purpose." If he replied (viii) that he moved his foot against the table in order to startle or distract me, then he would be explaining his act, not in terms of the cause of it, but in terms of his purpose or aim, or what he was trying to accomplish. It would be a clear way of indicating that he had done it "on purpose." That would not be a causal explanation at all, though it would certainly be an explanation. Or, finally (ix), if he said there was no reason at all, implying both that nothing caused him to do what he did (that he might just as easily have refrained) and that he did not do it for any reason (that there was no point to it, no purpose, motive, or aim), then while that answer might be somewhat implausible there would be no inherent absurdity in it. Men do sometimes act for no reason at all, with no purpose or aim; and the supposition that a given act is an instance of this does not entail that it is therefore something that is caused. It is perfectly possible that while the motion of the foot was caused by an agent, there was no cause of the agent's thus moving it. Such an act would be in every sense inexplicable, but not therefore impossible, for there is nothing whatever that is known to be true and which entails that no one can perform such a free but purposeless action.

Reasons and Causes

I have suggested that, while a man's actions may sometimes not be *caused* in the sense that events and states in inanimate nature are caused, it does not follow that they cannot be *explained*. A man's actions are sometimes—indeed, typically—explained in terms of *reasons* rather than *causes*. Now this, of course, presupposes that reasons, in the context of voluntary behavior, are quite different from causes, and this has long been highly controversial. The source of such controversy is that ordinary locutions typically used for explaining men's actions look for all the world like expressions of causality, and those who think they are not sometimes have great difficulty in actually showing this.

Suppose, for instance, that a given man goes to the pantry, and suppose this is correctly explained, by himself or another, by saying he did this because he wanted some salami, (or) because he desired salami, (or) because he wished to have some salami. Now the word "because" occurs very naturally in those statements, and in just such a way as to suggest that the agent's want, desire, or wish was the immediate *cause* of his action. It is easy enough to conclude, therefore, that a man's voluntary actions are caused, and in essentially the same way that other things are caused, the only difference being that the causes of a man's actions are of a special kind—namely, his wants, desires, wishes, and so forth.

This is utterly wrong. It is not just elliptical, incomplete, or partially wrong, but wholly wrong. Explanations of the sort just cited, which grammatically seem to assign causes for voluntary actions, assign instead reasons, reasons which are wholly different in kind from causes. To assimilate them to causes is simply to distort them and to create an entirely misleading conception of human agency.

Consider, for example, a set of statements such as the following, each of which is the expression of an ordinary causal connection between certain states or events:

    I. Jones fell from the stool because he slipped,

       Jones fell from the stool because he was pushed,

       Jones fell from the stool because it collapsed,

and so on. Now compare those with

    II. Jones went to the pantry because he wanted salami,

       Jones went to the pantry because he wished for some salami,

       Jones went to the pantry because he desired salami,

       Jones went to the pantry because he chose to have some salami,

and so on.

Now the statements of both sets are grammatically similar. The statements of both sets express a relationship between certain events conveyed by the word *because*. In the first set the relation is clearly that of causation, and it is, therefore, perfectly natural to suppose that the relationship in the second set, conveyed by the very same word, is likewise one of cause to effect.

Note first, however, that the statements in the second set are, in an ordinary context, equivalent. If any of them explains Jones' action—as each of them does, at least to the extent of indicating that it was not coerced, inadvertent, absent-minded, or unintentional—then the others also do. They all amount to saying essentially the same thing. Under ordinary circumstances one could not insist that one was true but another false. The same fact is expressed, indifferently, by any of them. Dispute over this could be only a quibble.

This is quite obviously *not* so with the first set, however. If a man's fall is correctly explained as the result of his slipping, then this is far from equivalent to explaining it as the result of his being pushed or his stool collapsing. The truth of any of the statements in the first set would ordinarily (though not necessarily) *exclude* the others, for these statements manifestly are not just different ways of saying essentially the same thing.

The second set, accordingly, does not, unlike the first set, constitute a variety of possible causal explanations for a given event. It constitutes, instead, a variety of ways of giving one and the same explanation, without tacitly or directly mentioning any causes at all. The second set, unlike the first, does not present us with a *choice* between possible causes. It gives no causal explanation whatsoever. If the statements of that set were causal explanations, then, given that they are in a normal context all one and the same explanation, we would have to conclude that wanting, wishing, desiring, and choosing are in this situation just alternative names for one and the same cause. That perhaps could be maintained without absurdity, except that it is thoroughly doubtful that they are names for any causes at all, much less alternative names for one and the same cause. Certainly they do not *normally* name the same thing. Wishing, desiring, choosing and wanting, when these denote anything at all, denote quite different things. A man often wishes for what he does not choose (e.g., an inheritance), wants what he does not in any plain sense wish for (e.g., food), and desires what he does not choose (e.g., another's death), and so on.

Note next, then, that the statements of the second set are entirely equivalent to

III. Jones went to the pantry in order to get some salami,

Jones went to the pantry for the purpose of getting salami,
or quite simply

Jones went to the pantry for some salami,
and so on. Now these statements do not even *look* like causal explanations. No causes are alluded to, even indirectly. Shall we say, then, that they are somehow *incomplete*? That the third one, for instance, must *really* mean something about some cause and its effect—for instance, that some state of desire (or want, or choice, or wish) caused Jones to behave as he did? But why should anyone say that at all? Why, indeed, except to coerce or jam these statements into a framework within which they can be construed as causal explanations? Whether they are causal explanations is, however, precisely the thing at issue. Apart from this there is not the least reason to say that these statements are incomplete, that the third one, for instance, is not perfectly correct

as it stands. The fact that these explanations do not even tacitly refer to any causes is not by itself any reason at all for assuming that, of course, they must tacitly refer to causes of some kind. To get *that* conclusion one needs a philosophical theory, and the very one that is here in question; the theory, namely, that *all* explanations must somehow be explanations in terms of causes.

Next note that there are no remotely similar locutions in which *any* of the statements of the first set can be expressed. These statements, which *are* explanations in terms of causes, in no way lend themselves to reformulation using such teleological locutions as "in order to," "for," and so on. Having said that a men fell because his stool collapsed, there simply is *no* statement containing such a teleological expression in which the same idea can be expressed. One cannot, for instance, say that the chair collapsed in order to dump him, for that would be senseless. It would at best be an inept way of saying that someone arranged for its collapse, in order to dump him; but that is far from equivalent to what we began with. It might, and normally would, be false, without this in the least suggesting that the cause of the man's fall was not the collapse of his stool.

Finally, compare the teleological statements of the last set with the following:

IV. Jones went to the pantry for some salami,

Jones went to the pantry for some cheese,

Jones went to the pantry to smoke,

and so on. Now these statements, *like* those of the first set but unlike those of the second, are *not* just alternative ways of saying essentially the same thing. The truth of any of them, like those of the first set, is perfectly consistent with the falsity of the others, and would ordinarily (though not necessarily) exclude the others as explanations for the agent's behavior. To say that a man goes to the pantry for salami is far from equivalent to saying that he goes there to smoke, for these would ordinarily be alternative rather than equivalent explanations for one and the same thing.

What, then, is the difference expressed in the statements of set IV? Is it a difference of causes? Plainly not, for no causes are in any way referred to or even hinted. They are simply differences of ends, differences in the possible states of affairs following upon the action which would or would not constitute the attainment of the purpose in question. One might go to the pantry for salami and end up with cheese, perhaps exactly as if he had gone there for cheese in the first place; but it would not follow from this that he had, after all, gone there for cheese—he only settled for it. Again one might, though he need not, go there for all three purposes at once, just as the man in our first set might have fallen from his stool as the result of all three causes acting together. Still, the difference in the ideas expressed by the two sets would remain. It is a difference that is expressed by saying that, in the first case, there were several causes, and evidently no end at all, for one and the same set of events (their *effect*), while in the second case there were several ends, and evidently no causes at all, for one and the same set of actions (their *means*).

The statements of the second set, then, being plainly equivalent to all those of the third set, explain an agent's action by citing his reason for so acting in terms of his end or goal. They say what the point of it was, what he was aiming to accomplish, and they refer to no cause at all. This of course does not entail that there *was* no cause of his action, but only that if there was, the explanation in any case gives no hint of it. They suggest nothing as to what, *if anything,* made the agent act as he did. They are therefore consistent with saying that *nothing* caused him to do this, though of course they do not entail this. It is perfectly possible that something caused him to act as he did—that he was driven to his action by fear, threats, a compulsive craving, or whatnot—though nothing of this sort is suggested by the statements before us. Their truth is therefore perfectly consistent with supposing that no such causal statements are true. If one nevertheless insists that there *must* (somehow) have been some cause of the agent's actions—his "desires," for instance—then it is not because this is suggested by the statements themselves, for it is not, nor is it because his actions would be left unexplained if this were not so, for they would not. The statements themselves explain them. Indeed, there is no basis whatever for such a claim, *except* the plausibility of the philosophical notion that *everything* is caused—which is, again, the very thing that is at issue.

To explain a man's action by saying he performed it *in order* that something else might happen is evidently to render a teleological account of it. It is to represent his action, not as the effect of a cause, but as the means to an end. It tells us what the point of his action was, what was the intention or aim of the agent, the purpose or goal he was trying to realize. To the extent that it does this it renders the behavior in question intelligible, and in the most straightforward sense tells us *why* he acted as he did. It thereby explains his action. It may not explain it completely, just as a causal explanation may be incomplete though nonetheless true, and it certainly does not explain it in such a way as to preclude a causal explanation. It does nevertheless constitute a real explanation, the force or explanatory value of which is in no way diminished by the lack of a causal explanation of the agent's actions (as distinct from his motions). It is an explanation which manifestly is not *reducible* to an explanation in terms of causes, for it is simply different in kind from that, and one which, moreover, in no way presupposes any *alternative* or *supplementary* causal explanation. It is, as far as it goes, independent of any questions of causation, just as the plainly causal explanations in our first set of statements are independent of any question of ends or goals.

These remarks introduce, of course, the concept of purpose, and all the related notions of means and ends, goals, aims, and "final causes," concepts which have been so troublesome in the history of thought that many have wanted to insist that they have no proper place in philosophy to begin with; but those ideas must be reserved for later discussion.

11

Mental Acts

The question whether there are such things as mental acts obviously cannot be decided empirically, experimentally, or introspectively; for the question is simply whether certain things, described in psychological terminology and perfectly familiar to everyone, are properly termed acts. The question whether a man can properly be said to be performing an act when, for instance, he solves a problem "in his head" is not one for which we need to seek evidence of any sort, additional to what we already have. It is not a matter of finding more facts, but rather one of interpreting certain facts with which we are already familiar.

The next step would therefore seem to be to appeal to the analysis of the concept of an act and see whether some of these things with which we are familiar are acts, as thus analyzed. This too is hopeless, however, for we have abundantly seen that there is no good, non-question-begging analysis of this concept. How one would analyze such a concept would surely depend, in part, on whether he believed there are such things as mental acts. We all know, or think we know, what is the difference between acting and being acted upon, between doing something and having something done to us, but it seems quite impossible to say, in any more philosophical way, just what that difference is.

I do not, then, want to raise all over again the apparently futile question of what an act "really is." Instead I shall outline two general conceptions of thought and suggest that one of them, which is a theory of mental acts, resolves certain philosophical perplexities that the other does not. This, I believe, will constitute a good reason for asserting that thought is sometimes an activity—or as some would prefer, that there are mental acts—and it will be all the better reason if, as I believe, this claim does not raise difficulties of its own which we do not already have on our hands from other considerations.

I again characterize an act, then, as anything that an agent does, as distinguished from things that are done to him. My raising my hand, for example, is an action of mine, whereas its being raised by any other thing or person is not. Or we can say in the case of anything which is an action of mine that I am the cause of it, I make it happen, originate it, or bring it about; that it depends, not just on my muscles, nerves, or whatnot, but in some well-understood but indefinable sense, on me. Events that are not my acts, on the other hand, occur as the result of causes with which I have nothing to do.

Three things now need to be noted.

The first is that while one would normally refer to some bodily motion in giving an example of an act, it might not be necessary to do so, for doing something need not entail doing something *with* something—for example, with one's body or some part of it. When I move a pencil I normally move it with my fingers, and when I am thinking I sometimes think with something—with pencil and paper, or with spoken words—and this involves bodily motions. It should, however, be left an open question whether one can think without doing anything with any part of his body. The common opinion that this cannot happen is derived, not from any facts that are known, but from certain speculative theories of metaphysics which are not known to be true.

Secondly, it should be noted again that there is always an essential reference to some person or agent whenever anything is described as an act. If, then, thought is an activity of an agent, then this same essential reference will appear in any description of such thought. Thus, the beating of my heart can be described without mentioning me at all, for this internal motion is not an act, either of myself or anything else. One would not, to be sure, know that it was *my* heart that was beating without somehow mentioning me, but one could know that it was the beating of a heart. My raising my hand, on the other hand, cannot be described or understood as an action without mentioning an agent—in this case, myself—as its cause. No description, however detailed, of what was involved in this motion and in its causal antecedents would convey the idea that it was my act until I was mentioned as the cause of it. This is perhaps as close as one can come to distinguishing acts from events. It is perhaps worth reiterating that whenever any inanimate thing is said to act— as, for instance, when sulphuric acid is said to "act" upon zinc, or a computing machine is said to be "doing" various things—we can *always* render a complete description of just what is happening without tacitly or otherwise mentioning the thing said to "act" at all, simply by describing what is happening in some of its parts or constituents. Thus when inanimate things are spoken of as *doing* various things, the word "doing" has not the same meaning as it has when used to refer to the actions of agents.

Third, we should note that a theory of mental acts need not, and surely does not, involve any claim that *all* thinking is activity, any more than a theory of physical acts implies that all bodily motions are acts. Just as some instances of bodily behavior are actions while others are instances of passive behavior, not within the control and direction of the agent, so also thinking is sometimes entirely passive, as in the case of dreams, reveries, and thoughts that are simply evoked by external stimuli. The question whether there are mental acts can, then, be understood as the question whether all thinking is passive.

Assuming, then, that we can with some confidence make these distinctions between activity and passivity, without having to say how we make them, we can now elicit two quite different conceptions of the nature of thought.

The Stream of Thoughts

The first theory, made familiar by Hume and more or less taken for granted by his successors, envisions thought to be a series or steam of things "within" one. My thinking, then, consists of my *having* various things, such as ideas, impressions, images, feelings, and other subjective or "private" things. It matters not what we call these things, or what we decide are the "ultimate constituents of consciousness." Some generic term, such as "ideas," in the sense given it by earlier empirical philosophers, or simply "thoughts," will do, letting it cover every sort of conscious state. The general picture is in any case clear enough. My thinking consists, on this view, of my having (say) thoughts, these following upon one another in a veritable stream. Consciousness is often thought to consist of just such a stream of thoughts, and the denial that certain things such as plants are "conscious" is thus usually interpreted to mean simply that no such stream of things occurs within them. To say that I am thinking or, alternatively, that I am conscious, is on this view simply to say that there is such a stream of things occurring within me or, more commonly, "within my mind." It is not, then, essential on this view to say that I am doing anything when I am thinking. It is enough to say that something is happening, namely, that thoughts are occurring within me, and that they collectively constitute a series or stream. Where these thoughts come from—whether from certain cerebral changes, as psychologists like to assume, or perhaps from "impressions" stamped upon my mind from within or without me, as earlier empiricists took for granted—is not a question that need concern us. My thoughts are, in any case, not literally created by me. In thinking, I do not make my own thoughts, I do not originate them—indeed, in terms of my earlier distinction, I need *do* nothing at all. My thinking consists simply in having something happen *to* me—that is, in my *having* thoughts, ideas, or whatever one chooses to call them.

Thought as Action

The other theory is to the effect that thinking is sometimes an activity, that my thoughts are not in the ordinary sense *things* that merely arise and subside in my mind, but that they are sometimes *acts* that I literally perform; that my thinking, in short, consists not in my *having* something, namely, thoughts or consciousness, but in my *doing* something, and indeed, doing various things. This doing perhaps need not, as noted before, involve doing something with my body, but sometimes it does. Thus, when one is working through mathematical problems he is doing something that may be properly called thinking, and he may be doing this with pencil and paper. Now on the stream of thought theory, the use of pencil and paper in such a case is quite ancillary to the processes of thinking, which is constituted entirely of the having of those thoughts, which come somehow to be "expressed" with pencil on paper, so that a person's thinking is one thing ("mental" in character) and his using pencil and paper quite another thing ("physical" in character). On the theory of mental acts, on the other hand, the use of pencil and paper in such a case is no more ancillary to the agent's thinking than the use of one's arm is ancillary to his throwing a ball. One might sometimes think *with* pencil and paper in precisely the sense in which one throws *with* his arm.

Two Implications.   The conception of thought as action, and not merely as a source or cause of action, has two fundamental consequences which serve best to distinguish it from the theory of the stream of thoughts. The first is that while thinking is sometimes, on this theory, doing something, that which is done is not a "thing" in the sense in which, on the theory of a stream of thoughts, a thought is a thing. Thus if one designs a pattern, the pattern is a "thing" in the most ordinary sense, but one's designing it, while this is something that is done, is not another "thing" in any comparable sense. It is instead an act. Or again, if one waltzes he does something, but there is not anything that is done. Waltzing a waltz is simply waltzing. And similarly, thinking *a thought* is simply thinking—the thought is not a *product* of thinking, nor something to which one is *related* by consciousness, nor something that one *has,* nor something which falls into a series or stream or bundle alongside other things. Thoughts, in short, are on this view not things that exist at all, any more than waltzes, throws, and checkmates are things that exist. They are rather, like these, sometimes acts that are performed. Contrariwise, the stream of thoughts theory puts thoughts on the level of things, though rather strange ones, which the mind does not create, but which proceed across the stage of consciousness and collectively constitute another thing, appropriately called a "stream" or more commonly "one's consciousness" or even "the mind." They are, according to certain old schools, derived from the "materials" of sensation and introspection, and they become related and associated with one another in various ways, according to supposed psychological laws. They are mysteriously correlated with certain states of the brain, according to the opinions of some writers, and sometimes enter causally into the observable behavior of bodies, according to others.

The second implication of the theory of thought as an activity is that thinking may sometimes be, in a sense inconceivable under the stream of thought theory, creative. This is simply a consequence of its being regarded as an activity in the first place, for any activity, particularly insofar as it may be regarded as free, is in a clear sense creative, that is, ultimately dependent upon an agent for being the kind of activity it is. Waltzing, for instance, is a creative activity, in the sense that something is thereby made to happen which would not happen were it not for the activity of an agent, and exactly what does then happen is sometimes determined by the agent himself. Composing a sonnet would perhaps be a better example. On the theory of the stream of thoughts, creative thinking could only consist in the creation of new thoughts, and thus in a new stream of things, which might or might not come to be "expressed" in some physical manifestation.

What I have said thus far is not intended as an argument in favor of one theory over the other, but only as a clarification of the two theories in contrast to each other. My argument in favor of the theory that thought is sometimes an activity, in the same sense that one's behavior is sometimes activity, will consist, first, of citing two or three questions of philosophy which, I think, a theory of thought as activity answers but which the alternative theory seems to render unanswerable; and second, of showing that certain entailment relations of statements expressing mental activity and passivity are exactly the same as those expressing bodily activity and passivity.

The " Mind "
and Its Thoughts

It has long been a question of philosophy just what might be the relation between oneself, or his "mind," and his thoughts. Those who presuppose a theory of the stream of thoughts usually answer this by saying that the relation is one of identity; that is, that the "self" or the "mind" simply *is* that stream of thoughts which constitutes one's mental life—just as a carriage is identical with the totality of its parts, or a university with the sum of its constituents. But there are two grave difficulties which, apparently, have never been resolved by this theory.

The first is that there is a seeming lack of continuity within the stream of thoughts, though not in oneself. Two thoughts, occurring one after the other, sometimes seem wholly disconnected—as, for instance, when my reverie is disrupted by the blast of a shotgun—though I seem to remain identically myself throughout this experience. Another way of expressing this difficulty is that the commencement of a new stream of thoughts, wholly unconnected with its predecessors, does not constitute the emergence of a new self.

The greater difficulty, however, in identifying the mind or the "self" with any stream of thoughts is that no one has ever been able to say what must be the relation between the various members of such a stream, such as to render them one stream—namely, that constituting oneself. This difficulty is sometimes just overlooked, and it does, in fact, take a while to appreciate it, but some analogies will help.

Consider, for example a length of rope. Now this rope *has* innumerable fibers, and this relation of *having* can be expressed simply by saying that the rope *consists* of fibers, suitably related to each other. Any fiber whatever, to be a fiber belonging to that rope, need only be related to the other fibers in a certain easily describable way, namely, to be twisted together with them. To say that the rope has many fibers, we need not suppose that the rope is one thing, its fibers something else, and that the rope has some special relation to these. The relation of the rope to its fibers is one of identity.

The difficulty of comparing the mind, however, conceived as a stream of thoughts, to such familiar unities of parts as this is that no one has ever said what must be the relationship between the constituents of any stream of thoughts, such as to render them a single unified stream. In the case of a rope, a carriage, or (to take a non-physical unity) a series of numbers, we can always say what the relationship between its constituents is, *by virtue of which* they collectively constitute a single thing. But in the case of thoughts no such relationship suggests itself. Consider, for example, the series of Peter's thoughts over a given period of time, together with the series of Paul's thoughts over the same period. Now there is no doubt but that this totality of thoughts, Peter's and Paul's, falls into two mutually exclusive streams, that no thought belonging to the one stream is, or perhaps even could be, a member of the other. But what relation does a member of one stream have to any other member of the same stream which it might not as easily have to some member of the other? The temporal relations can be the same. So also can the causal relations. If Peter and Paul are both watching a cinema screen, for instance, their thoughts might be very similar and arise from the same source. The only hope would seem to be to relate Peter's thoughts in some way, not to his other thoughts, but to his body—that is, his brain—and Paul's to Paul's body. This is seldom attempted, however, for it would make the respective identities of the two "minds" relative to the identity of their bodies. Besides, it has never been shown what relationship any thought must have to a given body in order to be a constituent of the "mind" or "self" with whom that body is associated. Memory is sometimes suggested as the connecting link, but this has the consequence that, in order for any thought to be a constituent of Peter's mind, it must either be or contain the memory of every preceding thought of Peter's, which seems absurd and contrary to fact. Besides, memory hardly seems to be a relationship between thoughts, but rather a relationship of men to certain things.

This problem, in fact, seems quite unanswerable on any view that identifies the mind or self with a stream of thoughts. Suppose, then, we now consider thinking to be, at least sometimes, the activity of an agent, meaning by "an agent" not a mind, soul, or whatnot, but simply a living, intelligent man. Viewing the matter this way, we are not in the least tempted to identify a man with his thoughts, any more than with another of his actions or passions. If we ask what the relation is between me and one of my acts—my act, for instance, of throwing a ball—we can only answer that it is something I did, something I made happen, as contrasted with something someone else initiated, or something that has simply happened. Similarly, we can say of my "thought," that is, of some more or less intelligent feat of mine, like an act of checkmating or solving a puzzle, that I did it, or that I was the author of it, in contrast to things done by other agents or by no one. It is also worth noting that we need not say that my *mind* did it—for example, that it was my mind that performed the checkmate, even though it may have been a clever one, or that my mind solved a puzzle, even though it may have been a difficult one. Such terminology is here, as in reference to bodily acts, superfluous. No one would feel tempted to say that it was my mind that threw a ball, even if it was done carefully and accurately, or my mind that waltzed, even though this was done gracefully, or my mind that operated a typewriter, even though this was done skillfully. It is enough to say in all such cases that a *man* did those things, and that I am that man. Some philosophers find it almost irresistible to say that men do, after all, have minds, and that it is because they have minds that they can do such things as throw balls accurately, perform clever checkmates, waltz gracefully, solve metaphysical problems, and so on. But such modes of expression only call attention to the fact that men, unlike other things, are capable of doing things of this sort.

The question, then, concerning the relationship between my various thoughts, such that they together constitute one stream of consciousness, or one mind or self, becomes analogous to, and indeed simply a version of, the question of what might be the relationship between my various deeds such as to render them one series, namely, the series constituting my voluntary behavior. We can only say, whether speaking of bodily acts or mental ones, that they are things that I do, as contrasted with things other people do, or things that happen without anyone doing them. Now we cannot, to be sure, analyze what it means to call some intellectual feat like a checkmate an *act,* as distinct from events that are not acts, beyond saying that some agent is the author or originator of it. But then we cannot analyze what it means to say of *any event whatever* that it is an act, so this is not a peculiar difficulty raised by the theory of mental acts.

The Ownership of Thoughts

On a theory that represents thoughts as things and the mind as a stream or bundle of such things it can always be reasonably asked why a member of one such stream could not have been the member of another or, indeed, of no stream at all. For in general, concerning any composite of existing things, there is nothing necessary about any part of it being a member of that composite rather than another, or a member of any composite at all. A fiber of rope, in terms of our previous example, can be removed and incorporated into another rope, or remain incorporated in none. Yet there seems to be an absurdity in the idea that one of my thoughts could have been yours instead, and a greater absurdity in supposing that it might have been no one's. You and I can both think of Mt. Monadnock, but it seems impossible that I should have had your thought of it and you mine. Similarly, we might both have headaches, but it seems senseless to suggest that I might have had your headache instead of the one I did have, and you have had mine, or that either might have been "had" by no one. On the theory of a stream of thoughts, however, there is not the slightest basis for any absurdity in such suppositions. Given that a thought or feeling is yours merely in virtue of its being related in some way to other thoughts, there is no reason why it should not have been related in the same way to different thoughts, or even lacked that relation to any thoughts.

If, however, we represent thoughts, not as things belonging to a larger composite, but as actions and passions, this queer sort of question does not even arise. If I ask whether some act of mine—my act of checkmating, for example, whether done on a chessboard or merely "in my head"—could have been someone else's act, I find that I am only asking whether someone else could have done it instead of me. And this is obviously not a metaphysical question, but simply one of human ability. Now if, to be sure, we allow to count as "my actions" and as "my passions" only those things that *I* do and those that are done to *me,* then it becomes logically impossible that my actions and passions should be done or suffered by anyone else; but this is trivial. For in the same manner we can say that if, for instance, I allow to count as *my* possessions only those things that *I* own, then it is logically impossible that anyone else should own them—but no philosophy turns upon that sort of sophism.

The Location
and Composition of Thoughts

I think it is fair to say that the location and composition of thoughts have never been described, except by the invention of terms that have *no* use *except* as answers to this sort of question. Thus, thoughts are sometimes said to be *in* the mind, as fibers of a rope are said to be *in* the rope; but no one can say what it is for something to be in the mind rather than outside it, other than to say in other words that the thing in question is something in the nature of a thought, idea, or feeling. Otherwise we could at least raise the question whether a body, particularly a very tiny one, might not be in the mind, alongside the thoughts that are there. But here we are apt to learn that the mind has no volume and hence cannot, of course, accommodate even tiny objects. If we ask *where* the mind is—or equivalently, where the stream of thoughts flows—we are apt to be told that it has no place either; but this makes us no wiser. The questions, What are thoughts "made of," and Whence are derived the materials of their composition, yield similar answers; for example, that they are mental things rather than physical, that they are composed of mind stuff or whatnot, and that they are derived from experience. Such expressions succeed only in telling us that thoughts are things like material things excepting only that they are not material and have none of the properties of bodies. In short, they tell us nothing.

Once thinking is conceived of as activity and passivity, however, the artificiality of all such questions is immediately perceived. Actions and passions, whether "mental" or "physical," are not composed of anything, and any question of their location is a disguised question of something else. Of what, for instance, would one say my act of raising my arm is composed? This is quite plainly a meaningless question. Any answer to it is odd, and we can see exactly why it is odd. And what sort of answer could be given to the question, Where did my act of raising my arm occur? If we say that it occurred "in my body" we are only calling attention to the point that it was a bodily act. Similarly, if we say that my act of recalling a name occurred "in my mind" we are stating that it was a mental act, and nothing more. Now ordinarily, to ask where a given act occurred—an act of murder, for instance, or of conspiracy—is only to ask where the *agent* was when he performed it. The answer to that is the one we ordinarily seek, and it matters not whether the event was an action or a passion, or whether it was "mental" or "physical." It was, in any case, a question of the location of an agent or a patient, that is, the location of a man.

Active and Passive Thinking

It is evident that a theory of mind that equates thinking with having a stream of thoughts, known collectively as the mind, cannot distinguish between thoughts that simply occur to one, as in reveries and dreams, and those creative thoughts and speculations that one thinks for himself, which appear to be within one's control and direction. If, however, we conceive of thoughts, not as things that flow in a stream, but as actions and passions—that is, as things *done,* either *by* an agent or *to* an agent—then the distinction we are seeking, between thoughts that merely occur to one and those that are within one's control and direction, is at hand: acting over against being acted upon, or, in the older terminology, action versus passion. Just *what* this difference is remains unknown, but this consequence arises not from a theory of mental acts but from the impossibility of defining action and passion with respect to any kind of behavior. What, for example, is the difference between my raising my arm and having my arm raised? If there is a good answer to that question, it is also the answer to the question: What is the difference between my thinking some thought and merely having the thought evoked? Perhaps we can only say, in either case, that it is a distinction between something I do, or make happen, and something that results from extraneous causes. Putting the matter this way raises grave problems, to be sure—but they are problems we already have, quite independently of any theory of mental acts.

Some Significant Entailments

In Chapter IX I elicited certain entailments between those statements which do and those which do not describe acts. If the same entailments apply to thoughts, they will serve well to distinguish mental activity and passivity. Of course, this assumes that the entailments worked out earlier are correct and do in fact distinguish active from passive behavior.

The four basic patterns of statements we considered before were these:

1. *e* occurs.
2. Something makes *e* occur.
3. A does *e*.
4. Something makes A do *e*.

We can, as before, for example, let A designate an agent, such as myself, and *e* some bodily motion, such as the motion of my finger, and the four statements can then be interpreted as (1) my finger moves, (2) something makes my finger move, (3) I move my finger, and (4) something makes me move my finger.

We noted before, then, that each of these statements logically entails all the statements above it, and that none of them entails any of the statements below it. From this it follows that no two such statements are identical in meaning, for there are no two which are such that, if either of them is true the other must be true and if either of them is false the other must be false.

Suppose, now, that we substitute for *e* something purely psychological in nature, such as solving a fairly simple puzzle or problem which is, we shall suppose, easily within my power to solve simply by "putting my mind to it." We shall thus get the following four statements, following the pattern set forth above:

1. The solution occurs to me.
2. Something makes the solution occur to me.
3. I solve the problem.
4. Something makes me solve the problem.

Now identically the same entailments hold with respect to these statements. Each entails every other statement above it, and none entails any of the statements below it. Thus, I might simply *find* the solution to the problem someplace where it is given, on the back of the sheet on which the problem is posed, for instance. In that case (1) and (2) would be true but (3) and (4) false, since in one clear sense I could hardly claim to have actually solved the problem. Or again, it is logically possible that the solution might simply occur to me —present itself to my mind—miraculously, without anything causing this to happen, and without my doing anything toward getting the solution. Doubtless this never happens, since it is very doubtful whether anything ever happens from no cause at all. At any rate this sort of thing probably could not happen in such a free and spontaneous way, but that is beside the point. For the point is that if this *were* to happen, which is certainly a logical possibility, then only (1) would be true. Or again, without the help of any answer sheet or miraculous occurrence, I might in the most straightforward sense *solve* the problem, by putting my mind to it, or by trying to solve it and succeeding. In that case (3) would be true, and (1) and (2) would likewise be true, but (4) would be problematical—for from the mere fact that I did this it would not follow that anything had made me do it. Or finally, something might make me solve the problem, in the sense of literally causing me to do so, assuming, as we are, that there is no question of my ability to solve it. I might be forced to solve it by threats of sufficient force, for example. In that case all four of the statements would be true, for the fourth would be true, and the truth of this one clearly entails that all the others are true.

We have here, then, precisely the same distinctions between activity and passivity that we had with respect to those actions which are expressed in bodily motions. The claim that actions are in a fundamental way distinct from bodily motions that are not actions can, in fact, be understood as being just the claim that these distinctions can be drawn. Accordingly, the claim that there are mental acts, or that mental activity is in a fundamental way distinct from otherwise similar mental states that are not actions, can be understood as being just the claim that these distinctions can be drawn with respect to thought, and it does seem quite clear that they can. *Having* a certain thought is not necessarily the same as *thinking*, for statements of the first two patterns above can be true, as in dreams, reveries, and the like, when corresponding statements of the last two are not.

We also noted in the earlier chapter that certain questions traditionally associated with the problem of free will can be expressed quite precisely in terms of these entailments. Thus, the thesis that there are "free and spontaneous events which are not acts" can be interpreted to mean that some statements of the first form are true when corresponding statements of the second form are not. This is, of course, a dubious or at least controversial thesis, but it can nevertheless be clearly expressed in just this way. Similarly, the libertarian thesis that there are "free actions," or actions not causally determined, can be interpreted to mean that some statements of the third form, and with these the corresponding interpretations of the first two forms, are true when corresponding statements of the fourth form are not. This, too, is a controversial thesis, but a clear one; it means only that agents are not always caused to do all the things that they do.

Now it is fairly obvious that these things all hold, whether *e* is interpreted as some bodily motion, as in the earlier chapter, or as some thought. The two questions, then, whether thinking is ever an activity, and if so whether it is ever a free activity, can be expressed by asking (i) whether, when *e* is interpreted as a certain thought, the first two statements can be true and the last two statements false, and (ii) whether the third might be true under circumstances in which the fourth is false. Affirmative answers to both of these questions can, then, be interpreted as a clear affirmation of the thesis that thinking is sometimes not only an activity, but sometimes also a free activity.

12

Deliberation

In spite of the current emphasis on problems of philosophical psychology rather little is ever said in contemporary philosophy about deliberation except in contexts of ethics. It should be fairly obvious, though, that deliberation is not itself a concept of ethics, since men often deliberate about matters having nothing whatever to do with moral choice. It is instead a concept of psychology. Yet one can search in vain through the literature of psychology for any thorough discussion of it; it is almost as if there were no such thing, so far as psychology is concerned. What is equally odd is that philosophers discuss it so little, for even the most cursory glance at what is involved in deliberation reveals enormous implications, not only with respect to the idea of the will, but with respect to human action generally. Typically, those writers who do touch on it at all confine themselves to observations of Aristotle's treatment of it, seemingly unaware of implications beyond the limited context of ethics in which Aristotle's treatment of it arose.

Deliberation and Purpose

Deliberation is clearly a teleological concept, since one can make no sense of it at all independently of the concepts of means and ends. That is to say, deliberation is always concerned either with the choice of alternative competing ends or, the end being given, with the choice of alternative means to the realization of it. It is for this reason that deliberation is never, as Aristotle noted, concerned with things past, for a man's present aims or goals can never be located in the past. It is this, too, which so sharply distinguishes deliberation from speculation, reason, and inference, though it is exceedingly common to find it confused with these in philosophy. It is sometimes even supposed that unless a man could somehow *infer* what he was going to do—from his intentions, for example—then he could have no way of *knowing* what he was going to do. The reason for this is no doubt partly that statements expressing intention, with respect to some means or end, have exactly the same verbal form as those expressing predictions, and it is the latter which philosophers somehow find natural, familiar, and intelligible. For example, "I shall volunteer for the service" and "I shall be drafted for the service" look very much alike. Yet the former is an expression of an intention, and might very well be the expression of an intention arrived at as a result of deliberation, whereas the latter would in most contexts be a mere prediction of an event concerning which it would, normally, make no sense to deliberate.

What Deliberation Is

Deliberation, as I am conceiving it, is a process of active, purposeful thought, having as its aim or goal a decision to act, under circumstances in which more than one action is, or at least is believed to be, possible for him who deliberates.

The elements of activity and purpose in this description are what are of primary significance. To say that deliberation is an activity means that it is something one does, not just a process that occurs, for which factors independent of the agent's activity are causally responsible. It would be impossible to describe a deliberative process of thought, thereby distinguishing it from such thought processes as are non-deliberative, without somehow referring to the agent as the author of those thoughts, or without qualifying its elements as thoughts which he himself evokes and considers. To say, further, that deliberative thought is purposive means that it is directed toward a goal, namely, toward a decision or the making up of one's mind. These two elements taken together—activity and purpose—distinguish deliberation from another familiar kind of thinking with which it is often confused; namely, vacillation between competing impulses, desires, or motives, which can be described entirely without teleological concepts and which need not involve the idea of agency at all.

To illustrate, suppose I am a guest for the evening in the house of a friend, some distance from home, and that while I had not thought of the possibility of spending the night there, I am now invited to do so. The most natural way of describing this situation is to say that two mutually exclusive alternatives are presented. Concerning each we can say that I can do it, for what I ultimately do will depend upon my decision, and my decision will depend upon me, in precisely the same way that any act depends upon its agent. Now the decision may require no thought, no deliberation at all—as, for example, if staying over has no appeal to me in the first place and I have, in addition, strong reasons for rejecting the idea. On the other hand, I might want to think about it—to deliberate, in the most straightforward sense. If, for example, my keenest desire is to stay over, and yet there are strong reasons, perhaps unconnected with anything I in any real sense desire, for not staying, the decision may not be easy. These reasons might have to do with certain obligations, for instance, and these might be obligations that are felt, but not at all felt as objects of desire. Finally, I make up my mind, I decide, as I surely might do after deliberation and in the conviction that I could have decided otherwise. If not, what would have been the point of the deliberation? And if not, how could it ever occur to me to reconsider the decision once made, which is nevertheless sometimes something that is done?

The foregoing kind of experience can be contrasted with another which it superficially resembles. Suppose, that is, that in the same circumstances I give no actual thought to the alternatives; I am aware both of my strong desire to stay over and of competing reasons for declining this, but I do not bring these into any active consideration, weigh no pros and cons, but just leave the matter to work itself out. At one moment, my desire to stay over prevailing, I shall decide in favor of staying, in case I decide at all. At another moment, my sense of my other obligations prevailing, I shall decline staying over, if the matter then comes to a head. Finally, when the decision cannot be put off any more and I have to make up my mind, I just decide, with little or no consideration, letting whatever impulse or inclination I happen to feel most acutely at that moment decide the matter for me.

Now while both of these continuing states of mind can in some sense be described as processes of thought, only the first is deliberative. The second is, simply, *vacillation* between competing inclinations. Both are, moreover, processes of *my* thinking. But in the first my thought is an activity, for I am intentionally calling it forth. In the second I do not call forth any thoughts or considerations; they simply occur to me, willy-nilly, with whatever force they may or may not have for deciding the matter for me. In the first my thinking is purposive, for thoughts are pursued with a view to making a decision, but in the second my thoughts have no purpose. They are only thoughts, impulses, or inclinations that occur in succession. The second situation can therefore be described without introducing the idea of my doing anything at all, except just deciding, whereas the first cannot, and there are accordingly all sort of locutions, mostly metaphorical, which are used to convey the element of activity involved in deliberation—such as "weighing" pros and cons, "turning" the thing over in my mind, and so on.

Deliberation and Speculation

Deliberation thus seems quite distinct in kind from vacillation in that it is both active and purposeful. Purposeless things which are not agents can vacillate but no sense can be made of their deliberating. Animals, too, can vacillate between competing impulses and stimuli but can hardly be supposed to deliberate.

Deliberation can also be differentiated from a second kind of thinking —the active processes of speculation and inference. In the remainder of this chapter, then, I shall point out some of the factors that are necessarily involved in deliberation but not in speculation, illustrating these with examples as I proceed. I shall proceed from the more obvious to the more controversial, basing the latter as much as I can on the former.

Deliberation and Future Action

It seems first of all evident that one cannot deliberate about anything except one's own possible future actions, conceived either as an end or as the means to the realization of an end. Speculation and inference, on the other hand, can be concerned with almost anything whatever about which there is ignorance.

Four restrictions are thus put at once upon deliberation, though not upon speculation and inference. These are (i) that the subject of one's deliberation is something conceived as future, never present or past; (ii) that the subject of deliberation is an action, and not some event unconnected with action; (iii) that this is always one's own action and never that of another agent; and (iv) that it is an action which is conceived as merely possible, and never as one that is either unavoidable or impossible.

With respect to acts of other people, for instance, one can speculate about them, try to predict them, or to infer what they are going to be; but one cannot deliberate about them. A statement such as "I am deliberating whether Jones will do E" cannot be true, unless it means "I am deliberating whether I shall have Jones do E," in which case it expresses deliberation about one's own possible future act. One can only deliberate about what he believes to be within his own power. Thus, "I am deliberating whether Smith shall be reprieved" entails "I believe it to be within my power alone to reprieve Smith." If I believe this to be within the power of another—the governor, for example—then I can speculate about what he will do, or I can deliberate about what I would do if I were governor; but I cannot deliberate about what to do.

Even with this condition satisfied there is a further stipulation—I cannot deliberate about what I have already done or am already doing; I can deliberate only about my possible *future* acts. I can regret things I have already done, take satisfaction in them, and so on. If I have forgotten what those acts were I can try to find out, infer, or guess; but I cannot deliberate about them. Though I may not know, for example, whether I took my vitamin pill yesterday, I can no longer deliberate about whether or not to take it *then*. Past and present things, even if they are my own acts, are no longer within my power to do or to forego, and I can deliberate only about things which are. Similarly, if I am sitting I cannot deliberate about whether to be sitting. I can only deliberate about whether to remain sitting; and this has to do with the future.

Now it would not, to be sure, be outrageously incongruous for one to say that he is deliberating or (synonymously) trying to decide whether he *ought* to have done something which he has in fact done, thus seeming to render doubtful the claim that deliberation is concerned only with the future. Deliberation in this sense, however, is both logically and psychologically different from what I am here concerned with. It is essentially no different from what a meteorologist would be doing if, studying his data and charts, he truly said that he was trying to *decide* what tomorrow's weather is going to be, or what a moralist would be doing if he truly said he was deliberating or trying to decide whether, say, Socrates should have taken the hemlock. In such cases one is, obviously, doing nothing more than trying to resolve a question or doubt of one kind or another. The meteorologist, unless he happens also to be a rainmaker, is not trying to decide whether to have it rain tomorrow, since this is not within his power, nor is the moralist trying to decide whether to have Socrates drink the hemlock. Similarly, in deliberating or trying to decide whether I ought to have done what I in fact did, I am not trying to decide whether to do it or not (it being no longer within my power to alter that fact), but only to resolve a doubt, which in this case happens to be a moral one. What I am doing is essentially no different from what the moralist pondering Socrates' behavior is doing. Thoughts and reflections which are aimed merely at the resolution of doubt, however, are essentially speculative rather than deliberative. When, unlike such cases, I am deliberating whether I ought *to do* something, which it is within my power to do or to forego, I am *not* merely trying to resolve a doubt or settle my opinion about something. Unlike the meteorologist who reflects about the weather, or the moralist who ponders the moral implications of Socrates' behavior, I *am* trying to decide whether to do something, or whether to leave it undone. I am trying, not merely to settle upon certain opinions, moral or otherwise, concerning what I do, but to decide just what it is that I shall do. Whatever may be the permissiveness of "ordinary usage," it is this which I prefer to call deliberation, in the strict sense, just to distinguish it from all those thoughts and reflections which are essentially intellectual and speculative.

Again, one cannot deliberate about such things as the future behavior of some heavenly body, even though this may be unknown to him, though he may make inferences or speculations concerning such things. One reason, of course, is, as Aristotle pointed out, that such things occur by necessity and are not within anyone's power to control. But there is another reason: Neither could one deliberate about, say, the outcome of the spin of a roulette wheel, assuming this to be causally undetermined. He could only guess, make bets on it, and so on—unless, of course, he thought he could influence this outcome. But then he would be deliberating on his own future activity—namely, whether or not to try influencing the outcome.

The final qualification, dictated by the preconditions of deliberation as well as by logic, is that deliberation is concerned with one's *possible* future actions. As we shall see shortly, an action which is believed to be inevitable cannot be the subject of deliberation nor, by the same token, can one which is believed impossible. Aside from this, however, if one is deliberating concerning certain *alternative* actions, then not all of them can be, simply, his future actions. Each can be no more than a *possible* action. If, for example, I am deliberating whether to leave the room or to stay, then not both of these can be my future actions, for on the supposition that either of them is my future action, it logically follows that the other is not.

Deliberation and Avoidability

It seems evident that one cannot deliberate even about his own future act in case he believes it is already inevitable or unavoidable. This, again, is a consequence of the fact that one can deliberate only about what he believes to be within his power both to do and to forego —which is, be it noted, something quite different from believing it to within one's power to both do and forego something, a self-contradictory belief which no one can hold. The very point, however, in calling something inevitable is to deny that this condition is fulfilled, for it can never be the case that it is within one's power both to do and to forego something which is inevitable, any more than it can be within one's power both to do and to forego something which is impossible.

Thus, one cannot deliberate about whether to (eventually) die; he can only deliberate on how to make the best of it, with insurance and so on. The husband of a pregnant woman cannot deliberate on whether to become a father, unless this is a question of whether to terminate the pregnancy. A passenger in an airplane cannot deliberate about whether or not to return to earth; he well knows that he will, in one way or another. He cannot even deliberate about when or where to come down, unless he is the pilot—that is, unless this is up to him, or within his power. In case such things are thought not to be "acts," we can add that a soldier cannot deliberate about whether or not to arm himself, in case he knows that there is a regulation requiring him to do so and that the regulation will be enforced. What to do is, in this case, not up to him.

Now of course one can deliberate whether to do this or that *if* a certain condition is fulfilled, not knowing whether that condition will be fulfilled but believing that it has already been rendered inevitable that it will be, or that it will not. One might, for example, deliberate whether to study in France or in Italy in case he gets a certain award, knowing that the awards have already been finally decided but not yet announced. In that case he can only guess, speculate, or even try by secret intelligence to find out whether he has won an award. But without doing any of this he can still deliberate about whether to go to France or to Italy, in case he does get it. In that case, however, he must believe that neither of these two alternatives is likewise already rendered inevitable, in case he has won the award. He cannot, for example, believe that the award, in case he has won it, will turn out to be one permitting him to study only in Italy, or only in France, and still deliberate about where to study on the award. At most he can then only deliberate about whether or not to accept the award, in case he turns out to have won it.

Deliberation
and One's Own Foreknowledge

Thirdly, I want to argue that an agent cannot deliberate about what to do, even though this may be something that is up to him and something that otherwise satisfies all the conditions so far elicited, in case he already knows what he is going to do. This is something that deliberation has in common with speculation, inference, and even guesswork; namely, that all presuppose ignorance, in the absence of which they can only be shammed. Inference about things future, however, has for its purpose the *discovery* of what is *going* to happen, whereas deliberation has for its purpose a *decision* about what to *make* happen. In this respect the two are utterly different.

There seem, in fact, to be only two ways in which one could know what he is going to do; namely, by *inferring* what he is going to do, or by *deciding* what he is going to do. In neither case can one deliberate about what he is going to do.

Thus, if a governor said, "I am, as a result of my forthcoming deliberations, going to reprieve Smith," he would indicate that his mind was already made up, and hence, that he was *not* going to deliberate about it—unless, of course, with a view to possibly changing his mind. But in that case he could not know that his statement was true. He could, of course, pretend to deliberate about it, discuss the matter with his assistants, perhaps publicly review the pros and cons once again, but if he did so he would be shamming deliberation. His purpose would not be to arrive at a decision, this having been already arrived at, but something else—perhaps that of conveying a desirable public image of himself.

Similarly, if anyone said, "I see, by reliable signs and portents, that I am about to do *e,* so I shall deliberate about it," he could not possibly be expressing himself accurately. If he does already know what he is going to do there is nothing there for him to decide, and hence nothing to deliberate about.

For example, it might be possible for a group of observers to infer reliably from certain signs that a certain man is about to be married. They see the flowers, witnesses assembled, preacher waiting, music playing, groom suitably attired, and so on. From the same evidence, which is apparent to the groom himself, he too can gather that he is about to be married, though for him, unless he doesn't realize what he has gotten himself into, such signs and portents are superfluous. If, however, he regards these signs as reliable evidence of what he is about to do, he cannot deliberate about what to do—he is past deliberation, and the die is cast. If, on the other hand, he still *does* deliberate about whether to get married—if he has last minute misgivings and second thoughts—then he obviously does not regard the signs as reliable evidence of what he is going to do. He is, in fact, contemplating confuting the very thing those signs point to, by walking right out of the church.

Of course deliberation is seldom if ever so pure as this. More commonly one finds himself partly trying to decide what to do, partly trying to predict what he is going to do, partly deliberating about what to do if the predictions turn out right and, perhaps in addition, deliberating about whether to hold to a decision that has been at least tentatively made, and so on. Mixed with our governor's deliberations, for instance, might be all sorts of attempts at predicting what his opponents will do, what he will be forced to do in response, and what, in the light of these, he ought to do about the reprieve, and so on. Still, deliberation about what *to* do is essentially different, both logically and psychologically, from prediction about what one is *going* to do, or what other people or things are going to do. One can deliberate, but not predict, about what to *make* happen, and one can predict, but not really deliberate, about what *is going* to happen. The fact that both can occur together and have significant connections with each other, and are for this and other reasons often confused in the minds of philosophers and others, does not at all obliterate the essential differences.

Deliberation
and the Awareness of Causes

From the foregoing it follows that a man cannot deliberate concerning some action of his if he believes that there are already conditions causally sufficient for his performing the act in question, or for his not performing it, and moreover knows what those conditions are and for what they are causally sufficient. If his act is caused in this sense —that is, if it is an inevitable consequence of certain conditions existing antecedently—then he can, simply by his awareness of those causes, know by inference what his act is going to be. Under such circumstances he cannot deliberate whether to do or forego the thing in question, for he already knows that he will, or else he knows that he will not.

Examples are supplied by compulsions, addictions, solemn agreements, and the like. Or consider some such act as sneezing, which is ordinarily performed involuntarily but which can be done deliberately. If one feels a sneeze coming on, in the sense that he is forewarned of this impending convulsion by a certain familiar nasal tickle, then he cannot deliberate whether to sneeze or not; he can only prepare for it. The only exception would be in case he thought he might be able to repress the sneeze; but in that case he would not, obviously, consider the felt irritation to be causally sufficient to make him sneeze. One might, on the other hand, have some occasion to deliberate whether to sneeze, if he were considering ways of attracting someone's attention, for example, or perhaps of feigning illness in order to avoid some irksome chore. His deliberation would have to cease, however, the moment he became aware of any condition sufficient either for his sneezing, or for his not sneezing, for he would then know what he was going to do.

From this it of course follows that one's deliberate acts cannot be caused, in the usual sense, or, if they are, then one cannot know that those causes exist at the time he deliberates. Like speculation about what is going to happen, then, deliberation about what one is going to make happen rests upon ignorance.

But now the question arises whether deliberation rests upon anything more; that is, whether it presupposes only an *ignorance* of the causes of one's deliberate act, or the actual *absence* of such causes. We shall return to this important question shortly, but here we can note that it is quite possible for one to deliberate about whether to do a certain thing even in the presence of conditions causally sufficient for his doing what he contemplates doing, provided, of course, that he is ignorant of the existence of such conditions. One might, for instance, be deliberating whether to sneeze, thinking that this might be an effective way of feigning illness, not knowing that a sneezing powder has been liberated into the room, the inevitable effect of which will soon be to cause everyone in the room to begin sneezing. Or one might be deliberating whether to leave a certain house, wholly unaware that the house is on fire and that he will shortly be forced to leave. One can hardly help noting, however, that in such cases one's deliberation is otiose and pointless, since what one then does is not the *result* of his deliberation at all. There was really nothing for him to decide; he only thought there was.

Deliberation and Causation

Fifthly, I maintain that even if one does not know what he is going to do, but nevertheless knows that conditions already exist which are causally sufficient for his doing whatever it is that he is going to do, then he cannot deliberate about what to do, even though he may not know what those conditions are. One can, in such a case, only guess or speculate about what he will do, or try to find out what it is that he will inevitably do. This is again a consequence of the fact that one can deliberate whether to do a certain act only if he believes it is up to him whether to do it or not, or, that it is within his power equally to do it, *and* to forego it.

For example, consider a soldier who knows that daily orders regarding the bearing of arms are enforced, and that he has no choice but to obey them. Suppose he does not know whether or not he shall be required to arm himself today, though he knows that the order has been posted. He cannot deliberate about whether to arm himself today. He can only check to see what order has been posted and, until then, perhaps try to guess. Of course he might deliberate whether to comply with his order; but if he did he would not be assuming that such orders are really *enforced*. He would be assuming only that there are strong, but perhaps insufficient, inducements for obedience.

Or consider a man—we'll call him Adam—who has spent the evening at the distant home of a friend and is then invited by his host to spend the night. This might call for careful consideration of the pros and cons on Adam's part, for weighing in his mind the pleasures of staying over against considerations of his responsibilities at home, and so on. Suppose further, however, that another guest—we'll call him Brown—knows that there exist conditions which render it causally impossible for Adam to go home. He knows, for instance, that the last train has left, and that there is no other way for Adam to get home. Now clearly, Adam can still deliberate about whether to remain or not, in ignorance of what Brown knows. But now suppose Brown announces that he knows what Adam is going to do, without giving any hint as to what this is, and that he knows it on the basis of certain unnamed conditions which are causally sufficient for Adam's doing what Brown knows he will do. If Adam *believes* this, he cannot any longer deliberate about what to do, even though he does not know what he is going to do and is not himself aware of any conditions sufficient for his doing either the one thing or the other. All he can do is speculate, guess, and wait to see what he will have to do, meanwhile exhorting Brown to tell him. He can no longer deliberate about the matter because, if he believes Brown, then he believes it is not up to him what he does; the matter has already been "decided," one way or the other, and there is no decision for Adam to make.

It is no good here, incidentally, to introduce such vague and familiar slogans as "Deliberation might, after all, be a natural process," or "Deliberation is only the way some, perhaps psychological, causes work themselves out," and so on. If such remarks are unpacked, and "natural processes" are found to be nothing but causal chains, and "causes" are understood to be causes of the usual kind, then far from being rejoinders to what has been said they only illustrate something that is painfully well known; namely, that philosophers are perfectly capable of holding speculative opinions that are inconsistent with some of their own beliefs of common sense.

Now I believe the principle involved here can be generalized, such that if a man believes that there are, or ever will be, conditions, not themselves within his control yet sufficient for his doing whatever it is that he is going to do, then he cannot deliberate about what to do, even though he may not have the slightest idea what this is, or what those conditions are, or will be, or what they will be sufficient for.

Consider a man at a cocktail party, for instance, who knows, in a cognitive sense—which entails that what he knows is true—that he will accept any standard cocktail that is offered provided it is made with gin, but that he will drink nothing alcoholic otherwise, having a nausea for any other type of spiritous beverage. Now this man cannot deliberate about whether to drink gin, for he already knows that he will, *if* it is offered. There is, then, nothing for him to decide. Nor can he deliberate about whether to drink at all, for he already knows that he will not, *unless* gin is offered. All he can do is try to speculate, or guess, whether gin will be served, this being, we are supposing, something that is not up to him. And it should be noted that under the conditions assumed it is impossible for him to deliberate even though he may not know what he is going to do, and may even doubt that conditions already exist which are sufficient for his doing whatever he is going to do.

This example is imperfect, however, for one can justly wonder how anyone could have such knowledge. One can "know" what he is going to do under certain and as yet undecided alternative circumstances, in the sense of having firmly made up his mind—and still, for instance, fall dead before having a chance to do it, showing that his "knowledge" was not of the kind that entails that what was thus "known" was true. This observation does not really affect the argument, but since the doubt raised about the illustration can easily transfer itself to the argument we should perhaps supply a better example. Consider, then, a man who is watching the spinning of a roulette wheel, and who knows (and has not merely resolved) that he will take the purse in case it stops on an even number, but that he will have to surrender his own stake if it stops on an odd number. Now he cannot deliberate about whether to take the purse or surrender his own, even though this has not been at all determined. And, it should be noted, this is still true even if he believes the behavior of the wheel to be causally undetermined with respect to where it stops, and hence believes that his own act is as yet causally undetermined as well, such that there are not yet any conditions sufficient either for his doing the one thing or the other. The reason for this is obvious; namely, that having got this far into the game it is no longer up to him what he does. It is entirely up to the roulette wheel, and there is nothing for him to decide. All he can do is guess, and hope.

Deliberation
and General Foreknowledge

Finally, I maintain that no one could in principle ever know what another man is going to do as a result of forthcoming deliberation. One can, of course, know what another is going to do as a result of deliberation that is already concluded, for that person can then simply announce what he is going to do. But one can make no such announcement while still deliberating, for he could not *himself* know that it was true. There is no way that he could possibly know, before he has decided, nor is there any way that anyone else could know.

If someone knew what another was going to do as a result of forthcoming deliberation, then he would know on the basis of some kind of evidence; that is, on the basis of his knowledge of certain conditions that were causally sufficient for the agent's doing the thing in question, and from which it could be inferred that he would do that. But if there were such conditions then they could also be known by, or made known to, the agent himself, such that he too could infer what he was going to do. This, however, is impossible, so long as the agent has not yet himself decided what to do. Indeed, the agent cannot even believe that any such conditions, known or unknown, exist, and at the same time believe that it is within his power both to do, and to forego doing, the thing in question. This, as we have seen, appears to be a necessary condition of deliberation.

The foregoing is not to be confused with a familiar type of fallacy, whereby one truly asserts what cannot happen in case something else happens, and then, ignoring this qualification, draws some categorical conclusion about what cannot happen. The point is rather, that no one can know by inference that a certain event is going to happen, except on the basis of his knowledge of certain conditions causally sufficient to produce that event. If no such conditions exist, then it obviously cannot be known by inference that the event in question is going to happen, and if it is so known, then there must be such conditions. If the event in question is the act of some agent, however, then that agent cannot deliberate about whether to do it, believing that any such conditions already exist, even though he may not know what they are; for the fact that *any* such conditions already exist would entail that it is no longer up to him what he is going to do. And moreover, if another person knows by inference what his act will be, then he cannot know that this act will be the result of deliberation still forthcoming. He will, on the contrary, know that it will be the result of conditions, known by him, sufficient to produce it.

Now I might, to be sure, know a person and his habits well enough to know that, whenever he is confronted with a certain choice—say, that of going to New York or to Boston—then he invariably decides the same way—say, by going to New York. And it is possible to suppose that, before deciding, he always or often deliberates about the matter. In that case I could predict with confidence what he was going to do, and this would be consistent with his always deliberating first. But then I would know what he was going to do, *not* as a result of his deliberation, but as a result of something else—of habit, for example. If, as a result of sheer habit, or as a result of some other condition that is always present when such a decision is made, the man invariably decides in the same way, then his decision is not the result of his deliberation, and not something that is really up to him. It is the result, or causal consequence, of something else; of habit, for example, or of whatever other condition we are supposing determines the matter.

If, moreover, I know that another person is deliberating about a certain choice that is before him, and know what his decision is going to be, on the basis of some consideration that is known to me and which must sooner or later also come to his attention and certainly decide the matter, then I know what he is going to do, not as a result of his deliberation, but as a result of this further consideration, which will terminate his deliberation. If, for instance, I know that someone is deliberating whether to remain in the room or leave, and I know, further, that the room is on fire, and that he will shortly notice this himself and leave as a consequence of this, then I know what he is going to do. But I know this only because I know that what he is going to do will *not* be the result of his deliberation, but of his knowledge of the circumstances. What he does is not up to him at all, assuming the fire to be of such a nature as leaves him no real alternative.

Deliberation and Determinism

One fairly obvious consequence of much of the foregoing is that deliberation is inconsistent with determinism. This does not mean that if men deliberate then determinism must be false; for it is perfectly possible that men do sometimes deliberate, whereas no one does know that determinism is false. What is inconsistent is for someone to affirm a theory of determinism and at the same time deliberate about some of his own future actions. For the thesis of determinism entails that, in the case of any action that any man ever performs, there are conditions antecedent to his action which render it causally impossible for him to perform any other. Deliberation on the other hand, presupposes that an action which one contemplates doing, and concerning which he deliberates, has been rendered neither causally impossible nor causally inevitable by any conditions obtaining at the time of deliberation. If any agent does not believe this, he cannot deliberate whether to do the action or not; he can only speculate or perhaps infer whether he is going to do it. Deliberation can only be aimed at a decision whether or not to act in a certain way, and is impossible if one believes that there is no decision to make or no rational connection between what one decides and what one then does.

Now if a man believes, concerning some of the actions he is going to perform, that there already exist conditions causally sufficient for his performing them, and conditions which therefore render them inevitable, then he cannot deliberate whether or not to perform them. If, accordingly, he believes this to be true of all the actions he ever performs, then he cannot, consistently with that belief, deliberate about any of them. Nor is it of any use to point out here that some philosophers do, after all, hold a theory that all human actions are causally determined and that these same philosophers do nevertheless deliberate about some of their own future actions. This only shows that it is perfectly possible, and in fact common, for philosophers to hold speculative theories which are inconsistent with some of their commonsense beliefs. If two things are inconsistent, then that inconsistency is by no means removed by the simple joint affirmation of both. Inconsistent views have often been widely held, particularly in philosophy and other areas of speculation, and here seems to me an excellent example of a philosophical view which, though consistent with itself, is not consistent with something that all men believe, including the defenders of that philosophical view. They have simply failed to see that inconsistency, which is, again, not so very uncommon.

Nor does it do to say that deliberation might, after all, itself be one of the causes of some human actions, namely, those that result from deliberation. To say that some agent does something as a result of deliberation is very far from saying that he is caused to do what he does by his deliberation. Indeed, to speak in such a fashion is entirely to misconceive what deliberation is. It is part of the very concept of deliberation that it applies to situations in which there are, or are at least believed to be, alternative possible courses of action, and that as a result of one's deliberation he might do either one. The very fact that a man is deliberating what to do, far from offering any assurance about what he is going to do, deprives one of that assurance.

Now deliberation can be illusory in either of two ways. In the first place, it might be illusory in the sense that a man deliberates about what he takes to be possible alternatives when in fact there are no alternatives—as in the case of a man who is trying to decide whether to stay in a room or to leave, being unaware that he will soon be forced to leave. Or in the second place, it might be illusory in the sense that a man thinks he is deliberating when in fact he is only rationalizing, or trying to find reasons for doing something which in fact he cannot help doing—as in the case of a man who is really incapable of a genuine act of generosity, but who nevertheless "deliberates" whether to perform such an act. In the first case deliberation is illusory because there is really nothing to deliberate about—the agent only thinks there is. The second is illusory because the agent does not really deliberate; he only thinks he does.

Now if it should happen to be true that all human actions are causally determined by conditions existing antecedently to them, as some philosophers maintain, then all deliberation must be illusory in one or the other of these two senses, and of course it is quite possible that it is. It is perfectly possible that no man ever does deliberate, that men only suppose that they deliberate, and perhaps flatter themselves that they do, when in fact they are only rationalizing their behavior in advance, like the selfish man who actually believes that he is deliberating whether to perform a genuine act of generosity. Or again, it is perfectly possible, and indeed not inherently implausible, that men do often deliberate, but that there is really never anything to deliberate about, every action being predetermined by factors that are for the most part unknown. We might, whenever we deliberate, be in a position similar to that of the man who will, unbeknown to him, soon be forced to leave a room, but who in the meantime deliberates whether to leave it or not.

If one consistently maintains a strong theory of determinism then he must, I think, also maintain that deliberation is always illusory in one or both of these senses. If, on the other hand, one believes that his deliberation is sometimes not an illusion—that is, that he does sometimes deliberate, and not merely fancy that he deliberates, and that his actions do sometimes actually result from deliberation—then he cannot consistently maintain that *those* actions are causally determined by conditions existing antecedently to his deliberation.

No one, I think, can categorically *say* whether or not determinism is true, or whether or not deliberation is sometimes not an illusion in either sense. Whatever view one takes is a matter of opinion or, if firmly put forth, of sheer dogmatism. One can show, however, that some views are not logically consistent with others, and I have tried to show that it is at any rate inconsistent to hold both that determinism is true and that men are sometimes not under illusion when they deliberate. It is regrettably, however, an inconsistency that philosophers have often failed to see or even, it seems, to consider.

13

Prevention
and
Purpose*

In an earlier chapter I briefly considered, incidental to other questions, why causes are never thought of as "working backward," that is, why no events can sensibly be conceived as having effects prior to themselves in time. This question, as I there noted, is not answered, except on a very superficial level, by any observations about the meanings of words as they are ordinarily used.

In the present chapter I am going to consider, incidental to a larger purpose, the somewhat similar question why causal agency cannot sensibly be conceived as directed toward things past. This is not exactly the same question that I raised before, because I am here concerned with agency rather than the very different concept of causal connection found between states and events. Another way of putting my present question would be: Why do we have no corollary to the concept of prevention? Or, taking the word "postvention" to be the verbal complement of "prevention," we may ask: Why does "postvention" not even occur in our language?

*This chapter, in somewhat different form, appeared first in *Freedom and Determinism,* edited by Keith Lehrer, © Copyright, 1966 by Random House, Inc.

Now such a question, considered in isolation from other problems, is surely more curious than wise, but I am introducing it in order to call attention to a fundamental and insufficiently noted difference in the way men view future things as opposed to the way they view past things, at least insofar as these bear upon their weal or woe. I believe that this difference does not result from the way we happen to use words, but conversely that we use certain words as we do because of this difference. Our views of past and of future things largely arises, I shall maintain, from our more fundamental concept of ourselves as purposeful beings, and of our actions as being, at least ordinarily, not merely the causes of effects but the means to ends or goals, which is something quite different. If this notion of means and ends were banished from men's thinking then we would, I believe, have as little use for the idea of preventing things as we have for the idea of postventing them. Finally, I shall try to show what bearing these observations have on the notion of the will, and particularly on the idea of freedom.

Prevention

To have *prevented* some event is, precisely, to have done something that was, under the conditions then and thereafter prevailing, both sufficient and necessary for, though logically independent of, the subsequent non-occurrence of that event. We shall see, in terms of the types of inference warranted by prevention statements, why an action that was genuinely preventive must have been both sufficient and necessary for the non-occurrence of what was thus prevented. Here we need only note that a preventive action and the event it prevents are always logically independent of each other, or such that it is not a logical contradiction, though it is false, to assert that both of them occurred. Some might want to say that they can be brought into logical relationships with each other by conjoining true statements about them with certain statements of the laws of nature, and that is all right, at least so far as any points in the present discussion are concerned. Some persons, too, might prefer such expressions as "guaranteed" or "insured" for "was sufficient for," and such expressions as "was essential for" or "was indispensable to" for "was necessary for," just to make clear that the relationships involved are not those involving any logical necessity or impossibility, but this need not detain us. The foregoing definition of prevention already stipulates that a preventive action and what it prevents are at least logically independent of each other.

To illustrate this, suppose that a physician rightly claims to have prevented another man's death by a timely operation. This means that he did something—performed a certain operation with scalpel and other instruments—which was, under the other conditions then and thereafter prevailing, sufficient for the non-occurrence of that man's death, and also necessary, or such that the man would not have lived had he, the physician, not done what he did. Now of course the physician does not claim to have thereby prevented the man's *eventual* death, since no man can prevent that. In saving his patient's life he did not render him immortal, and did not claim to. He only claimed to have prevented a death that was otherwise impending.

Again, suppose a policeman rightly claims to have prevented another man from murdering someone by secretly removing the bullets from that man's gun with his fingers. This amounts to saying that he eliminated a certain condition which was, under the other conditions then and thereafter prevailing, necessary for that murder and also, under those same conditions, sufficient for that murder, or such that, all else then happening just as it did, the man would not have failed in his attempt at murder had the policeman not taken this timely precaution. Again, of course, this preventive action does not guarantee that the man shall never again try murdering someone and perhaps succeed, but the policeman does not claim to have prevented all that. He only prevented *this* otherwise impending murder, by rendering the weapon harmless for the time being.

Prevention
and Counter-factual Inferences

Statements like these, to the effect that certain actions have prevented the occurrence of certain other events later on, warrant a certain familiar type of counter-factual inference expressed in subjunctives, though they are not, of course, the only statements that warrant such inference.

Thus, if it is true that a physician has prevented someone's death by a timely operation, then we can say that had he (contrary to fact) not performed the operation, the man would have soon died. Indeed, this is precisely what the physician would be claiming in saying that he thus prevented the man's death. Similarly, in our second example, if the policeman claimed to have prevented a murder by removing the bullets from a certain gun, precisely what he would be asserting is that had he (contrary to fact) not removed the bullets, the murder would surely have occurred. It is because these inferences are justified, at least in any strong and justified claim to have prevented something (and not merely to have helped to prevent it) that preventive action must be considered as something that was, under the conditions then and thereafter prevailing, not only sufficient but also necessary for the non-occurrence of the event thereby prevented. If conditions were such that the first man would not have died even if (contrary to fact) there had been no such operation, and the second man would not have committed murder even if (contrary to fact) the gun had been left loaded, then neither event could truly be said to have been prevented. They would be things that were not going to happen anyway, and the ostensibly preventive actions would not really have been necessary at all. The physician's operation would have been a waste of time and the bullet removal a wasted, superfluous ceremony, so far as preventing anything was concerned.

Besides being necessary, however, a preventive action must also be something that was, under the conditions then and thereafter prevailing, sufficient for the subsequent non-occurrence of the event thereby prevented. This scarcely needs argument. Had the first man, for example, somehow managed to die soon anyway, in spite of the operation, and had the second man somehow managed to commit the murder anyway, in spite of his gun being empty, then obviously neither event could truly be claimed to have been prevented.

Postvention

The word "postvention" does not occur in our language, even though it can be so defined as to be the exact complement of "prevention." This latter expression has a perfectly clear and common meaning which seems to lend itself to straightforward definition, as we have just seen, and the former can be given a similarly clear meaning. Not only that, but perfectly ordinary situations can be described in which the idea of postvention would seem to be entirely applicable; and yet no such word or any word expressing a similar idea is in fact ever applied in such situations. This at first seems odd, in the same way that it would be odd to find a language in which there was a word for future but none for past, or a word for north but none for south. The reason "postvention" does not occur in our language is, of course, that we have no use for it, but that is not interesting. What is philosophically interesting is to see just *why* we have no use for it. The most natural answers to this are quite unsatisfactory.

Thus, to have *postvented* some event is, precisely, to have done something which was, under the conditions then and theretofore prevailing, both sufficient and necessary for, though logically independent of, the antecedent non-occurrence of that event. Again, of course, some persons might prefer such expressions as "guaranteed," "insured," "was essential for," and so on to express these relationships, but that is neither here nor there.

But *do* men ever postvent things in this sense? Clearly, they often do, though for some reason this is never referred to as postvention. Indeed, whenever a man does anything whatever under conditions which are such that the prior non-occurrence of some event was both necessary and sufficient for his doing it, he postvents that event. The relationship between what he does and the event thus postvented is exactly the same, save only for the temporal relation, as the relationship between what any man does and the event he thereby prevents. Any event that is postvented does not, of course, occur, so there is a certain strangeness in speaking of its relationship to someone's subsequent postventive action, but similar remarks can be made about any event that is prevented. It, too, does not occur, and yet the very explanation of its non-occurrence is found in its connection with someone's preventive action.

We have, in fact, superficial examples of postvention already before us, for in our first example the patient postvents the physician's not having operated on him simply by recovering, and in our second example our would-be murderer postvents his gun's having been left loaded simply by not committing the murder. Better examples can be made up, however, for it might be objected here, perhaps rightly, that in the examples considered, the first man's recovering is not really any action he performs, and the second man's merely failing in his murder attempt is, similarly, no action he performs.

Suppose, then, that a certain woman breakfasts with her husband as usual on some given morning. Well, clearly, his not having overslept might well be a necessary condition for her doing that, and we can suppose that all the other conditions are such that his not having overslept is also sufficient for her doing that, or, that nothing else occurs to prevent husband and wife from breakfasting together as usual that day. By breakfasting with him in the usual way and at the usual time the wife guarantees, in the best possible way, that he has not overslept, and his not oversleeping also guarantees, under the conditions we are assuming to prevail, that he breakfasts with her as usual. The wife, accordingly, can properly claim to have postvented his oversleeping by breakfasting with him in the usual way. If she did claim to have done this, and if she meant by "postvented" exactly what we all mean by "prevented," except with the time reversed, she would appear to be right. Of course by breakfasting with him that morning she does not postvent his *ever* having overslept, but she does not claim to. She only claims to have postvented it this time.

Again, suppose a woman has breakfasted alone on some given morning. Suppose further that conditions were such that, had her husband not gone on a trip the day before, he would have been there too, having breakfast with her as usual. Well clearly, she has managed to put herself in a situation—breakfasting alone—which is sufficient, under the other conditions then and theretofore prevailing, for his not having foregone the trip the day before. His having gone on a trip is also, under the conditions we are assuming, sufficient for her then breakfasting alone, there being no one else for her to have breakfast with, and so on. (This corresponds with the murder example, wherein we assumed that the would-be murder had no other weapon to kill with, etc.) This wife, then, under the analysis given, postvented her husband's hanving stayed home. This should not suggest that she has thereby postvented his *ever* having foregone such trips, however. She only postvented him from staying home that time.

It is worthwhile noting that statements like these, to the effect that certain actions have served to postvent he occurrence of certain other events earlier on, warrant exactly the same familiar type of counterfactual inference that statements about prevention permit.

Thus, if it is true that a woman has (on the analysis given) postvented her husband's oversleeping that morning by breakfasting with him, then we can say that had she (contrary to fact) not breakfasted with him, we would be warranted in concluding that he had overslept —which is but another way of saying that his not oversleeping was, under the totality of conditions assumed, sufficient for her breakfasting with him. Similarly, if the second woman has by breakfasting alone postvented her husband's staying home instead of going on his trip, then we can say that had she (contrary to fact) not breakfasted alone, then we would be justified in concluding that, conditions having been such as they were, she had breakfasted with him, and hence that he had stayed home after all. This, again, is but another way of saying that his having gone on the trip was sufficient, given that the other conditions were such as they were, for her breakfasting alone. If conditions were such that the first husband would not have overslept even if (contrary to fact) his wife had not breakfasted with him, and the second husband would not have stayed home even if (contrary to fact) his wife had not breakfasted alone, then neither event could truly be said to have been postvented. They would be things that had not happened anyway, and the ostensibly postventive actions would not really be necessary at all. The first woman's breakfasting with her husband would have been a waste of time, and the second woman's breakfasting alone a wasted, superfluous ceremony, so far as postventing anything was concerned.

Besides being subsequent necessary conditions, however, a postventive action must also be something that was, under the conditions then and theretofore prevailing, *sufficient* for the antecedent non-occurrence of the event thereby postvented. This scarcely needs argument. Had the first man, for example, somehow managed to oversleep and still have breakfast with his wife as usual, and had the second man somehow managed to stay home and still leave his wife to breakfast alone, then obviously neither event could truly be claimed to have been postvented.

Four Obvious
But Wrong Answers

Why, then, if postvention and prevention are such exactly analogous concepts, differing only in the tenses in which examples are described, do we have no use for the concept of postvention? It is not at all easy to see what the answer to this is, but it is certainly worth noting some considerations that are apt to occur to one very quickly, but which do not provide the slightest answer to this question.

In the first place, there is no point whatever in suggesting that, while we are sometimes able to prevent certain things, we are unable to postvent anything—"the past is unalterable," and that sort of thing. For we must surely take it for granted that anything whatever that anyone *does* do, is something he *is able* to do. Now the first wife we described *did* breakfast with her husband on a given occasion, and the second wife *did* breakfast alone, from which it surely follows that these were things they were *able* to do. And by doing these things they did perform certain actions which were, under the conditions assumed to prevail and to have until then prevailed, necessary and sufficient for the non-occurrence of certain events earlier on, and in precisely the way that the actions of our physician and our policeman were sufficient and necessary for the non-occurrence of certain events later on.

Second, it does no good to point out that nothing in the history of the universe has ever been postvented. Absolutely nothing in the history of the universe has ever been prevented either. This is analytic. To say of any event whatever that it is a past event logically entails that it was not and never will be postvented. But similarly, to say of any event that it is a future event logically entails that it was not and never will be prevented. No one can name a past event that he will postvent, but neither can anyone name a future event that he will prevent. All these seemingly grave observations are really utterly trivial, expressing only what is analytically true. In speaking of postventing events of the past or preventing events of the future, however, one is not saying anything the least trivial or logically odd. He is only claiming the legitimacy of such counter-factual inferences as I have illustrated. Those inferences are equally good, whether one is speaking of post-vention or of prevention.

Third, there is no point in noting that we can only cause things to occur in the future, not in the past. This is true enough, but only because that is the way the word "cause" happens to be used. If a meaning can be given to the idea of postventing things, then there is no reason why the use of the word "cause" should be restricted the way it is. Indeed, the question of why its use is thus restricted to antecedent necessary and sufficient conditions is as good as the question with which we began; namely why the word "postvent" has no use at all. Given the notion of antecedent necessary and sufficient conditions, on the one hand, and subsequent necessary and sufficient conditions, on the other—and it is impossible to have either of these notions without the other—we can easily define both prevention and postvention, as I have done, without speaking of causes at all. Examples of postvention can be readily supplied, which seem in every way identical to examples of prevention, save only that the temporal relations are reversed. The other relations can be described in terms of the concepts of necessary or sufficient antecedent or subsequent conditions or, what amounts to the same thing, in terms of certain true conditional statements in the subjunctive whose antecedents or consequents are contrary to fact.

And finally, it looks as though no light is going to be thrown on this question by any observations about what does, and what does not, count as a human action, or by any distinctions between actions and "mere events." Sometimes a man, stricken with a serious malady, is prevented from dying by the automatic production of certain antibodies in his blood, without any intervention by a physician. A man setting about to commit murder can be prevented from doing it by a sudden, unexpected and surprising eclipse of the sun. Many dreadful accidents have been prevented by automatic flashing lights at railway crossings, or by the sun melting the ice from the highway, which is to say that such accidents would have happened had not these preventive events happened first. Trees are sometimes prevented from blooming just by contamination in the earth, which need not have been introduced by human agency. None of these preventive events is a human action, or even an action at all. They are all just mere events, which do, however, sometimes serve to prevent other events.

Preventive Actions
as Means to Ends

I do not think we should suppose that the absence of the word "postvent" from our vocabulary represents any odd lacuna. I think the notion is truly useless. However clearly it can be explicated and however similar it may at first appear to the notion of prevention, one can hardly help feeling that there is something highly artificial in my foregoing discussion, something significant that has been left out of account. I want now to show that this is indeed so, and to bring forth the missing element that has thus far been ignored.

The first thing to note is that the two examples I gave of typically preventive actions are both aptly described as actions performed as the means to achieving some end or, what amounts to the same thing, as means for the avoidance of something. Thus, the physician operated as a means of preserving someone's life, and the policeman removed the bullets as a means to protecting someone. The same cannot be said of the postventive actions I cited. Thus, it is plainly untrue that the first woman breakfasted with her husband as a means of getting him up on time, or that the second breakfasted alone as a means of getting her husband off on a trip. Even if we suppose these two women to have had such goals or purposes, we cannot represent *these* actions as suitable or even intelligible means to their accomplishment.

Does not this, however, merely make the trivial point that, as a matter of customary usage, anything which is a means to some end must *precede* that end in time? And hence, that no postventive actions are means to ends for the simple reason that they must, by definition, succeed in time those negative states of affairs to which they are postventively related? Anyone wishing to press this suggestion could certainly make a dialectically subtle case for it. The counterpart to the concept of an *end,* for example, is obviously that of a *beginning.* Having then characterized preventive actions in terms of their relationship to certain ends, one could then characterize postventive actions as related in precisely the same way to beginnings. The policeman's preventive action, for example, was performed for the end of preserving a certain man's life. The housewife's postventive action of eating with her husband was performed for the beginning of getting him up on time; and so on.

The analogy is fascinating but, quite apart from its apparent artificiality, it does not really hold up. For in the first place, it is not true that the ends of actions, even when realized, always succeed those actions in time. For example, one might walk, simply for the purpose of walking, with no end or goal beyond that. Here means and ends are identical and hence contemporaneous. Again, one might move his hand for the purpose of drawing a line. Means and end are here not identical, though they are certainly contemporaneous—the line does not appear *after* the hand has moved, but *as* it moves. But more interesting than these are certain purposeful actions, the ends or goals of which seem actually to *precede* those actions. For example, if it is one's purpose to flex a certain arm muscle, the only way he can accomplish this, normally, is by moving his arm. The arm is *caused* to move by the motion of the muscle, but the arm is moved *in order* to move the muscle, not vice versa. The motion of the muscle does not follow upon the motion of the arm, however; if anything, it precedes it slightly. Or consider nerve impulses. Part of the cause of the motion of a man's arm, when he moves it, is certainly a certain nerve impulse from his brain, but it is false that he moves his arm *by means* of the nerve impulse. It is the other way around. Thus, if a man learns of these nerve impulses—and many go to their graves without ever suspecting they exist—and then has some occasion to produce one of them—perhaps for the purposes of some experiment in physiological psychology—he can do so only by moving his arm. The purposeful action in such a case—namely, the man's moving his arm—is the means to a certain end—the production of a certain nerve impulse—which actually precedes that purposeful action in time. And this, incidentally, is the *only* kind of case I can think of in which one apparently does something, truly as a *means* to the occurrence or non-occurrence of some prior event. It is thus the only kind of case I can imagine of changing the past *at will*, or of having some event in the past literally within one's voluntary control. The example is frightfully puzzling, however, and I shall henceforth disregard it.

To say, in any case, that some action is the means to a certain end cannot mean simply that it is antecedently necessary and sufficient for that end. It need not be antecedent to its end. Besides this, there are many actions which are antecedently necessary and sufficient for the occurrence of certain events which are, however, in no sense the means to the realization of those events. When one sits on a sofa he depresses the springs, but that is not ordinarily one's purpose, though it could be. When one brakes his automobile he wears down the brake drum, but again, that is not ordinarily his purpose.

A preventive action, then, is something *more* than an action that is antecedently necessary and sufficient for whatever it prevents. It is easy to supply examples of actions which fit that description but which are not preventive, and also easy to supply examples of preventive actions which do not fit it. To say, however, that one's action is *postventive* is *not* to say anything more than that it is subsequently necessary and sufficient for the non-occurrence of what it postvents.

Doing Something
with Something

Having described preventive actions as means to the realization of ends, we find now another striking disanalogy in our examples. It concerns the senses of the word "with" in those examples. The physician, I said, operated upon a man *with* a scalpel, the policeman removed some bullets *with* his fingers, and the housewife ate breakfast *with* her husband. These statements are all grammatically similar, but the third "with" is utterly different in meaning from the first two. The first conveys the idea that the physician operated, using the scalpel as a tool or means to his end. The second, similarly, means that the policeman removed the bullets, using his fingers for this. But the third certainly does not mean that the housewife ate breakfast by means of her husband, that she used him in the way another person might use a fork. This "with" expresses only the idea of accompaniment. The wife merely ate in the presence of her husband.

It is thus misleading to describe the wife's *action* as eating with her husband. Her action consisted solely of eating, and would have been no different had her husband not been there. It is not, however, misleading to describe the policeman's action as removing bullets with his fingers. This is a different action than removing them with one's teeth—though it is still true that he removes them in the presence of, even if not by means of, his teeth.

These observations are meant to reinforce the point already made, that preventive actions, unlike postventive ones, can only be understood as involving the idea of means and ends. The word "with" as it sometimes figures in the description of a preventive action has no other function than to convey this idea of a means. Postventive actions, on the other hand, cannot be so understood, and when the word "with" is introduced into the description of such an action it does not convey the idea of a means-end relation. No philosophical ingenuity can contrive descriptions in which it has any meaning remotely analogous to that of a means—with the possible exception of those rare cases in which one might move a limb, or hold it still, literally as a *means* to the prior occurrence or non-occurrence of a nerve impulse.

Preventive States
and Events Which Are Not Actions

So far I have labored the point that preventive actions are always, or at least typically, means to ends. This, of course, does not entail that nothing can be described as preventive *unless* it is an action and, in fact, many things that are preventive are not actions at all.

Thus, a man can be prevented from leaving a burning building by smoke, even though no one is making the smoke; a man can be prevented from reaching a mountaintop by a landslide, even though no one starts the landslide; and so on. Examples are easy to multiply, and they all show that not all states and events which are preventive of something are preventive actions.

What is still left, however, even in those cases, is the notion of an end or purpose, and I want to insist that this notion is still essential to the description of anything whatever as preventive. Thus, the smoke could not be described as *preventing* a man from leaving a burning building except on the supposition that it was his purpose, goal, or intention to leave, and the landslide can be considered as preventing a man from reaching a mountaintop only on the supposition that he was trying to reach it. Had the first man, for example, intended to stay in the burning building all the while, had this been his purpose— perhaps in order to test some fireproof suit—then he could not be said to have been prevented by the smoke from leaving. The most one could say is that he would have been prevented, in case he had tried.

One further observation should make this last point perfectly obvious. I have said that the idea of prevention is unintelligible apart from the idea of a purpose or goal, and that this is what distinguishes preventive events and states of affairs from those that are merely necessary and sufficient for the subsequent non-occurrence of something. Now if this were *not* so, then, in the case of every event that does not occur and for which there are antecedent conditions necessary and sufficient for its non-occurrence, we would have to say that it was *prevented* from occurring. And this would be an absurd thing to say. There are, for example, infinitely many things that are *not* happening in my room now. The carpet is not disintegrating, the ash tray is not changing color, the dust mote that is drifting toward the door is not drifting toward the window, and so on, *ad infinitum*. It can hardly be said that all those things are being *prevented* from happening, even though it can be said, presumably, that there are antecedent conditions necessary and sufficient for their not happening. To say they were being prevented would imply that it was someone's purpose or goal either that they should happen or that they should not.

Again, however, no such notion of a purpose or goal of any agent is required for the understanding of postvention, nor is there any intelligible way to fit such a notion into the concept of postvention. Everything that does not happen and for which there are subsequent conditions necessary and sufficient for its not happening—which probably includes, simply, everything that does not happen—is thereby postvented from happening.

Here it will be well to remark upon something I said earlier. I said that a man is sometimes prevented from dying by the automatic production of antibodies in his blood, that automobile accidents are sometimes prevented by automatic signals, that trees are sometimes prevented from blossoming by a natural contamination in the earth, and so on. Now this first statement, I think, makes sense only on the supposition that it is the man's elementary purpose to remain alive. The second statement makes sense only on the supposition that the signals were put there in order to prevent accidents, and that it is presumably contrary to men's purposes to have accidents. With respect to the tree, I believe the statement makes sense only on the supposition, doubtless erroneous, that it is the tree's purpose to blossom. If, as I believe, this is metaphorical or poetical and not strictly true, then I believe it is also not strictly true that the tree was prevented from blossoming. All we can say is that it normally would have blossomed, but that conditions in this case were not normal.

The Will

We have now to see what bearing the foregoing might have on the notion of free will. I have already indicated that the thesis of determinism, as I understand it, cannot, in my opinion, be either proved or disproved. It is the thesis to the effect that in the case of every event, and hence every human action, and hence every action that is purposeful or goal-directed, and hence every preventive action, there are antecedent conditions (causes) sufficient for the performance of just that action and for the avoidance of any and every alternative action. This is a perfectly *general* thesis, and I do not know how anyone could profess to know that it is true, or that it is false. Most purported proofs of its truth amount to maintaining that it is implied by the basic beliefs and conceptions that all men have. Well, it is certainly not implied by the conception of a preventive action and is, I think, rendered somewhat implausible in the light of that conception.

Not every preventive state of affairs, I have maintained, is itself purposeful or goal-directed, though it cannot be conceived as preventive except in relation to the purpose or goal of some agent. The smoke that obstructs a passageway may not be of purposeful origin, but it cannot be spoken of as preventing anything except on the supposition that it frustrates some agent's purpose. I have also maintained, however, that every preventive action *is* purposeful or goal-directed. This should perhaps be qualified by saying that every action which is *as such* preventive is also purposeful, in order to allow for those actions which prevent, but which are not as such preventive. A man might, for instance, incidentally to making a smoke screen, unintentionally prevent another man from leaving a building, in which case his action is preventive, but not as such. It is only preventive *per accidens,* and may be quite purposeless. Typically preventive actions are, in any case, distinguished from postventive actions in being purposeful, for nothing remotely like the idea of purpose can be fitted into the idea of postvention.

Goals and Causes

This entails that the idea of a preventive action cannot be analyzed in terms of necessary and sufficient conditions. Postventive actions can be so analyzed—indeed, they are simply defined in those terms. There is an additional element contained in the very idea of a preventive action, and that is the idea of a purpose, goal, or end. Nor will it do simply to add this as another necessary causal condition—by saying, for instance, that an action is preventive in case one of the conditions constituting part of the cause of it is an agent's purpose. A purpose, end, or goal is no part of the *cause* of a preventive action. It is part of the very *concept* of such an action, just as being a sibling is part of the concept, but no part of the cause, of being a twin.

Besides this, it would seem artificial in the extreme to suppose that preventive actions are causally explained in terms of purposes or goals. Preventive actions can, indeed, be *explained* in terms of goals or purposes—indeed, that is the standard and normal way of explaining them—but there is no reason whatever for thinking that such explanations fit the pattern of causal explanation. If the policeman of our earlier example were asked to explain why he removed the bullets from the gun, he would say what his purpose was, what he was trying to accomplish, but this is very far from saying or implying that his behavior was antecedently rendered unavoidable by, among other things, his having or resolving upon such a purpose or goal. There is not the slightest appearance of absurdity in supposing that, while he did act from such a purpose or goal, he might have declined to act upon it, or might have sought to realize it by some other means.

But does the supposition that men sometimes act preventively, and hence purposefully, entail that determinism is false? Some persons have thought so. It seems to some that the very idea of pursuing an end or goal, particularly over a long period of time, implies that the end is freely chosen, as well as the means to its achievement.

I believe this is clearly not true, however. The supposition that men sometimes act preventively, and hence purposefully, does not by itself entail that determinism is false. The further supposition that such actions are sometimes the result of deliberation does, I have maintained, entail that they are at least believed to be free, in the sense of being not causally determined, but that is a question I have already gone into. All that follows, I think, from the supposition that men sometimes act preventively is that they sometimes act in ways that cannot be *analyzed* in terms of antecedent necessary and sufficient conditions. This does not by itself by any means imply that, when they so act, there sometimes do not *exist* such conditions.

The Metaphysical Meaning of "Free"

To say that a given preventive act was free means, I take it, that the agent who performed it was free with respect to that act. And this, I take it, means that, under the onditions then and theretofore prevailing, he was able to perform that act *and* he was also able to refrain from performing it. To say, on the other hand, that he was *not* free with respect to that act means, I take it, that he was not able to refrain from performing it, or, that circumstances rendered his action unavoidable.

Prevention Consistent with
Determinism and Indeterminism

Any statement of the form "I prevented X by doing A" is clearly *consistent* with "Something made (or caused) me to do A, thereby preventing X." These must be consistent, since the second entails the first. It is important to note, however, that the first does not in the least entail the second. It may be, as I suspect it is, that in some cases a statement of the first form is *true* and the corresponding statement of the second form is *false*. They are nevertheless not inconsistent with each other. In other words, I suspect that men sometimes prevent certain things by certain of their actions when nothing makes them perform just those actions to the exclusion of any others. Certainly there is no evidence that this cannot be true. The supposition is not itself inconsistent, nor is it inconsistent with anything else that anyone knows to be true. It is inconsistent with the thesis of determinism, to be sure, but while many philosophers believe in that thesis, no one knows that it is true. It seems to me, in any case, that the thesis just enunciated —that men sometimes prevent certain things by their actions when nothing makes them perform those actions—is more likely to be true than the metaphysical thesis of determinism, with which it is inconsistent.

The supposition, then, that men sometimes act preventively, is consistent both with the affirmation and the denial of determinism. "I prevented X by doing A" is consistent with "Something made (or caused) me to do A, thereby preventing X," but it is equally consistent with "Nothing made (or caused) me to do A, thereby preventing X." Nor can anyone argue, I think, that in case a statement of the second form were true—that is, in case someone were free with respect to a preventive act he performed—then that act would be "inexplicable." A preventive act can still be explained, or rendered intelligible, in terms of the very purpose or goal by virtue of which it is a preventive act, even if that act, as distinguished from the bodily behavior associated with it, is uncaused. Such a statement, for example, as "He removed the bullets in order to prevent that man from killing someone" renders the act of removing the bullets quite intelligible and at least partially explained. That explanation is not in the least wiped out if one makes the further supposition that the agent in question was free with respect to that act, or, that nothing made him do it.

The Doubtful Status
of Determinism

Can we, then, draw any conclusion concerning the truth or falsity of determinism from this? We cannot, on the basis of anything I have said, conclude that determinism must be false. If, on the other hand, anyone maintains that determinism is true, and that, accordingly, no preventive act is free, in the sense defined, then I think his position is at least doubtful. He cannot, I feel sure, *analyze* the concept of a preventive act in such a way as to make it even *look* like an act which is, by its very nature, metaphysically unfree or causally determined. Moreover, he will be in the position of maintaining that in the case of *every* true statement of the form, "O prevented X by doing A," there is a corresponding statement of the form "Something made O do A, thereby preventing X," which is also true. And this, to say the very least, is something I think no one has the slightest reason for believing.

14

Explanation and Purpose

I have, especially in the last chapter, repeatedly alluded to the notion of purposeful behavior, or of acting with the view to attaining some goal or end, and suggested that this may provide the clue to the understanding of certain kinds of human behavior which cannot, perhaps, be understood in terms of the more familiar notions of cause and effect. Here I want to concentrate on this idea, which seems to me one of the most neglected in both philosophy and science, in order to show that explanations in terms of purposes and goals are sometimes genuine explanations. In the chapters following I shall elicit more carefully the difference between behavior that is and behavior that is not purposeful and, most important of all, show that purposeful behavior cannot be analyzed in terms of, or reduced to, behavior that is adequately described in terms of the concepts of physical science. It is, I believe, the neglect of these concepts in contemporary philosophy that has given rise to so much strange speculation about minds and machines, about whether certain machines can "think," and so on, as if the questions at the bottom of those speculations were quite clearly understood.

Purposeful *vs.*
Causal Explanation

If it should be true that purposeful behavior cannot be understood in terms of explanatory concepts borrowed from physical science then the consequences are fairly momentous. For one thing, in case certain typical human behavior is purposeful, as it most certainly is, then it will follow that much of the science of human behavior is simply on the wrong track. It has long been customary in experimental psychology, for example, to assume that unless human behavior can be understood in terms of what is observable and verifiable, and unless, moreover, it can be interpreted in the light of theories which permit of prediction—unless, in short, it can be understood within the framework of the concepts and methods familiar to the physical sciences—then it cannot be scientifically understood at all. Now this is all doubtless true. But it is generally assumed by those teachers and students of the anthropological sciences—empirical psychology, sociology, and so on—that the consequent of this hypothetical assertion is false. It is generally assumed, in other words, that human behavior *can* be scientifically understood. It is therefore also assumed that it can be understood within the framework of the concepts and methods familiar to the physical sciences—which is precisely what I expect to show is false.

Thus, empirical and behavioral psychologists experience a justified sense of discovery when they find that some aspect of human behavior is explicable in terms of certain observable or verifiable conditions which permit of predictions. Again, they have a deep interest in describing the workings of the brain and nervous system in terms of the concepts of chemistry and biochemistry. Much of a certain sort has been learned by proceeding along this path, which consists of describing human nature, or at least the living human organism, in terms of the concepts and theories borrowed from the physical sciences or modeled after these. It must nevertheless be obvious to everyone that this approach has yielded nothing whatsoever toward the understanding of human action, wherein lie all the interesting questions concerning human nature itself. Little peripheral things are turned up now and then, but the simplest and most obvious questions remain in the same deep and total darkness as before. The supposition made in the sciences is that their inquiries just have not been pushed quite far enough, that the subject is complex and yields itself very slowly to understanding. My suggestion, on the contrary, is that progress has been slow because the inquiry is in an essential way misguided. Students of man have sought an understanding of human nature within the limitations of concepts which human behavior does not fit. Those concepts which are useful for the understanding of human nature, on the other hand, such as the concept of purpose or goal-directed behavior, are either avoided as "unscientific," that is, of no use to the physical sciences, or the vain and futile attempt is made to reduce them to concepts that are "scientific."

Consider, for example, such a familiar and simple thing as moving one's limb. Now what sort of thing would count as a scientific explanation of this simple fact? Well, if a physiological psychologist could discover some set of conditions which are logically unconnected with a man's moving his finger, or such that it would not logically follow from the mere description of them that he moves his finger, but which are nevertheless invariably present when he does move it and absent when he does not, and which could therefore be deemed causally sufficient for his moving it, then the occurrence of those conditions would constitute a scientific explanation of the fact in question. That, moreover, is the *only* thing that would count as a scientific explanation. Anything, to count as an explanation, would have to fit that general schema. In addition, most investigators would insist that the presence or absence of such conditions must be verifiable by some sort of test or observation, that they should be verifiable by more than one person, and so on, but those are details too obvious to dwell on.

Note now, however, that if, as we are assuming, the fact to be explained is an act of an agent, such as the simple act of moving one's finger, then that kind of explanation is simply impossible, just in the light of the points previously developed. It is not impossible in the sense that the difficulty of it exceeds the present level of scientific achievement. It is not such that it might fall within the limits of the possible with time, patience, and the gradual increase of knowledge. It is impossible in the very conception of it. Nor is this a result of the fact itself being recondite or rare, for it is neither—hardly anything could be more familiar than the simple act of moving one's finger. Nor is it the result of the fact's being frightfully complex. Doubtless the events involved in moving one's finger—the motions of muscles and all the changes within the cells of these, the changes within the nervous system, and so on—are terribly numerous and complex; but the act itself is as simple as any act could possibly be. Probably no act could be any simpler.

The reason that no such explanation is possible and the search for it therefore vain is that if it were given it could not possibly be the explanation of an *act*. The very supposition that any such purported explanation was *true* would by itself entail that the thing thereby explained was no act at all, but something else. It *logically* could not, therefore, explain what it would purport to explain.

Suppose, for example, that someone were to suggest, on the basis of whatever evidence, that a certain set of antecedent conditions, *a, b,* and *c,* are always present whenever a certain finger moves and absent when it does not, and he thus proposed this as the explanation of that motion. The supposition would be that those conditions, whatever they might be, are causally necessary and sufficient for that finger motion and can therefore be cited as the explanation of that motion. Given that they are present, it can be reliably predicted that the finger will move, and given that they are absent, that the finger will not move. If, moreover, the origin of those conditions can be discovered, as consisting of some further, earlier set of conditions, then earlier predictions will be made possible by determining the presence of that earlier set of conditions; and so on.

Now this might in fact work as an explanation for a finger's moving. Indeed, explanations of this kind are well known. But it could not possibly be an explanation of a man's moving his finger. We know, for instance, that normally a man's finger does not move unless certain muscles and tendons move, that these do not normally move unless certain changes take place within the cells of those muscles, that those changes do not occur except when brought about by certain changes in the nerves, and so on. Such changes as these, then, once fully described, can be given as the explanation of the finger's moving, and they do in fact constitute an explanation of sorts. Indeed, if a complete explanation of an event consists of no more than a description of some set of conditions necessary and sufficient for it, but logically unconnected with it, then something like the foregoing can be regarded as a complete explanation of the motion in question, since those changes in the muscles, nerves, and so on are sufficient and necessary for the motion of a normal finger.

Is it not obvious, however, that no such recital of antecedent conditions can be the explanation of a man's moving his finger? If it is not, then it can be made obvious by the following considerations.

Suppose that, by an electrical stimulus or something of that sort, I bring about within the nerves or muscles of some man those changes which are necessary and sufficient for his finger's moving. This being accomplished, it follows that his finger does move. It also follows, however, that he does *not* move it, but rather that *I* move it for him. The motion of his finger is my act and not his, just as fully as if I had simply grasped it and moved it. He had nothing to do with it. He was simply the passive spectator of my activity, a patient upon whom I performed certain simple operations to make his finger move.

Nor will this result be altered if we seek out, as our explanation of his moving his finger, some set of conditions more recondite and remote. It will be no different if we go way back into his very mind or soul, as empirical psychology has no business doing, and set forth, as those conditions explanatory of his moving his finger, certain changes or states occurring very deep in his innermost self. So long as these are logically unconnected with the act to be explained—so long, that is, as they do not include such things as "the desire to move that finger," "a finger-moving act of will," and so on—then their remoteness helps things not in the least. Whatever they are, whether relatively obvious and verifiable things such as muscle motions and nerve impulses or more dubious things such as desires or thoughts or mental events, it will always remain a possibility for these to be induced by the machinations of another person and that, having been thus brought about by that other person, the finger will move in response. But that motion will never be the act of the man whose finger moves. It will be only the causal consequence of those changes within him, and if these are wrought by another person, as it is always possible that they might be, then the motion of that finger will of necessity be that other person's act.

The Causation of Acts

Here it is possible to get a bit more sophisticated and seek some set of conditions necessary and sufficient, not merely for the finger's motion, but for a man's moving his finger. Now such a set of conditions would indeed constitute an explanation of an act, and not merely of a bodily change that need not be an act. Such an approach, if paraded as a scientific explanation of an act, bristles with difficulties, however.

There are, in the first place, innumerable ways in which a man can be made to move his finger. He can be made to so act by threats, for example, or by habit, or by conditioning, or by appealing to his greed, or by frightening him, and so on. Now these are surely not concepts that have any proper place in the physical sciences. They are quite utterly different from the motions of muscles and chemical changes within the nerve cells.

One might, to be sure, disregard this, broaden the notion of "scientific" a bit, and treat such concepts as belonging uniquely to the *science* of psychology. Here, though, a fresh difficulty arises; namely, that the kinds of thing that can induce a man to perform even the simplest act, such as moving his finger, are frightfully numerous and varied. One can sometimes be made to act in some specified way by being requested to do so by a physician, being ordered by a commander, being threatened by a bandit, and so on. Such inducements are sometimes sufficient, but not one of them is necessary, and this ought to suggest the hopelessness of seeking a scientific explanation of a man's acts in this direction. Even if such an explanation should be put in the form of a disjunction, and the disjunction should be allowed to be ever so wide and copious, it is doubtful whether it would ever be complete. If, for instance, someone claimed to explain a man's act by saying that *either a, or b, or c, or*...and so on occurred and was sufficient for his acting in that way, it certainly appears always possible to find some condition that was in fact what made him act as he did, but which was not mentioned in the purported explanation.

But even overlooking these difficulties—the strange, nebulous, and disjunctive character of such an explanation, and its remoteness from what is ordinarily deemed worthy of consideration in the sciences— such an explanation is logically impossible anyway. For suppose someone were to suggest, as the explanation of my moving my finger, in case I do move it, some elaborate and disjunctive set of conditions, the satisfaction of any one of which would be sufficient for my so acting. He is no longer, we are supposing, trying to explain merely why my finger moves, but rather, why I move it, in case I do. Now surely it will always be possible for me to arrange that not one of those conditions is satisfied—to arrange a time and place such that I am not threatened, not ordered, not frightened, and so on—and then, in the absence of any sufficient condition mentioned in the explanation, to move my finger anyway. Nor will it do to say that, in this case, the set of conditions proposed needs only to be enlarged, so as to include whatever it is that makes me move my finger on this occasion. For I am pointing out, what is surely true, that however numerous might be the disjunctive list of sufficient conditions thus mentioned, it will *always* be possible for me to arrange that not one of them is fulfilled and still, in the absence of all of them, simply to move my finger. This is not, of course, to suggest that no conditions are antecedently *necessary* for my so acting. I must have a finger to move, for example, and it must be unparalyzed, connected with certain muscles in the usual way, and son on. But I am saying that no set of such conditions, each necessary for my moving my finger, is enough to make me move it—I can refrain from moving it even though nothing prevents me from moving it. Further, I can move it, even though not one of the conditions mentioned in the explanation, any one of which is admittedly sufficient for my moving it, is fulfilled. This, at least, follows from the fact that I can always *arrange* that not one of those individually sufficient conditions is satisfied and still move my finger in their absence. Surely nothing could be simpler. The temptation is to say that, in case I did so, then the list of alternative sufficient conditions needs only to be enlarged to include whatever made me move my finger in those circumstances. But this is of no use, for even if this were done I could then arrange that this further condition, too, did not obtain, and still move my finger in the absence of it. Again, nothing could be any simpler, and *that is a step that can always be taken.*

Now there is a fairly familiar argument against the foregoing, and it is one that is apt to occur to anyone; namely, that there are *always* certain conditions antecedently necessary for an agent's performing any action whatever. If, then, all the conditions necessary for an agent's performing a given action are satisfied, then that set of conditions must be sufficient for his performing it since, by hypothesis, no *further* conditions are necessary. To say, then, as I have said above, that all the conditions necessary for the performance of a certain act may be fulfilled, and that the agent might nevertheless refrain from performing that action, amounts to a contradiction, for it amounts to saying that something can fail to occur even in the presence of conditions sufficient for its occurrence.

This argument involves a simple amphiboly, however, in the notion of sufficiency. For on the one hand, a set of conditions is described as "sufficient," meaning by this *only* that no further conditions are necessary; and on the other hand, that set is described as "sufficient *for*" a given action, meaning now that it renders the performance of that action inevitable. The argument, moreover, begs the question at issue, for it simply *assumes* that, certain conditions always being necessary for the performance of any given action, the totality of those conditions will also be sufficient (in the second sense) for the performance of that action. To see this, we need only to ask what the argument would amount to in case it should be *false* that every action is performed under conditions which are such that they are sufficient for the occurrence of the action in question. On such an assumption the argument obviously would have no force whatsoever—though it might still be true that certain conditions are antecedently necessary for the performance of any action whatever. The argument must, then, already *presuppose* the truth of the very thing it purports to prove; namely, that if any conditions are antecedently necessary for the performance of a given action, which is doubtless always the case, then the entire set of such conditions will turn out to be sufficient for the performance of that action.

Actions and Goals

I noted earlier the great difference in kind between two such statements as

>   1. This match started the forest fire,

and

>   2. This man started the forest fire.

These two statements are identical except for their subjects, but they are utterly different in meaning. The first cannot be literally true, though the second might be.

The first statement expresses the idea that the ignition of the match in question was significantly involved in the beginnings of the fire mentioned; more precisely, that its igniting was, under only those other conditions that are assumed to have existed, necessary for the beginning of that fire, and also sufficient. It does not suggest that the match actually did anything, or that it performed any act. It, or its igniting, was simply a necessary link in a whole series of causes and effects. The statement does not suggest that the match ignited its own head, and in that sense literally *started* something that spread to the magnitude of a forest fire.

The second statement, however, might be literally true, conveying the idea that the man in question did perform an act, that he literally did *start* the fire, presumably by means of a match or something of that sort. He, or some event in which he was significantly involved, was not merely a link in a whole series of causes and effects; that series itself was presumably started by him. And unlike the match, which did not ignite its own head, the man did, presumably, move his own arm, or perform some other simple act, thus starting what the statement alleges he started.

Both statements, it is clear, are incomplete as explanations of the fire, but they are incomplete in totally different ways. An explanation involving the first statement would be completed by stating how the match came to be where it was in the first place, what conditions raised the temperature of its head to its igniting point, and so on. Disregarding the fact that matches themselves are the products of human agency, this explanation might be completely given, as a "natural catastrophe," without implying any agency anywhere—by noting, for example, that the match was ignited by the heat of the sun, or by being blown by the wind against a stone, or whatnot.

An explanation involving the second statement would not ordinarily be completed in the same way. It might be the case, for example, that nothing other than the man himself made him be where he was, that nothing put him there, nothing carried him there, but that, unlike the match, he went there himself—for a *reason,* perhaps, but from no ordinary *cause.* It might be the case that, unlike the match, nothing other than the man himself caused his body to move as it did, thus igniting a match or whatever and, by its means, starting a fire. The explanation involving this second statement would, however, be completed by discovering the man's motive or purpose, by finding out *why,* in that sense, he did what the statement affirms that he did. This, however, would be an explanation in terms of his purpose or goal, a kind of explanation that is so radically different from the other that it would be senseless if the explanation involving the first statement were expanded in such terms. There is, or normally would be, an answer to the question why the man started the fire, but there can be no *similar* answer to the question why the match started the fire.

It was also remarked earlier that the second statement, but normally not the first, might constitute an ultimate causal explanation, even though neither statement is a complete explanation. It is now fairly easy to see how this is so.

If we begin with the first statement it is perfectly reasonable to wonder what caused the match to ignite. This is a question concerning those conditions, whatever they were, that occurred and were causally necessary and sufficient for that igniting. Having found such conditions, it would be perfectly reasonable to inquire what caused these, that is, what further conditions occurred and were causally necessary and sufficient for them, and so on. Sooner or later such a quest for causes might become hopeless, due simply to the limits of our possible knowledge, but it need not otherwise be the least unreasonable.

If we begin with the second statement, however, it might, and normally would, be unreasonable to seek further causes lying behind the one mentioned, namely, a certain agent himself. There is here no question about what caused the man's body to move as it did, grasping a match, presumably, and striking it against something. The supposition is that he caused these motions himself, that they were his own actions. Something *may* literally have caused him to act in this fashion, but it is by no means necessary to think so. If we ask *why* he behaved in that way, the explanation sought would ordinarily be a teleological rather than a causal one. If we were given true statements about his aims or goals, about what he was trying to accomplish, and if his actions could be properly viewed as his means of attaining those aims, then we would have an explanation of that behavior. It would not, however, be an explanation in terms of what had caused his behavior, for that, it is already assumed, or might reasonably be assumed, was the man himself.

This suggests that the explanation of human behavior, or rather of some human actions, should be sought in terms of purposes or goals rather than causes. Indeed, it is purposeful explanations that are usually sought and accepted in all areas except, curiously, certain of the anthropological sciences, where explanations of a more "scientific" character are vainly desired. In these areas of science, however, the term "scientific" has become a commendatory adjective, and at the same time has somewhat uncritically come to suggest those types of explanation which the physical sciences have yielded in such abundance. In these such notions as purposes, ends, or goals have, quite rightly, no place whatsoever. We can admit at once that considerations of purpose have no place in the understanding of inanimate things. It hardly follows that, in order to be scientific, we must pretend that they have no place in the understanding of human behavior. Indeed, it is naïve even to entertain such an idea, for the actions of men can often be understood in no other way. To explain human actions in the manner in which the behavior of inanimate things is explained is, as I have tried to show, not merely difficult, but logically impossible. No such explanation can be true unless what is explained is in fact *not* the act of an agent.

" In Order That "

A purposeful explanation of an event or series of events is some statement that represents the events in question as the *means* to some *end* or goal. A natural way of expressing such a statement is by use of the locution "in order that" or " in order to." Indeed, this can probably serve as a criterion of a purposeful explanation; namely, whether it can naturally and easily be expressed in those terms.

For example, such statements as "He is running in order to catch the train," "He raised his hand to get the speaker's attention," "He burned the woods in order to destroy the evidence," are all clearly purposeful. They would, moreover, ordinarily be considered explanatory—they explain why the agents referred to did the things they are said to have done. They describe actions which are performed with some near or remote goal or end in mind, things that are done in order that certain results may be achieved. Different thinkers interpret such statements variously; some even seem to have wanted to maintain that no such statements can be really true. It is nevertheless clear that, whatever they might mean, such statements as these *are* sometimes true. Raising one's hand, for example, is a way of gaining someone's attention, and it is a way that is frequently employed. On learning, moreover, that a given man has performed such an act in order to get that result, one does not doubt that his action has been at least partially explained; one knows, in the most straightforward sense, why he did it.

Some statements—indeed, probably most of those referring to the actions of men—are implicitly purposeful, in the sense that it is natural to construe them as referring indirectly to the purpose of some agent or agents. Thus, "She has gone shopping" would ordinarily convey the idea that the person in question has gone somewhere in order to make purchases, and this expresses a purpose or goal, for the accomplishment of which something is done. Such similar statements as "He has gone to his grave" or "He has gone to prison" would not ordinarily be so construed, however, and in fact these do not, at least on the most natural interpretation of them, lend themselves to being re-expressed in terms of the locution, "in order that." There are *some* circumstances in which they might—for example, in case a man has gone to prison in order to visit an inmate there, or gone to his previously prepared grave to see whether it is ready to receive him at the appropriate time, and so on. But that is not how one would ordinarily understand those statements. A man is carried to his grave, is sent and transported to a prison—for a purpose, no doubt, but for no purpose of his. A housewife, however, can go shopping without being sent or transported thither. If one said she was sent by her avarice and transported by her legs he would only speak whimsically.

Any statement embodying the purposeful locution "in order that," in the way that it is ordinarily used, is of course a purposeful statement, but not all such statements, it seems needless to say, are true. Like any other statements they can be false. Thus, to say that rain is falling in order to make the corn grow, that the river is rushing to join the sea, that the plant is opening its leaves in order to capture the sunlight, and so on, is to make statements expressive of purposes, but false ones. They are at best only poetic.

This suggests, which I believe to be true, that only the actions of agents can be purposeful, although, of course, the converse does not follow. A man might do something quite purposelessly, for no reason, without any aim or goal. It is not necessary to say whether this ever happens or not. In any case, any true assertion that something *does* occur *in order that* some result may be achieved does seem to entail that the event in question is not merely an event, but the act of some agent. This suggests why the odd statements considered in the previous paragraph are poetic; in ascribing purposes to inanimate things one is enabled to view them in a false but charming light. To say, for example, that the river is rusing to join the sea suggests that the waters are not being merely carried along, passively, by the force of gravity, but that they are active, that they are moving themselves, perhaps in the face of obstacles, toward some goal.

We cannot here, however, treat it as a foregone conclusion that purposeful events necessarily represent the actions of agents, for it has been maintained that inanimate things which are not agents—target-seeking missiles, thermostats, and the like—are nevertheless things that behave purposefully. This claim cannot be summarily dismissed, but I shall show subsequently that it cannot really be true.

This suggests further, I think, one reason why purposeful statements are viewed with such abhorrence in the sciences, including, quite marvelously, even the sciences of human behavior; namely, that they carry with them the suggestion of agency, even in those cases where no agent is apparent. If one proposes, for example, that the heart beats in order to circulate the blood, or that the pupil of the eye dilates in order to admit more light, and so on, then he seems to suggest that these occurrences are the acts of an agent. Since, however, neither the heart nor the eye is an agent—neither acts with a view to attaining any ends or goals of its own—such descriptions or "explanations" suggest agency on the part of some other being—some god, for instance. That is, a purposeful explanation of such behavior intimates that the things in question, not themselves agents, were designed or constructed by some agent for the purpose of achieving some end or goal of that agent. And such a hypothesis is, needless to say, quite useless for scientific understanding of events.

It is nevertheless wonderful that this abhorrence of purposeful explanations, which is so appropriate an attitude in the study of things that are *not* agents, should be carried over into the study of men, who *are* agents. It may indeed be true that the behavior of inanimate things cannot be understood teleologically or purposefully, it may be true that to view inanimate things from a perspective of purposes or ends would be to presuppose, or at least to suggest, all sorts of anthropomorphic and even theological notions, and it may also be true that no understanding of the organs of living things can be gained by the postulation of goals and purposes. It nevertheless remains that *men,* at least, are sometimes agents, that they do sometimes act purposefully, that their behavior can sometimes be understood through an understanding of their purposes, aims, and goals. Indeed, this seems to be the only way it can be understood, in case it is purposeful. To rule out purposeful explanations in human psychology, accordingly, where such explanations can have no possible theological implications is to rule out the only kind of explanation that renders certain kinds of human behavior intelligible.

The Adequacy of a Purposeful Explanation

A purposeful explanation of someone's behavior does not interpret it in the same way that, for example, a causal explanation would.

Nevertheless it is sometimes perfectly adequate in that it renders intelligible what no other explanation possibly could.

Suppose, for example, I see a friend hurrying along the walk, and I ask for an explanation of his behavior. He replies, we can suppose, that he needs some cigarettes, and the store closes in two minutes. Now here is a bit of perfectly typical human behavior, and the answer given to my question, it must be obvious, *explains* that behavior. Having heard that answer I then know, assuming the answer to be true, exactly why he is doing what he is doing—his behavior is intelligible to me. And the explanation is clearly purposeful; it has, or at least appears to have, nothing whatever to do with causes and effects, but only with a goal and the means thereto. Whether it can be reduced to an explanation in terms of causes and effects is another question, and an important one, which I shall turn to shortly.

There are two obvious remarks to make on this simple illustration before contrasting it with another. The first is that the explanation, and its truth, are not affected in the slightest in case the goal referred to is never attained, or did not even exist in the first place. If the store had closed before my friend reached it, such that he failed to achieve his end, it would still be true, if it was true in the first place, that his behavior was goal-directed or purposeful. A true statement to the effect that an agent is behaving in a certain way in order to realize a certain result does not entail that he realizes it. Purposeful behavior that is frustrated is no less purposeful for that. Indeed, even if there had been no cigarettes in that store to begin with, and even if there had been no such store, and hence no actual goal to attain, his behavior would have been no less purposeful, no less goal-directed. It would only have been misdirected.

The second observation, already implied in what was just said, is that there is nothing in such an explanation to imply that goals or ends are causes that come after their effects, which is a fairly standard misunderstanding of purposeful explanations. It is, accordingly, no criticism whatever of a purposeful explanation to say that it represents causes as "working backward," of following their effects in time, and so on, for no such notion is implied in the least. If a man explains his behavior by saying that he is doing something in order that a certain end may be achieved, he does not at all imply that this end, which does not yet and may never exist, is causing him to behave that way. Such a criticism, in short, is simply irrelevant.

Sometimes (but not always) the *cause* of an effect is the *means* to that effect, but an end or goal of an action is never in any kindred sense the *cause* of that action. It is for this reason that the expression "final cause" is misleading, though it need not mislead anyone who understands it.

Next contrast the situation just described with this one. We suppose that I am watching the turbulent flow of a stream, and I somewhat naïvely ask someone for an explanation of this behavior. Now if this were explained to me by saying that the water is hurrying to join the sea, the author of such an explanation would be speaking absurdly. The absurdity does not arise, however, from an inherent meaninglessness or uselessness in the purposeful explanation but only from the absurdity of the application. A purposeful explanation is not useless or meaningless as applied to the behavior of a man, as we have just seen. On the contrary, it is sometimes the best explanation that can be given, and a perfectly adequate one. This suggests what should be fairly obvious; namely, that streams and similar inanimate things are not agents, whereas men sometimes are. If such things as streams really acted, there is no reason why they might not do so purposefully. But the behavior they exhibit is in fact never purposeful just because it is always the passive effect of something else. A purposeful explanation applied to an inanimate, inactive thing is for this reason never more than a poetic, metaphorical utterance which may charm with its allusion to activity and purpose, but which is nevertheless never a true explanation. Here is why purposeful explanations are so utterly out of place in any physical science, and rightly scorned in those areas. It is not because they never explain anything, but rather because they never explain certain things, namely, the behavior of inanimate and inactive things. The fault, then, lies not with purposeful explanations as such, but in the misapplication of them.

Now there are some apparent exceptions, for sometimes it does appear meaningful and informative, up to a point, to explain the behavior of certain inanimate things in teleological terms. Thus one might say of a telephone that it is ringing in order to summon its owner; that a whistle is blowing in order to release the workmen from their labors for the day; or that water is flowing into a lock in order to lift a ship therein to the level of another lock, and so on. In every such case, however, the implied purposefulness of the behavior in question has only a borrowed meaning, which is derived from the activity of some agent or agents, who have arranged that the inanimate things should behave as they do. Thus the telephone does not literally ring in order to summon its owner; but another person literally makes it ring, or arranges for it to ring, for that purpose. Similarly, the water does not literally flow into a lock in order to raise a vessel, but some agent makes it behave thus, with the view to attaining some purpose of his. Remove the element of agency that is presupposed as part of the context or background of all such examples and the element of purpose simultaneously disappears. Of course, these observations do not exclude the possibility that an inanimate thing might behave purposefully, in the same sense in which men do; but to that larger question I shall shortly return.

It seems hardly doubtful, then, that purposeful explanations are often useful, true, and adequate in the realm of human behavior. Indeed, it is precisely the kind of explanation that is usually sought in almost every aspect of life. If one asks why a given man has, for example, ignited some leaves, he wants to know what he was trying to accomplish by that behavior, what his goal or purpose was. This is not what he would want to know if he asked why a given match or bolt of lightning has ignited some leaves. Normally, whenever we ask for the why's of human behavior—why this man did that, why this group of men are doing whatever they are doing, and so forth—we are asking for some indication of purposes or goals, some intended result. We are asking for an explanation that will represent the behavior in question as the means to some end. When such explanations are given, they are sometimes *adequate;* they set curiosity at rest, they render the behavior inquired about intelligible. They may, in fact they certainly do, differ radically from other types of explanation—from those sought in the physical sciences, for instance —but they do not differ by explaining nothing. The answers they provide are sometimes the only possible answers to the questions that are asked.

Explanation and Prediction

Now there is, to be sure, a sense of "explanation" much in vogue according to which teleological explanations, even in the realm of human behavior, are not real explanations, or are at least dubious as such. According to this interpretation, something is alleged to be "explained" only if it was *predictable;* that is, only if there is some general *law* from which, together with certain data consisting of the observable occurrences of other things, the thing in question could have been predicted. Now it is doubtful whether the purposeful behavior of men, or at least of individuals, is always explicable in that sense. Apart from the behavior of fairly large groups of men in certain situations having a common pattern, there seem to be no such laws. If there are, they certainly are not known. There are, for example, no laws in terms of which the purposeful behavior of an individual man from one moment to the next can in fact be predicted. It is doubtful, moreover, whether there could be such laws, because typically a man is able to pursue his various ends or goals in a variety of ways, and there seems to be no way anyone could predict which of these ways, to the exclusion of every other, a given man might choose on a given occasion.

Suppose, however, that this should all be true; suppose, that is, that at least some instances of purposeful behavior are in principle unpredictable, that there are no laws, known or unknown, under which a given purposeful act could be subsumed. We need not affirm that this *is* so, but let us for the moment suppose it is. What follows? Does it follow that such a purposeful act would be inexplicable? Hardly. All that follows is that it would not be predictable. If it could nevertheless be explained, it would follow that explanation does not consist simply of predictability.

And that is, in any case, obvious from what has already been said. Predictability is *one* sense of explanation, very useful in the study and understanding of inanimate things, but utterly out of place in the understanding of *some* cases of human behavior. I am not here saying that human behavior is in principle unpredictable, for to some extent, of course, it is. I am saying instead that in some cases the question whether it is predictable is irrelevant to the question whether it is explained. The behavior of the man hurrying down the walk to get some cigarettes, for example, is explained as soon as we know what his purpose is, what he is trying to accomplish, and are able to view that behavior as an appropriate *means* to that *end*. This has absolutely nothing to do with the predictability of his or any other man's behavior. If his actions were quite unprecedented, they would nevertheless be understood, intelligible, and in that sense explained, if they satisfied these conditions—that is, if they could be truly represented as an appropriate means to some end. It is in courts of law often of the highest importance to understand why a given crime was committed. Now this kind of understanding *never* takes the form of subsuming the crime in question under some general law of behavior which would have enabled anyone to predict it. This would simply be irrelevant. It is understood, instead, in terms of the *motive* of him who committed it—in terms of what the criminal was trying to accomplish. It is thus, and thus only, that it becomes intelligible. The question whether any similar man in similar circumstances and with similar purposes or motives would have done the same thing is an interesting philosophical question, the answer to which is not known by anyone, but it has absolutely no relevance whatever to understanding in this way, and in that sense explaining, why this man performed the acts he did perform. If this were not so, then we would be forced to conclude that hardly any crime, if indeed any crime at all, has ever really been explained by any detective or prosecuting attorney; for *in fact* no general laws are known to such people in terms of which the specific crimes coming to their attention could have been predicted. If such laws exist, they are in any case not known, and hence are not invoked for explanations. It is nevertheless true that ever so many individual crimes, which no one was in fact able to predict, and which have accordingly never been "explained" in the sense of having been shown to have been predictable, *have* been explained, in the sense that they have been quite thoroughly understood. Courts have been satisfied, and rightly satisfied, that they knew exactly why those crimes were committed by those who committed them. The explanations of them that were produced were explanations in terms of motives, purposes, ends, or goals of certain individual agents. For one to insist that they were not *genuine* explanations, since they were not in fact explanations in terms of any laws of human behavior, would only show that one was trying to cram the whole concept of explanation into the specialized meaning it has in areas far removed from human behavior, a sense that is often wholly irrelevant to the explanation of certain individual instances of human behavior.

The Irrelevance of Causes in Purposeful Explanations

Revert now to my earlier example, the man who is hurrying along the walk to get some cigarettes. Suppose that, in response to my request for an explanation of that behavior, he had attempted a causal explanation. This is perhaps possible, but what would such an explanation be like? Well, he could say, truly, that he was being moved along quickly because his legs were moving quickly, that these were moving in that way because certain muscles were behaving in such and such a way, that the motions of the muscles were the effects of changes still more remote, ultimately, perhaps, even changes deep within his very soul, the advent of certain desires, wants, and so on. Now clearly, while this would be perfectly all right as a rough causal explanation of his behavior, needing only to be filled out with certain data of physiology, it would be an extraordinary kind of answer, and certainly very far from any sort of information I was seeking. Rather than giving me an explanation for his behavior, he would only be getting farther and farther away from it. Sooner or later he must get around to saying that some of these things that are happening are things that he is causing to happen, things that he is doing—and then I shall need to ask my first question all over again; namely, why is he doing that? And here he cannot just start repeating what he has already said, for *no* answer will do now except a purposeful one; namely, that he is doing those things in order to achieve a certain result—to supply himself with cigarettes, for example, as we were supposing.

Of course another type of causal explanation would be in principle possible, and that would be one which causally explained, not just the observable behavior of his body, but his actions; that is to say, one that set forth what was causing him to do whatever he was doing. The general form of such an explanation would be the enumeration of certain conditions, either within himself or outside himself, which are such that, given these, it is causally impossible that he should avoid doing whatever it is that he is doing.

The difficulty with this, though, is that there may not be any such conditions. It might perfectly well be, for instance, that there are no such conditions inside or outside of himself, that he could neither point nor allude to any circumstances which are such that, given these, he cannot help doing what he is doing, that no internal or external conditions are causing him to behave in that way, that nothing makes him do so, and that his behavior is in this sense quite free. There might, to be sure, be certain external inducements— the fact that he is out of cigarettes, for example, and that the store can presumably supply more, and so on—but these things can hardly be represented as causes of his behavior in any usual sense. It is exceedingly doubtful whether these circumstances are such that, given them, it is causally impossible for him to behave in any manner other than precisely the way he is behaving. They would equally "explain" entirely different behavior—his using his pipe instead of cigarettes, for example, or his soliciting cigarettes from someone else, and so on—and a causal "explanation" which can be used as an explanation of any of a variety of things incompatible with each other is an explanation of none of them.

Nor will it help here to cite conditions within the agent himself, and to suggest that these are, together with certain external circumstances that obtain, causally sufficient for his doing whatever he is doing. The only "internal" conditions that suggest themselves are certain desires, beliefs, and the like. Thus, one might say that the agent is caused to hurry down the walk in the direction of the store by, among other things, his desire for cigarettes. But this is to relate his behavior, not to the desire as such, but to the *object* of that desire. It does not represent his actions as the effects of the desire within him, for it would be a very strange example of a cause and effect connection if it did. Rather, it presents his behavior as a means to the attainment of a certain end, the object of that desire, and is accordingly nothing but a disguised explanation in terms of a purpose or goal. To say that a man is being caused to run by his desire is, if literally understood, about as whimsical as saying that a shopper is being driven toward the shops by his avarice, or that a lover is being impelled by his lust to that part of the city where dwells his mistress. Such explanations make sense only because they are not literally understood. They are as poetic as the purposeful explanations of inanimate things to which I have alluded. They are taken to represent certain specimens of human behavior as the chosen means to the attainment of certain goals. They indicate that the behavior in question has a point or a purpose, that something is intended to be achieved by it. They are, in short, disguised purposeful explanations, and not really explanations in terms of cause and effect at all.

It need hardly be remarked, moreover, that such a purported causal explanation of behavior, which represents one's actions as the literal effects of certain inner or subjective states, is nothing but a variant of the theory of volitions all over again. There is no way, for example, of characterizing the desire for tobacco without in one way or another referring to tobacco. Considered merely as a subjective state, such a desire is characterless, with nothing to distinguish it from, say, the desire for alcohol. And there is no way of connecting any particular behavior with such a desire except by representing it as a means to the attainment of the object of that desire, which is no cause and effect relationship at all. The supposed causal connection, then, between one's desires and what one does to fulfill them is no causal connection but a logical and semantical one. The inferences guaranteed by such a connection—such as, that if so-and-so had not had a desire for cigarettes he would not have gone out to buy some—are not guaranteed by any real relation of cause and effect, but simply by considerations of meaning. They become completely empty if one refers to the desire without mentioning what it is a desire for. Such inferences are thus utterly different in kind from such genuinely causal inferences as that a certain fire would not have occurred if a certain match had not ignited, or that a certain pot of water would not have boiled if the stove had not been turned on, and so on. This indicates, too, why inferences connecting actual causes with actual effects, are sometimes worthwhile and informative, while ostensibly causal inferences connecting behavior with desires are not. To say that a man is caused to run looking for cigarettes by his desire for cigarettes is about as useless as saying that a man raises his arm in response to a volition—an arm-raising volition, of course.

15

Mechanism and Purpose

I have claimed that purposeful behavior is uniquely characteristic of agents, and that it cannot be understood or even described using only the concepts of physical science. A serious implication, as I have noted, is that if human behavior is ever purposeful, as in fact it usually is, then it can never be understood in terms of the concepts of physical science. In that sense, but in that sense only it cannot be understood "scientifically" at all. Since, however, such understanding is the only kind sought or even countenanced in whole areas of science, including most anthropological sciences such as empirical or behavioral psychology, it follows, if what I have claimed is correct, that those sciences can never truly understand or explain even the most simple purposeful behavior, but must rest content with descriptions in terms of conditioning and similar concepts—in short, with "explanations" which are simply off the subject. This is not to suggest that those empirical sciences of human behavior are not scientific nor that their conclusions are untrue. It is only to say that their conclusions and inferences are mostly irrelevant. The futility of explanation here, engendered by a too narrow and dogmatic conception of what is allowable by a scientific method, does not result from the complexity of the subject matter nor the present limitations of human knowledge. It is a logical difficulty, a difficulty of trying to understand certain facts, including facts of the simplest kind, in terms of concepts into which they simply fail to fit.

My task now is to show that purposeful behavior cannot be explained by the model employed in the physical sciences. Any descriptions of purposeful behavior must represent it as the *means* to some *end* or goal; no description or analysis of that relationship in terms of the concepts of physical science will work. This is in part a consequence of the fact that behavior can be goal-directed even though the goal toward which it is directed may never exist. From this it follows, first, that no inanimate or mechanical thing, whose behavior can be entirely understood and described in terms of the concepts of physical science, ever exhibits purposeful behavior as men, for example, sometimes do, and that no such inanimate thing could possibly be fabricated. To view as purposeful certain things whose behavior strikingly resembles that of men—chess-playing machines, for instance, or computers, or target-seeking missiles—is an absolute error and an illusion. It follows, secondly, that purposeful behavior cannot be understood in terms of any concepts remotely like those familiar to the physical sciences, that it cannot be described behavioristically, for example, nor in terms of such concepts as cause and effect, observable correlation, and so on. Nor is this a consequence of the notion that men "have minds" while machines ("by definition") do not, for no such supposition is needed. Even if we were to suppose that men "have minds" and that inanimate things do not, we still could not translate a purposeful explanation of a man's behavior into any other terms—causes or antecedent sufficient conditions, for example.

The Idea of
" Goal-directedness "

It is fairly natural to suppose that purposeful behavior is directed toward some goal. But what does "directed" mean here? And what is this concept of a "goal?" We can consider these two questions in turn, although the answers are not independent of each other.

Anything that is in any sense *directed* toward something must be so directed either by itself or by something else. A man, for example, can direct himself toward some end, toward the attainment of a certain goal. He can, for instance, direct his steps—literally propel his own body—to that part of the city where dwells his mistress, and that sort of thing. If, on the other hand, a man throws a stone at some object, or directs a gun toward a target, then the stone or the gun can clearly be said to be directed toward something, but it is directed by something other than itself—by a man, for example. Now in this latter case the behavior of the object in question—the stone's moving in the direction of some intended object, or the gun's coming into line with some target—represents nothing purposeful on the part of the object itself. Though the stone can properly be said to be directed toward an object, it cannot be said to be any purpose of the stone's to hit that object. Without reference to the thrower it is senseless to describe the stone as directed towards anything. The purpose is entirely on the part of the man who throws it. The stone's behavior is goal-directed only in the derivative or borrowed sense that it is used by the man for the attainment of some goal of *his*. The stone moves through the air only because it was thrown. But the man who throws it at some selected target has a purpose or goal, in the light of which one can understand why he threw it as he did. It makes perfect sense to say that he threw it in order to hit a cat, for instance, but it would be absurd to say, without any reference to this fact, that the stone itself is moving as it is *in order* to hit anything—as absurd, at least, as saying that a certain river is flowing through the meadows in order to join the sea.

An object can be regarded as behaving purposefully, then, only in case it *directs itself* toward some goal. Objects which are directed toward goals or ends by other things—by men, for example—do not thereby become purposeful or exhibit purposeful behavior in any but a derivative sense. They come only to be *used* for some purpose. Stones, hammers, clocks, and other inanimate things, whether simple or complex, are not in themselves purposeful beings, nor is there anything purposeful about their behavior as such, though such things may be used for a variety of purposes. It is never literally true, for instance, that an alarm clock rings in order to awaken some sleeper—not true in the same sense in which, for instance, someone might shake a sleeper in order to awaken him. The clock is set and adjusted by a purposeful being, and it is his behavior, not that of the clock, that is purposeful. The case here is no different from that of the stone aimed at a cat, whose motion becomes purposeful or goal-directed only when it subserves the purpose of a goal-directed agent. It cannot be of the least significance to the clock or to its functioning whether this or any other result is achieved by its ringing. It has no purpose or goal. The behavior of the clock has effects—many of them —but no purpose. Should the effect of its ringing be not to awaken the sleeper, but only to annoy the neighbors, or only to disturb the air around it, no purpose would be *frustrated* except perhaps that of some agent or agents. It is, in fact, only in relation to their purposes that any distinction can be drawn between the mere *effects* of the clock's ringing and the *purpose* of its ringing. In relationship to the clock by itself one can only distinguish causes and effects. One cannot further distinguish, among these, means and ends. Men, on the other hand, are not merely used for various purposes; though they sometimes are. They also sometimes use things, such as stones and clocks, or direct themselves to the attainment of various ends. In relationship to a purposefully behaving man, one can distinguish not merely causes and effects, but also means and ends. Some, though not all, of a man's behavior is a means to an end, and sometimes some, though not all, of the effects of his behavior are his purposes or goals.

Goal-seeking Mechanisms

What, then, of an inanimate, mechanical object that *does* direct itself toward some goal? Can such an object exist? Can such things be fabricated? So it seems; but let us look more closely at alleged examples.

As more and more interesting machines are invented and as these gradually replace men in the doing of various tasks, the idea easily spreads that they can be thought of as purposeful beings, purposeful in somewhat the same sense that men are. The intriguing idea thus germinates that inanimate things are much more like men than some have supposed or, what amounts to the same thing, that men are not different in principle from certain inanimate things, and that human behavior can, accordingly, be explained and understood in terms of the concepts of physics—the only concepts needed for the under-standing of any machines, however complex and wonderful. This idea is not only fruitful for the writers of science fiction but sometimes even seduces the learned, confirming in their minds the idea that, with time and patience and industrious inquiry, human behavior too will lend itself to explanation in terms of the concepts of physics. It has, in fact, even become somewhat unfashionable to doubt this, so seductive are the solicitations of these ideas. Learned and critical men thus find increasing fascination and satisfaction in comparing men with computing machines and other fabricated and sometimes self-regulating devices; they seek persistently to bridge the gap of knowledge, as though the differences between men and machines were only of degree rather than of kind. In back of this is the undoubted truth that self-regulating and ostensibly purposeful mechanisms can be fully understood and explained in terms of the concepts of physics. They are, indeed, the very fruit of those concepts. The intriguing implication, then, is that human behavior, and with it human nature, can eventually be similarly understood. It is time to repeat, however, that if the obstacles to such understanding are conceptual and logical, and not merely obstacles presented by a nature who surrenders her secrets slowly and in small bits, then those obstacles cannot be overcome simply by increasing our knowledge, and certainly not by continually dwelling in fascination on superficial comparisons, analogies, and metaphorical descriptions.

Let us consider, then, a target-seeking missile—a purposeful mechanical object if ever there was one. We suppose a missile—an underwater torpedo, for example—which is such that it rests quietly and unattended in its haven until, perchance, a suitable target wanders into its range, whereupon it sets itself off, doggedly pursues its target, continually adjusts and readjusts its course to compensate for evasive tactics on the part of its prey and then, in case it does not fail in the achievement of its goal, hits and perhaps destroys it. Now it does certainly act as if it were a purposeful being, it does appear to behave as it does in order to hit and destroy a certain object. Moreover, no agent directs it to that target. It fires and directs itself, frequently redirecting itself in accordance with the evasions of its prey, exactly as if it were behaving that way "on purpose." Now then, it might reasonably be asked, if this object *behaves* like a purposeful being, if its behavior is to observation indistinguishable from that of some being which is admittedly purposeful, what reason can exist for refusing to describe it in just that way? Clearly, if the *criteria* of purposeful behavior are to be empirical or behavioral, as physical science must require in case it is to have any place for the notion of purpose at all, then no such reason can possibly exist.

The answer to this is, quite simply, that there do not and logically cannot exist any behavioral criteria for purposeful behavior, an important point to which we shall shortly return. For now we need to look more closely at this missile and remind ourselves of how, in general, it works. There is, of course, nothing the least *mysterious* about this; it is only terribly complex, and appears mysterious and wonderful only to ignorance. An engineer of suitable training can describe and explain the mechanics of such a missile without needing any concepts whatever except those of physical science, and in particular, he can give a *complete* and adequate explanation without once introducing the idea of a purpose or goal.

Let us suppose, then, that the torpedo is designed to "seek out," under water, any propeller-driven ship, being guided to this by the sound waves of the propellers. The behavior of the missile can, then, be correctly, though superficially, described as follows. The sound waves emanating from the target's propellers act upon a sonic mechanism in the torpedo, and changes within this, in turn, act through complicated intermediary devices on the steering mechanism of the missile. To say that such changes "act," however, means nothing more than that they are causes, or that they causally suffice for certain other changes. If, accordingly, the torpedo is diverted by currents or whatnot from its course, relative to the sound waves from the propellers, the resulting change in those sound waves relative to the missile's sonic device suffices to reorient it through changes effected in the steering mechanism. Similarly, if the target itself moves then the correlation between the sound waves and the missile is likewise upset and this, again, suffices to alter the course of the torpedo. This is simply the way the torpedo is made. Of course a full and adequate description of just what goes on is by no means so simple, but such a description would consist only in the addition of details to the general picture. It should be noted, however, that the torpedo does not in any strict sense *direct* itself to any target. It is purposefully designed, by men, to be guided *by* the sound waves of propellers. If similar sound waves were produced by something else—if they were deliberately simulated, for example, in the effort to "fool" the torpedo —the result would be exactly the same. The torpedo would in this case in no sense be "fooled." It would be doing exactly what it was designed to do, to behave in a certain way in response to a certain kind of causal influence, and it cannot be of the slightest significance to the torpedo what happens after that. No one would be fooled, foiled, or frustrated except those who intended and designed the torpedo to hit a propeller-driven ship; and those are purposeful men.

To make this even more evident, let us compare this missile with a somewhat simpler one. Suppose this simpler missile is a torpedo designed to be guided, not by sound waves, but by a cable someone has attached to the target itself. All the torpedo has to do, then, is propel itself through the water; the cable will guide it to its target. Now the behavior of this missile, with respect to its target, is the same as that of the more sophisticated one described before, the only significant difference being that while the first was guided in a clever and complicated manner by sound waves between itself and the target, this one is guided by the more gross and simple means of a cable. If this second torpedo is diverted from its path, by currents or whatnot, then this change in its alignment, relative to the cable and thus to the target, suffices to reorient it. The same is true if the target itself moves; again the missile veers toward it, doggedly pursuing it as before. The only significant difference between the two missiles is, then, one of mechanical complexity. If one were observing the second, cable-guided missile but were unaware of the cable he would, in fact, have the same impression of a purposeful, "self-directed" missile as he has in the case of the first, but it would be no less an illusion in either case.

To the two foregoing "self-directing" mechanisms we can compare an even simpler one, namely, a bomb that has been fastened with a length of rope to the stern of a moving ship, with the idea that when the ship stops, the bomb will drift up to it—"seek it," if one pleases—and explode upon impact. This device, too, will exhibit "purposeful behavior," turning this way and that as its target changes course, doggedly "pursuing" it despite evasive maneuvers, then finally overtaking and destroying it. The only significant difference between this primitive "target-seeking" missile and the second one described is that, while the second is self-propelled, this one is propelled by the large propellers of the target.

Now clearly, none of these devices exhibits purposeful behavior. The last mechanism is passively drawn this way and that by the target itself, and cannot possibly be viewed as behaving as it does in order that it may sooner or later destroy the target—though of course one might have the *illusion* of purposeful behavior here too if he did not realize that the bomb was attached to the ship with a rope. But the other two missiles are also simply drawn this way and that by the target, one by the mechanism of a more or less cleverly arranged cable, the other by enormously cleverly arranged sonic devices. The same possibilities of the illusion of purpose exist for these devices, though deception becomes easier and more tempting as the complexity, and hence the ignorance of the observer, increases.

All these devices are purposeful only in the sense that they are all set up and arranged to satisfy certain goals or purposes of certain men. They are used for a purpose, and so arranged and designed, but no more exhibit self-direction than does a stone hurled at a cat. The failure of any of them to function "correctly" can be nothing but a failure to function as it was meant and intended by certain purposeful men to function, and its failure to attain a given "goal" can only be a failure to attain that goal that is aimed at or intended by men. Suppose, for example, a wire should get crossed in the mechanism of the first missile, with the result that it should turn around in mid-course, return with great vigor and determination, and explode in its own haven, to the consternation of its designers. This would be no malfunction on its part. It would be behaving exactly as such a device, with that wire crossed, might be expected to behave, and might conceivably be designed to behave by some saboteur whose purpose was to destroy the haven. Whether its behavior is considered the result of a "malfunction" is, accordingly, something entirely relative to the agent's purpose, and is in no sense relative to any imaginary purpose of its own. Similarly, if the same missile should be diverted from its intended course by the sound waves emanating from a school of fish, with the result that the fishes, and not the ship, were blown up, this would in no sense represent erratic, inept, or misguided behavior on the part of the missile. It would be behaving exactly as it was designed to behave, namely, to move in the direction of certain sources of sound. The outcome of such behavior in this case could in no way be viewed as the frustration of any goal or purpose of the missile—which has no goal or purpose—but only of a purposeful agent who presumably had more interest in destroying a ship than in disrupting a school of fish.

The whole concept of purpose in this context is, then, derivative from and relative to the purposes and intentions of agents. Even the word "target" has no meaning aside from denoting some object a man intends to hit by means of a crude or perhaps a sophisticated missile. The missile cannot intelligibly be spoken of as having any "target," being as indifferent to one as to another. Indeed, if anyone is for any reasons tempted to view target-seeking missiles as displaying purposeful behavior, or behavior that is performed as a means to the attainment of some goal or end, he will find exactly the same reasons for so viewing numberless other things fabricated by men— trains that are guided by tracks, for example, or automatic elevators, or indeed, almost any machine whatever.

From the foregoing we can derive the important conclusion that there can be no *behavioral* or *observational* criteria for saying that anything, whether it be a man or a machine, is directing itself toward the attainment of an end or a goal. The behavior of self-directed mechanisms is in every relevant respect exactly the same as that of a self-directed and truly purposeful agent. On the basis of observation alone we sometimes *impute* ends and goals to whatever displays such behavior, but this is *always* an illusion in case the thing in question is an inanimate object. It is, as we shall see shortly, only *sometimes* an illusion in the case of men. If a mechanism, such as a target-seeking missile, behaves exactly *as if* it were pursuing a goal of its own, and if, nevertheless, it never does, then it follows that the criteria for goal-directed behavior are not susceptible to observation. Similarly, if men *do* sometimes behave in certain ways pursuant to certain goals, aims, or purposes, and if their behavior is then indistinguishable in any significant respect from that of certain purposeless mechanisms, it again follows that the criteria for goal-directed behavior cannot be found in behavior itself: Behavior, by itself, affords no final determination. We can only observe *what* something, whether man or machine, is doing; we can never observe *why* it is behaving as it is, if this "why" is meant to ask what *for.* The purposes of things are read *into* them on the basis of clues afforded by their behavior. Such imputation of purposes is always false in case the behavior is that of a machine—unless, of course, it is behavior that suggests some end or goal of a man who uses the machine in question as a means to some goal of his. A similar imputation of purpose is *not* always false in case the behavior is that of a man, though sometimes it is. For men, unlike machines, do sometimes act intentionally and purposefully, *in order* that certain results may obtain. It is, in fact, only *because* this is true that we can even speak, in a derivative sense, of human artifacts as ever behaving purposefully in the first place.

The Concept of a " Goal "

The concept of purposeful behavior and the concept of a goal are obviously related, since the former is identical with the concept of behavior that is goal-directed. Much of what needs to be said concerning the latter is therefore implicit in what has been said about the former, and yet some additional important points must be made.

I have said that the criteria of goal-directed behavior cannot be found in such behavior itself, nor can it be described in the vocabulary of physical science, that is, without reintroducing teleological concepts. The behavior of two different things, such as a target-seeking missile (so called) and a goal-seeking man, may be significantly alike even though not both are goal-directed in the same primary sense. And further, when such ostensibly purposeful beings as target-seeking missiles are described, and adequately described, without the use of teleological language, they are found not to differ significantly from certain other simple objects whose behavior is never in any sense deemed purposeful. Such descriptions invariably tend, in fact, to eliminate every appearance of their being purposeful in the first place, showing clearly enough that such words as "strives," "pursues," "endeavors to reach," and so on are entirely metaphorical in such contexts.

Suppose, however, that the notion of a *goal* or *end* could be given some perfectly straightforward meaning in terms of what is observable and in terms, accordingly, of what is scientifically ascertainable. In that case there would be no ultimate difference, or no difference in kind, between purposeful behavior and the behavior of certain things that can be described entirely in terms of the concepts of physics. For if such an analysis of a goal were given, we could then say that any behavior is goal-directed just in case it is directed toward a goal, as so conceived. This, of course, is something that could be ascertained by observation. Suppose, for example, it could be shown that something is a goal, provided it has some simple or complex characteristic, the presence or absence of which can be ascertained by scientific observation, or that something is a goal provided it is related to certain other things by some simple or complex relationship, the existence or non-existence of which could similarly be ascertained by observations of some sort. Suppose, that is, that something's being a goal consisted simply of its having some characteristic, or some relationship to something else for which it is a goal. If this were so, then obviously the difference between purposeful and non-purposeful behavior would be at most only a difference of degree and not of kind, contrary to what has been said so far; for there is no reason why, for instance, inanimate things might not be directed toward—that is, in some sense simply move toward—objects having such characteristics or relations. This would suffice to declare them goal-directed, in precisely the sense that the behavior of men, for example, is sometimes goal-directed, since in either case their being such would consist of nothing but their being directed to objects of that kind.

It is my purpose now to show the hopelessness of such an idea. It cannot, of course, be proved false by way of philosophical demonstration, but can nevertheless be revealed as vain and hopeless just by showing how *any* such purported analysis must inevitably admit of counter-examples of all sorts—simply because such an analysis equates differences of kind with differences of degree.

Ends as Culminating States

Aristotle often spoke as though the end or goal of a process or activity were simply the normal or usual outcome of such a process or activity, the state in which it usually culminates. Now this, of course, is something one can often determine just by an examination of cases, so if this suggestion were right, we would have a perfectly empirical definition of a goal—one that would easily fit purposeful behavior into the framework of physics.

What Aristotle had in mind, evidently, is that some processes are orderly; like the growth of trees from seeds they follow a more or less fixed pattern. The developmental histories of such seeds are more or less similar, culminating in trees, so Aristotle thought of their becoming trees as their ends, goals, or "final causes." Similarly, the end or goal of a sculptor's activity is the production of statuary, this being, in fact, the normal culmination of such activity. Purposive behavior, then, on such a conception as this, is by no means unique to animate things; indeed there is no reason why goal-directed things might not be fabricated by men, since it is a simple matter to fabricate something whose behavior normally culminates in a certain state.

This conception of purposive behavior is by no means archaic, for learned men of our own day, particularly those who have been impressed by servomechanisms and other self-regulating devices, have proposed essentially the same idea. Indeed, any purely behavioral conception of a goal can be nothing but a variation upon this basic idea. Things such as target-seeking missiles, self-aiming guns and the like are sometimes, apparently in perfect seriousness, described as purposeful objects for no other reason than that, when functioning "normally," their behavior culminates in certain significant and interesting correlations with other things, similar to certain end results of purposeful activities of men. The fact that they were cleverly designed to behave in just this way is generally regarded as something quite ancillary, at least so far as their exhibiting purposiveness is concerned. The whole conception is, nevertheless, utterly inadequate, and for three reasons, each of which seems entirely conclusive.

The first reason is that *all* behavior culminates in some final state, and the similar behavior patterns of classes of individual things often culminate in similar states or final correlations, though it would be absurd to speak of those culminating states as the goals or purposes of such behavior. The behavior of every living thing, for instance, culminates in death, but shall we say that this is the purpose of such behavior, or the goal at which it is aimed? Smoke from tobacco pipes normally wends upwards towards the ceiling, and stones released above the earth normally fall back to the earth, but one can hardly be so absurd as to regard these as examples of purposeful, goal-directed behavior. Nor will it help at all to say that behavior is goal-directed in case the culminating state is attained even in the face of obstacles, or under conditions that divert the behaving object away from that final state or goal. This is, of course, often true of purposeful behavior, but unfortunately it is equally true of behavior that no one would describe as purposeful. The smoke from one's tobacco pipe, for instance, must sometimes circumvent obstacles in its path toward the ceiling, and rivers must often do the same in their paths to the sea, but this hardly makes these latter the goals or purposes of their behavior. A compass needle that is deflected from its alignment with the gravitational forces normally vacillates for a while, gradually reassuming that alignment; but to describe this as its purpose or goal is an outrageous metaphor. Similar remarks can, of course, be made concerning the most everyday things, such as rocking chairs and pendula. A weighted roulette wheel may normally end its spin on the same number, but can scarcely be said to have this as its purpose—though it could with no appearance of absurdity be given as the purpose or goal of whomever, if anyone, attached the weight to it in the first place.

To conceive goals in any such manner is, then, plainly worthless, for it merely obfuscates the very distinction it was to clarify. That a given process culminates in some final state or some normally repeated correlation with other things is not a defining condition of its being purposeful. One must add that the behaving object behaves as it does *in order* that such a final state or correlation may result, which is merely stating that such a final state or correlation is the goal, end, or purpose of its behavior. With this observation the futility of this whole approach becomes very obvious. A man who wends his way, by diverse routes and in the face of numerous obstacles, to that part of the city where dwells his mistress can indeed be described as a being whose behavior culminates in a certain final state or correlation with other objects, and he can *further* be described as a being whose end or goal that final state is, which is saying something more. It may be, though I do not declare that it is, that when salmon fishes leave the ocean and find their way, with enormous struggle and in the face of overwhelming obstacles, to the inland waters where they spawn, they do this *in order* to spawn. In any case, this is absolutely implied if their behavior is described as purposeful or goal-directed. It is not implied when their behavior, perhaps with similar struggle and in the face of similar obstacles, culminates in their finding their way into a fisherman's net, which might happen more often than not, precisely because no one supposes that they behave as they do *in order* that this final state or correlation may result.

The difficulty here seems to beset any purely behavioral or otherwise empirical definition of, or criteria for, a goal. If, that is, one specifies any such criteria whatsoever, it seems quite easy to find simple instances of processes which no one would ordinarily call purposeful or goal-directed—rising smoke, falling stones, rushing rivers, and the like—but which nevertheless satisfy the definition or criteria given.

The second reason why such a conception seems hopeless is that, even with respect to processes and activities which *are* undoubtedly purposeful or goal-directed, there are no behavioral or otherwise empirical criteria by means of which one can say with certainty *what* the goal of such activities might be, even when there is no doubt that the criteria are satisfied. This is simply a consequence of the fact that two such processes or activities which are behaviorially and physically identical may nevertheless be directed toward entirely different ends or goals.

Consider, for example, a man who on one occasion takes aim at a partridge with his gun, fires, and misses, hitting instead a nearby tree, and who on another occasion aims at that tree, fires, and hits it as before. The behavior and its effects in both cases are the same, yet the goals are not. Any behavioral criteria of a goal which permitted us to say, correctly, that it was the hunter's goal to hit the tree on the second occasion, would require us also to say, incorrectly, that this was likewise his goal on the first occasion. Or consider a man who, seeking out in the semi-darkness what he takes to be a burglar, fires his gun and shatters a mirror, mistaking his own image for his victim. His purpose is to fire upon an intruder, yet his *behavior* is precisely that of a man whose purpose is to shatter a mirror with a bullet. Examples like these readily come to mind, indicating that there is something more to goal-directed behavior than just the behavior itself. If, indeed, this were not so, then there would be no possibility for such a thing as *dissimulating* one's aims or purposes. Dissimulation consists precisely in acting *as if* one thing were one's purpose or end while all the while the true goal is concealed. Now if one's true goal were something for which behavioral or otherwise empirical criteria existed, then it would of necessity be displayed in any goal-directed behavior; and yet when one's purposes are successfully dissimulated, it is just this true goal that cannot be displayed.

The third and perhaps clearest reason why empirical or behavioral criteria cannot possibly be supplied for applying the concept of a goal is, simply, that the end or goal of purposeful activity sometimes does not exist. Now as a matter of logic, the properties of *all* unreal things are identical and, in any case, equally unfit to serve as observable things. From this it follows that on any empirical conception of a goal, any two instances of purposeful behavior whatever must have the same ends or goals, in the event that their goals happen not to exist.

Diogenes, for example, is supposed to have spent much of his life looking for an honest man, finally concluding, perhaps rightly, that none exists. Others have as strenuously sought the philosopher's stone, and many a man has gone to the cupboard for food only to find it empty. Now in any strictly empirical sense, we are forced to say that the ends or goals of all such activities did not exist, that is, that there were no such ends or goals. Or, equivalently, we can say on empirical criteria that the goals of all such activities were one and the same, namely, nothing—since that is in fact what they were. And yet it is equally obvious that their goals were not the same, that these activities are not all directed to the same end or goal, though there are no empirical criteria of goals which permit us to say that at all. More importantly, it is no part of the notion of goal-directed behavior that its goal must exist, for almost *any* such activity is capable of being frustrated—and frustrated, not just because the goal is not reached, but because it was never there in the first place. It is quite clear, however, that such activity is nonetheless goal-directed for that.

This, incidentally, exhibits once again the folly of speaking of machines as purposeful or goal-directed beings. Missiles can be made whose behavior astonishingly resembles that of a purposeful being, as we have noted. Guns can be elaborately designed to follow their targets, and mechanical dogs can be made to chase real or mechanical rabbits. A missile of this sort might sometimes "make a mistake," as some would put it, setting off in pursuit of the "wrong" target, as in pursuing a school of fish; a self-aiming gun might sometimes "err" and fire upon "friendly" targets, and a mechanical hound might, like a live one, go off in dogged pursuit of a chipmunk that was not supposed to be there. These things can all happen easily. But no such missile can set out, like Diogenes, in pursuit of something which, as it is later discovered, did not exist to be found. The purpose of a mechanical hound can never be so misguided that it goes seeking a moving object which, as it later turns out, was never there to be pursued. An astronomer might search with his glass for the planet Vulcan, but no sense can be made of the idea of an automatic, self-guiding, and self-adjusting telescope, of whatever complexity or elaborate design, undertaking a search of the skies for *that* planet; for no such planet exists.

Could not, however, a self-operating telescope be *designed* to search for the planet Vulcan? That is, could not one be made which was of sufficient refinement that it would stop searching the skies if, but only if, it found a heavenly body exactly fitting the description of Vulcan? The fact that no planet of that description exists does not imply that a telescope of that kind could not exist and search for it; it only implies that its search would be vain. Similarly, could not one design a unicorn trap—a trap, that is, of sufficient complexity and refinement that it would spring only upon an animal exactly fitting the description of a unicorn? Such a trap would never catch anything, but that would indicate no fault or error on the part of the trap. Again, it might seem that a self-aiming gun might be designed to follow enemy targets of a certain precise description and no others. If no such target appeared, or if none existed to begin with, the mechanism might nevertheless have as its goal to shoot such a target in case it were to appear. Such a gun would be useless or to no purpose only in the sense of being superfluous or not needed—but in the same sense, *men* trained and posted to shoot only at enemy targets would be useless in case none appeared. Such men could nevertheless claim, correctly, that it was their purpose to shoot at such targets.

The difficulty with all such examples is, again, that they are examples of mechanisms designed only to subserve certain purposes of men, having none of their own, and can thus be described as having goals or purposes only in this borrowed sense. There is no difference, for example, between two self-operating telescopes, one of which is designed to "search" the skies endlessly, stopping at nothing, and the other of which is designed to "search" the skies, stopping only if it chances upon the planet Vulcan. The two might in fact, though they need not, be of exactly the same design, and could then with equal truth be described as both having the one purpose, or the other, or no purpose at all of their own. The case is no different from, say, two roulette wheels, one of which just happens as a result of age, warping, or wear to be unbalanced in such a way that it usually stops on the number seven, and the other of which has been purposefully set off balance in such a way as to produce the same result. Without any reference to the aim or purpose of some man, there is no way of distinguishing which has as its "purpose" to stop on number seven, and which just happens, as a result of its being unbalanced, usually to stop on that number. The two wheels might, indeed, be identical. Either can then be *used* for one and the same purpose; but if one of them, independently of the purpose of any man, has no purpose in behaving as it does, which by hypothesis one of them has not, then neither has the other.

An Example

A single rather graphic example should make this last point clear. Let us suppose a little old lady is employed in an assembly line to thread needles as they pass in front of her. We shall suppose that her skill and efficiency are quite good, so that she gets the thread through the eye on the first try, let us say, on the average nineteen times out of twenty. But now let us suppose that, for reasons of her own—a grudge against her employer, perhaps, or as a tactic for extracting better wages from him—she begins missing *on purpose*. Hitherto it was her goal or purpose to get the thread through every time, a goal she more or less achieved, since she missed, quite unintentionally, only about five per cent of the time. Now, however, she misses fully fifty per cent of the time—but she does this on purpose, this being her very goal and one which, moreover, she achieves perfectly. All this makes perfectly good sense, and the *difference* between the lady's two behaviors—which can be understood only in reference to her purpose or intentions—is entirely intelligible.

Now, to continue the example, let us suppose that with the increase of automation this little lady is replaced by a needle-threading machine which, we can suppose, works with about the same efficiency as the lady when she was trying to poke the thread through the eye every time. The machine, that is, works well, though imperfectly, since it too misses about five per cent of the time. Are there any circumstances under which we can say here, as we could in the case of the lady, that it is the machine's *purpose* to get the thread through the eye every time, and that this goal is more or less achieved, though imperfectly? The behavior of the two beings is essentially the same, and so is the result.

Yet there is a difference, and it consists precisely in the fact that while the lady can be correctly described as *trying* to accomplish a certain result, and thus as having an end or goal for her behavior, the machine cannot possibly be so described. The lady prior to her slowdown gesture tries every time and occasionally misses; but all we can say of the machine is that it occasionally misses. No sense can be made of its *trying* and missing.

This becomes perfectly obvious when we imagine the machine duplicating the still purposeful behavior of the little lady after she starts trying to *miss* half the time, and succeeding. Now the machine could, to be sure, start missing half the time; but such a performance could not result from its trying to miss. It could not, unlike the lady, miss on purpose. Suppose an engineer were told to construct such a machine; what could he do? What, that is, other than to construct a machine that worked fairly badly, or one that was in need of adjustment? Now the lady, as we described her, was not merely in need of adjustment when she began missing half the time. She *could* do much better; she was still perfectly *able* to get the needle through almost every time; she was only missing intentionally, and perhaps pretending otherwise. But what would a machine be like which performed in the same way, but which was still, without any adjustment, *able* to do better, one which *could* get the needle through almost every time but instead missed half the time, on purpose? Suppose an engineer were told to construct *two* needle-threading machines, each of which missed half the time, but which were nevertheless different in this one respect: that while one of them would be such that it simply missed half the time, the other would be such that, like the lady, it missed half of the time on purpose. How would the two machines differ? What could the engineer *add* to the second to achieve such a difference? It seems perfectly obvious that there would be nothing whatever to add; the two machines might as well be exactly alike. Anything added to the second machine—any extra vacuum tubes, wiring, or whatnot—would be entirely superfluous. If any such additional parts made any difference, it would be a difference in how the machines performed and behaved, and this is precisely a differences that is not wanted. The engineer could, to be sure, make the machines very different—such that, for instance, one worked by electricity and the other by steam, or such that one had double the number of parts, and so on. But then it would be perfectly arbitrary which to call the one which merely missed half of the time, and which to call the one which missed half of the time on purpose. No mechanical elaboration can produce such a difference. The two machines, whatever their construction and design, are equally purposeful and equally lacking in purpose; like every other mechanism they can sensibly be spoken of as having purposes and goals only in a borrowed sense, or only, that is, in relation to the purposes for which they are used by truly purposeful beings. In this respect the two machines are the same, whatever other differences there might be, each being as good as the other for getting threads through needles half of the time and for missing the other half of the time.

The Futility
of Behavioral Criteria

It should be obvious by now that the difficulties in such behavioral and empirical criteria for goals and goal-directedness as we have been considering do not result merely from the simplicity or crudeness of such criteria. The difficulties are not such that they might be overcome by the introduction of still more behavioral or physical concepts, or by refining and elaborating the criteria so as to meet obvious counter-examples. The error lies in trying to render a conception of purpose in terms of such concepts in the first place. Men would never have attempted this had it not been for the fact that certain inanimate things, and especially certain highly sophisticated things fabricated by men for their own purposes, strikingly resemble in their behavior and in their effects certain actions of men which are performed as a means to achieving similar effects. Struck by such similarities, men have unabashedly ascribed purposes to such fabrications, describing them as though they were veritable agents in their own right, speaking of them as, for example, trying, sometimes succeeding, sometimes blundering, sometimes making mistakes, becoming tired, inept, and so on. The metaphors have then been taken for real descriptions, and the gulf between purposeful agents and their tools has been treated as though it did not exist or was, in any case, constantly decreasing. Sometimes, carried away by all this and with the very minimum of philosophical criticism, men have even spoken as though their metaphorical uses of teleological terms constituted some new and overwhelmingly important *insight* into human nature and human behavior. Some machines are very much like men—astonishingly like men; hence, men are very much like certain machines—that follows; but men *made* those machines...and so on. Once started on that exhilarating train of thought, there is no end to it.

The gulf between a thing which acts *as if* it were a purposeful being because its behavior strikingly resembles that of the latter, and one which acts similarly because it *is* a purposeful being, is not a gap that can be narrowed by multiplying concepts derived from observation or from physics. Physics does not arbitrarily exclude anything by eschewing teleological notions; rather such notions simply have no place in a physical explanation. We cannot say, for example, that a thing is behaving purposefully provided, among other things, it more often than not reaches its "goal." Smoke more often than not rises, but has no goal. We cannot qualify this by saying that it "tends" to continue toward its "goal" in the face of "obstacles." The water in a riverbed strewn with rocks does that, but has no goal. We cannot qualify this by adding that in any case it "strives" toward its goal, thus "striving" perhaps unsuccessfully to overcome obstacles; for "striving" is no concept of physics and no concept that can be defined in terms of behavior. There is no difference between two alarm clocks, one of which merely awakens a sleeper and the other of which does the same thing through striving to awaken him. Similarly, there is no difference between two rivers, one of which merely fails to overflow a dam (its "obstacle") and the other of which strives to overflow its dam but fails. Multiply concepts as one will, he finds he gets not one whit closer to an understanding of purposeful behavior, for such concepts are either empirical ones, whose applicability can be determined on purely observational criteria, in which case they always apply to numberless things which it would be absurd to call purposeful, or they are, like the concept of "striving," disguised purposeful concepts to begin with, in which case there are found to be no observational criteria for their application. They are notions that are *read into* a situation—as when a missile is said to be "striving" in the face of "obstacles" and "evasions" to reach its target—and never concepts that are empirically *derived* from any situation. They are, in fact, derived entirely from one's own understanding of himself as a purposeful being. But one never *observes* —notes, notices, infers from signs—that he himself is trying to accomplish something, that he is striving toward an end or goal. He sometimes knows that he is, but not *that* way.

16

Purpose and Subjective Causation

Many philosophers have supposed that, when an agent is correctly described as behaving purposefully, all that is meant is that his behavior is caused by certain subjective psychological states, such as specific desires or beliefs. And this, it is imagined, is why inanimate things such as clocks and missiles and computers cannot properly be described as behaving purposefully. They happen to lack "minds," the requisite causal antecedents to purposeful behavior, and hence have no desires, beliefs, and the like. This view is so commonplace in philosophy that it is quite generally thought to remove any puzzlement in the notion of purposeful behavior, and is largely responsible for the neglect of this notion. We are told that purposeful behavior is simply behavior that is *caused* by certain desires together, perhaps, with certain beliefs, the implication being that it differs from the non-purposeful behavior of inanimate things only in this, that its *causes* are somewhat different. They are "subjective," "private," "mental" causes which lie in the mind or soul. Since machines have no minds or souls, it should not be surprising that they do not really seek goals, however much they may sometimes appear to. They do not have within them the right kinds of causes.

Now there is a truly stupifying thought. It is not stupifying because it is patently absurd, for it is not. It takes a bit of reflecting on it to see that it is absurd. Nor is it because it is so manifestly contrary to our experience. It is contrary to no experience, for experience, observation, trial, or experiment have nothing to do with it at all. No one ever *discovered* that purposeful behavior is subjectively caused by private "mental" events in the soul. No one ever discovered that certain events or states occurring in his mind or soul appeared to be quite regularly followed by certain motions of his body, concluded that the former must be causing the latter, and baptized the former "desires for the results of those motions" and the latter "purposeful behavior." The thought is stupifying because it fits fairly well into the semi-mechanical model of explanation men generally presuppose when dealing with inanimate things and appears to give content to certain customary modes of speech—"ordinary language"—that are reflections of that model. Thus it permits men to say what they are accustomed to saying—without requiring them to look to see whether what they are saying has any semblance to facts. There is no need to look, because there is nothing to look for—the causes of purposeful behavior lie too deep within the soul, are too subjective and private to be found by anyone except, perhaps, him in whose mind they transpire.

The Nature
of This Theory

The way to see the absurdity of this whole conception is to see just what it is really saying. We are to suppose that when a man, say, is behaving purposefully, then his behavior is literally being caused by his desire for a certain goal, and also, perhaps, by his belief that the behavior in question constitutes a promising means of achieving that goal. In order to have desires and beliefs, however, one must first have a mind, for believing and desiring are, of course, things done by the mind. Machines do not have minds—they are purely physical things. That, everyone knows, is why machines do not behave purposefully—they lack the requisite spiritual organ or part.

The "explanation," then, is of the sort that might be given for the fact, say, that Mexican cave fish do not see (because they do not have eyes), or for the fact that a given radio produces no sound (because it lacks a necessary vacuum tube), and so on.

Disregarding for the moment the question what it *means* to say that men have, but machines lack, minds, it is worth asking how anyone professes to know this. It has never been discovered that men, along with hearts, brains, and livers, also have minds, nor has anyone ever discovered such a thing within himself. Moreover, there is no good reason to suppose that machines, even the simplest of them, do *not* have minds, once we assume the existence of such things. Why *not* say that the alarm clock is ringing because it is striving to awaken the sleeper, that it has this desire and is acting in accordance with it? Why not say its very works are its mind, and the thing that makes it ring is its desire to ring? The only reason for not saying this is, obviously, that we have another explanation for the clock's behavior, namely an explanation in terms of simple mechanics, which is quite complete without introducing desires as additional causal factors. But if that is so, then all one is saying in asserting that a man's behavior, when he awakens a sleeper by shaking him, is caused by his desire that the man should wake up, is that we do *not* have a similar explanation for this. There must, then, it is easy for a simple person to say, be a slightly different cause and effect explanation—so a "desire" is postulated just in order to supply the missing element. That, I believe, is substantially the reasoning that underlies the thesis that desires within men's minds cause some of their behavior but that machines have no desires to cause theirs, though it is not always put so bluntly.

What "Having a Mind" Means

This introduces the more fundamental question, bypassed a moment ago, of what after all it *means* to say that men have minds. Clearly it does not mean that, in addition to a man's visible organs—his heart, limbs, and so on—there is still another, invisible one called his mind—though some philosophers have appeared to mean something like this. We should perhaps then say that *if* it is supposed to mean that, then there is in any case not the slightest reason to think any such part exists; for clearly there is not.

I take it that what it means to say that men have minds is that they are capable of doing all sorts of things which machines, for example, cannot do, just because they are only machines; that men are capable, for example, of deliberating about what they are going to do, as contrasted with merely vacillating between alternate forces; of choosing, skillfully or ineptly, means to ends, as contrasted with automatically hitting upon certain causes of certain effects; of acting in certain ways in order that certain results may obtain, as contrasted with behaving in certain ways which do in fact have certain effects or results; of remembering their past and guiding the future behavior in terms of such memories, as contrasted with merely undergoing certain changes as a result of what has happened in the past; of making intelligible discourse that is suitable for expressing their thoughts, as contrasted with mechanical or phonograph-like production of certain noises, intelligible or otherwise; of setting up goals or ends and striving toward them, as contrasted with merely culminating, like clockwork, in certain final states or relationships; and so on.

Now obviously, it is only because men are capable of doing such things that philosophers have ever said they "have minds" in the first place. The fact that men are capable of such things has, in other words, functioned as *evidence* that they "have minds." And the only reason it has ever seemed good evidence for this is that philosophers have found it incomprehensible that men's *bodies* could do all those things—for men's bodies, after all, are not significantly different from machines, being perfectly physical and mechanical.

What I am suggesting, however, is that such facts are not merely *evidence* that men have minds. They only express what it *means* to say that men have minds. They are just the sort of fact to which one calls attention by saying that men have minds. The claim that men have minds is, in other words, nothing but the claim that they are capable of doing all sorts of things, a small sample of which has been given, which machines and other inanimate things cannot do—of deliberating, acting in certain ways in order that certain results may obtain, choosing means to ends, and so on. That men are capable of doing such things is doubtless mysterious, inasmuch as it so sharply *distinguishes* them from machines and other inanimate things; but it is no explanation of how they can do such things, and hence no dispelling of any mystery, to say that they "have minds," but only a restatement in other words that they are unlike machines. To *explain* how men can do all those things by saying they "have minds" would be like "explaining" how a clock is able to do all the things that it does by simply listing the

things that it does, asserting on the basis of this that it "has _____,"
and then filling in the blank with some contrived word that is henceforth to be understood as meaning that the clock is capable of doing
the things previously listed. It is not, in other words, an explanation
of any facts, but only a funny and misleading way of calling attention
to those very facts.

If this is so, the philosophical theory before us shrinks to nothing.
If having a mind just means, among other things, being able to do
such things as lay plans, deliberate, select appropriate means to ends,
pursue goals, make certain things happen in oneself and his environment in order that certain other things may happen, and so on, then
it is no real *explanation* of how men are able to do such things, to say
that they have minds. It is only a strange way of saying the same
thing again.

Desires as Causes

Still, the theory that purposeful action is simply behavior caused
by certain subjective, psychological states is not likely to go down
just from those observations. The rather metaphysical question whether
or not men have minds can, it will be claimed, be disregarded. It
nevertheless remains that purposeful action is just a variety of caused
behavior, and that what distinguishes it from other behavior—from
purposeless behavior, for example, and from all inanimate behavior—is
that it is caused by one's desires together, perhaps, with his beliefs.
If, for example, someone truly says that he raised his hand in order to
attract another person's attention, he is explaining his behavior as
purposeful. At the same time, all he is really saying is that his arm
was caused to rise by his desire to attract that person's attention,
together with his belief that this would be a suitable means to that
end. One can perhaps say this without committing himself on the
further question whether men, in some special sense, have minds.

There are many enormous difficulties with this general picture,
however. For one thing, purposeful behavior must certainly be purposeful action, as distinguished from simple automatic response, and the
theory before us does not even make that distinction. Desires are
capable of literally *causing* all sorts of changes in the body, and some
of these have, and are believed to have, certain good effects, that is,
effects that one wants; but not all such bodily changes qualify as
purposeful *actions*. Hunger, for example, which is the desire for

nourishment, sometimes causes salivation and other changes which are, moreover, useful to nourishment; but one does not salivate in order to be nourished, or at least, it would be odd to say so. It is not even an action that one performs; it is only an automatic response to a stimulus. Similarly, sexual desire sometimes literally *causes* very definite and manifest physiological changes upon its onset, particularly in a man, and these changes, too, are useful and even necessary to the gratification of such desire. But again it would be odd, and indeed false, to represent such changes as actions that are performed in order that such a goal might be achieved. They are not actions at all, but mere physiological responses. They are not things that one does in order to achieve a certain result, but only things that happen to him and which are, in fact, useful to the attainment of that result—which, indeed, he may not even actively seek, though nonetheless desiring it.

The theory might be modified to take account of this by saying that purposeful *actions,* as distinguished from useful responses and other non-voluntary behavior, are in any case caused by one's desires for certain results, together with one's beliefs that such actions are appropriate means to achieving those results. Thus, raising one's hand is sometimes an action, and not just a response, and one might be caused to raise his hand, as distinguished from one's hand being caused to rise, by his desire to attract another person's attention, together with his belief that raising his hand would have this effect.

We can ignore for the moment the extreme artificiality of this general picture. Even if it were not artificial and extremely dubious from the standpoint of what does actually happen when one performs a purposeful action, it would not do. For it is not difficult to find examples of behavior which fit that description, in case anything fits it, but which nevertheless are *not* purposeful actions, or in any case not purposeful in the way the theory requires. Suppose, for example, that a member of an audience keenly desires to attract the speaker's attention but, being shy, only fidgets uncomfortably in his seat and blushes. We may suppose, further, that he does attract the speaker's attention by his very fidgeting; but he did not fidget *in order* to catch the speaker's attention, even though he desired that result and might well have realized that such behavior was going to produce it. Again, suppose a man has a keen desire to see his friend and believes that telephoning him to arrange a meeting is a fit means to this end. He is thus caused by his desire to go to a telephone booth, where he happens to find his friend sitting in the booth. His action was caused by his desire to see his friend and he believed—correctly, as it turned out—that it was a fit means to this goal; but he did not go to the phone booth in order to see his friend there.

The Strangeness
of This Conception

Such criticisms are superficial, however, and almost as contrived as the theory itself. To see the truly absurd character of the theory, we must suppose that one's actions, when purposeful, are literally *caused* by desires within him for certain goals as well as by his beliefs that the actions in question are suitable means to these goals; that these desires and beliefs do not merely cause his body to behave in certain ways, which would be a strange enough notion, but that they cause him to make his body move in the ways he moves it.

This is a peculiar sort of cause and, what is less likely to be noticed, a peculiar kind of effect. Let us first note, for example, that the desire in question, and the belief in question, cannot be anything very simple. Even the minimal description of either must be something hideously complex. Consider the man, for example, who raised his hand to attract the speaker's attention—a fairly simple specimen of behavior, one would suppose. Can we say, simply, that it is caused by his desire to catch the speaker's attention and by his belief that raising his hand will accomplish this? Hardly, for there are numerous ways he could accomplish the same result—by waving a handkerchief, for example, or by coughing, or by speaking, or by raising his right hand instead of his left, or his left instead of his right, or by standing, or by raising his hand a little higher, or a little less high than he does, and so on. Any of these are things he might have done to catch the speaker's attention. Probably all are actions he believed would be effective means to that end. Yet he did not and could not do all of them. To say simply, then, that whatever action he performed was caused by his desire to catch the speaker's attention and by his belief that this action would do it, does *not* explain the occurrence of *that* action. It would equally have explained any of a variety of alternative actions. An "explanation" which serves equally to explain any of several mutually incompatible occurrences is an explanation of none of them.

What we should have to say, then, is that his action of raising (say) his right hand, in just the manner and at just the time he did raise it, was jointly caused, not merely by his desire to catch the speaker's attention and his belief that this would do it, but by (i) a desire to catch the speaker's attention by raising his right hand at a certain time and in a certain way, namely, at the time and in the way that he did, together with (ii) his belief that raising his right hand at that time and in that way would attract the speaker's attention, or would at least have some chance of doing so. If it is not spelled out this way, we have no more explanation for his raising his hand than, say, for his standing or waving a handkerchief, which are things he did not do. But even disregarding the element of belief in this alleged cause, what kind of *desire* is that? Has anyone ever felt such a desire, in any manner remotely like feeling a headache or a twinge of remorse? Can anyone ever say of such a desire when he first began to feel the onset of it, as distinguished from when he first formed a certain intention? Or when it began to abate, or when it reached its peak of intensity? If anyone *said* that he "felt" such a desire, would he be telling us anything more than that he wanted or intended or had as his purpose to catch the speaker's attention by raising his hand in that way? That, however, is precisely the notion we were supposed to be getting rid of by reducing it to *simpler* and more readily intelligible terms. Far from reducing the basic idea of acting purposefully to something simpler and easier to grasp, we have by following this approach only re-expressed that very idea in terms that must eventually be translated back into the language of purpose. No *causal* explanation has been given at all. All that has been given is a frightfully cumbersome locution for saying over again the very thing that was said simply and clearly in the first place.

The theory of the causation of purposive actions by desires and beliefs is, then, a fairly complex and unbelievable thing when applied even to the simplest actions, like raising one's hand. What does it look like when applied to rather complex and protracted purposeful behavior, such as playing on a musical instrument or weaving a basket? Shall we say that each stroke of the pianist's fingers is caused by a fresh desire to move that finger, together with his belief that, by so doing, a certain desired effect will ensue? We could say that, but then we would not be describing anything that actually happens, for a pianist does not in fact experience a torrent of desires and beliefs following one upon the other with the rapidity and variety of the notes that flow from his instrument. Shall we then say that the sudden onset of a *single* desire and belief, just prior to this flow of melody, produces the whole works? Well, we saw a moment ago that the desires and beliefs involved in so simple a thing as raising one's hand would have to be terribly complex things, but what must be the complexity of a belief and desire such as this one? The expression of the belief by itself would require a small volume. It is no belief that the pianist could possibly entertain, for he could not even comprehend it all at once. Simply sitting down and playing the melody through is a simple feat in comparison.

I said that not only the causes, but also the effects, as conceived by this theory, are very strange animals, and it is time now to consider these. We must first point out again that what, under this theory, is caused by certain beliefs and desires is not simply a bit of behavior or bodily motion, but an act of an agent. In our example it is not merely the man's hand that is caused to rise, but the man who is caused to raise his hand. This is already a very complicated sort of effect. In raising his hand, however, the man did many other things as well. He raised his fingers aloft, for instance, and also his finger nails, and also, perhaps, the ring on his finger. Yet the desires and beliefs which are supposed to be the causes of his action had nothing to do with these, despite the fact that they did, if they caused the man to raise his hand, cause him to do these things as well, since these are assuredly things that he did, *just* by raising his hand. In what sense, then, do they not causally explain them? Ordinarily a bona fide *causal* explanation of any complex event is equally a causal explanation of every *part* of that complex event, but not here. Why not? The obvious answer is that, in raising his hand, it was no part of the agent's purpose or intention to elevate his finger nails, his ring, and so on, even though these are things he did, while it was his purpose to raise his hand. But that, again, simply reintroduces the very concept of purpose which this allegedly causal explanation was meant to obviate. It is of no value as an explanation, even as a causal explanation, until we have qualified it suitably by references to the agent's purposes; and with such qualifications it is hardly a good *substitute* for the purposive explanation with which we began. We might as well have said at the outset that the agent raised his hand in order to catch the speaker's attention, and simply let it go at that, for the implication of purpose contained in the expression, "in order that," has by no means been dissolved or reduced by this theory to any such notions as cause and effect, or to anything remotely like these.

An Example

To see this better, compare the following three situations: (i) a man raises his hand in order to attract the speaker's attention, and thereby both attracts the speaker's attention and drives off a fly; (ii) he raises his hand in the same way in order to attract the chairman's attention, and thereby attracts the speaker's attention and drives off a fly; (iii) he raises his hand in the same way in order to drive off a fly, and thereby attracts the speaker's attention and drives off a fly. Now exactly the same things happen in each situation. The effects that actually occur are all the same, though not all these effects are the *ends* or purposes of the man's action in each case. Similarly, the causes that actually occur are all the same in each case, though not all these causes are the *means* to the effects that happen. The situations are distinguishable, then, not in terms of causes and effects, but only in terms of means and ends. Now of course one can say that the causes are not the same in each case, since the "desires" are not the same and these desires are causes. But obviously, all that really amounts to saying is that the *ends* are not the same, since the "desires" are distinguishable from each other *only* in terms of what they are desires *for*. Apart from that, there is no reason whatever why they might not be exactly alike. Indeed one should suppose they must be alike, for if they really differed as *causes* it is quite impossible to see how, in exactly the same circumstances, they could have identical effects. One might as well say that the three motions of the arm are different causes, since in the first case it is a gesture for catching one man's attention, in the second a gesture for catching another's attention, and in the third a gesture for shooing a fly. This would not describe any difference in the gestures themselves, which are identical in all three cases and which have identical effects in each case, but only a difference in the ends or purposes for which those gestures are performed. The differences in the three situations are not, then, differences of causes or effects, whether these be of the observable or unobservable kind, but simply and solely differences of means and ends. This, however, is a difference that can be understood only in terms of the concept of purposes, ends, or goals. It is, in short, an irreducibly teleological distinction.

The Teleological Character
of This Theory

It should be evident by now that this theory, which purports to eliminate the need of teleological concepts in describing purposeful behavior, cannot be spelled out without larding it very heavily with just such concepts. Worse than that, the theory cannot even be stated, however inadequately, without introducing such concepts. The theory, in its simplest and grossly inadequate formulation, says that a purposeful action is caused by a desire *for* something, and by certain beliefs concerning *means and ends*. The concept of means and ends is itself, however, a teleological concept, and is by no means coextensive with causes and effects. Not all causes are means, nor are all effects ends. There is no way of distinguishing, from among causes and effects, which are means and ends except by reference to someone's purpose. An action has many effects—raising my hand to catch the speaker's attention, for example, also has the *effect* of attracting the attention of other persons, of elevating my ring, of disturbing the air nearby, and so on, but the *end* of my action is catching the speaker's attention rather than any of these other things. It is distinguished from them as an end, however, only in relation to my purpose. Similarly, in case this end is achieved, it has many causes—the conditions being such that my hand is visible to the speaker, the speaker's being so placed that he sees my hand, and so on. But these *causes* of his attention being attracted to me are not the *means* by which that end is achieved. The means, which is my raising my hand, is distinguished from the other causes only in relation to some purpose of some agent—in the present case, in relation to my purpose or intention of achieving a certain effect.

Similarly, to speak of having a desire *for* something is, in the context of such a theory as this, no less a teleological concept than that of means and ends. Such a "desire," as the term is here used, can only be a desire for some goal or end, and is absolutely indistinguishable from other "desires" of the same sort except by reference to this very end or goal. What, for example, distinguishes my desire to catch the speaker's attention by raising my hand from my desire to catch the chairman's attention by the same act? These are two quite different desires, since I can desire either without the other, and yet there is nothing whatever to distinguish one from the other except by reference to my purpose or goal. The act is the same in either case. So, then, are its effects. But whether or not my "desire" is frustrated can be determined only by reference to whether my action achieves its *intended* result, whether the end or purpose for which I performed it is accomplished. Like "volitions," which are characterless apart from those actions of which they are the alleged causes, "desires" of this kind are equally characterless. Apart from the ends that are their objects there is nothing to distinguish one from another. Similar remarks cannot be made about genuine causes, however, which are never characterless or indescribable apart from their effects; and from this we can conclude that desires, as they are represented in the theory before us, are not even fit candidates for *causes* of actions, which the theory nevertheless requires them to be.

All of this shows, finally, that the theory in question, to the effect that purposeful actions are caused by desires and beliefs, is no causal theory at all, but only a cumbersome circumlocution. It in no sense renders purposeful behavior more intelligible, nor does it explicate such behavior in terms of the more seemingly empirical or scientific notions of cause and effect. It is not in the least empirical or scientific, but amounts only to rephrasing a familiar mode of description, namely, a teleological one, in terms of cause and effect. One has to realize, though, that the kinds of "causes" involved (desires for certain ends or goals) are not really causes in the sense in which the term is used in other contexts, and the kinds of "effects" involved (certain ends or goals) are likewise not effects of a kind that we ever speak of in other contexts. Indeed, the theory is intelligible, as a description of a purposeful action, only if we *first* understand quite clearly what a purposeful action is, independently of that theory. We understand the theory, then, only in the light of our prior understanding of a purposeful action. Indeed, to say that a given agent performed a certain action because he desired a certain result is just a misleading way of saying that he did the action in order to achieve that result. It is misleading because it tempts one to suppose that the notions of purpose and goal have been replaced by the more acceptable notions of cause and effect, whereas this has not, in fact, been accomplished. The notions of purpose and goal are still there. They are only concealed, and rather ineptly at that.

To say, then, that certain behavior is goal-directed or purposeful seems to be, first of all, sometimes *true,* and secondly, it seems to be an ultimate or irreducible fact about such behavior. That is, it is something that cannot be expressed in any other, non-teleological way. If this is so, then the concept of *purpose* is as basic a category as that of cause and effect. Neither can be "reduced" to the other. There is, then, no point in trying to *understand* purposeful behavior in terms of such concepts as cause and effect, nor in terms of any other concepts of empirical science, such as correlation and whatnot. Further, (1) if human behavior is sometimes irreducibly purposeful or goal-directed, and (2) if the sciences of human behavior are in any sense "committed" to the exclusion of teleological concepts in their descriptions and explanations, then (3) it is logically impossible that such sciences should ever explain or even adequately describe some of the simplest examples of human behavior; for purposeful actions need not be things the least extraordinary or recondite. Scholars can, of course, go right on eschewing teleological concepts, rigorously excluding them from any statements they make in their capacities as scientific inquirers, and thus preening themselves that, however meager and often irrelevant may be the fruits of their inquiries, they are, nevertheless, *scientific.* That is pretty much what they do when issues like this come up for serious attention, pointing with boundless pride to their *method,* thereby at least seeming to join the coveted ranks of those inquirers into inanimate or physical nature whose researches have yielded the most awesome results. It should be obvious, however, that from the fact that there is no *need* and indeed not even the slightest temptation, except on the part of the poetically minded, to introduce teleological concepts into the study of inanimate nature, it hardly *follows* that there is no need for such concepts for the understanding of human behavior.

I have suggested that the concept of a purposeful action is a basic and irreducible one. Although it cannot be analyzed or defined in non-teleological terms, it nevertheless has certain implications, the most important of which is: that if a given specimen of behavior of a given being is genuinely purposeful, and not merely purposeful in the borrowed sense that it subserves the purpose of a purposeful being, then that behavior is the act of an agent, or is the product of such an act. There can be no purposeful behavior apart from such agency; that is to say, no behavior as such is either purposeful or non-purposeful, except in relation to action. If, moreover, as I have suggested earlier, the action of an agent is self-originated behavior, as distinct from behavior which is only the causal consequence of things happening to or within that agent, then purposeful behavior will likewise be self-originated. To say that a given specimen of behavior is purposeful, however, implies a further condition, for it is not logically necessary that every act of an agent be purposeful or directed toward some goal. This further condition is that such behavior be a *means to some end*; and there is, I have maintained, *no* way of expressing that idea except in terms of concepts that are themselves purposeful, that is, intelligible only as expressing teleological concepts.

17

Conclusion

In many ways the results of my inquiry leave human nature as mysterious as before. Indeed, it has been part of my purpose to convey the idea that human nature is not a simple subject, and to inveigh against that tendency of thought, older than philosophy, to try making things understandable by first representing them as quite different than they are. When a man understands one thing well and another ill, and yet finds a certain semblance between them, the temptation to represent the unknown in terms of the known is almost irresistible. Thus he prides himself on understanding what remains an enigma. It is said that savages have a tendency to think of storms and the like as expressing the moods of powerful unseen beings—for they understand how the moods of men can be expressed in this way. Analogously, learned men have a tendency to think of human nature and particularly human behavior as being very much like the nature and behavior of inanimate things—for they understand the latter well, and want badly to understand the former.

The crucial step in philosophy is more often than not a clear understanding of what the problems are and why certain issues are problematical. I suggested at the beginning that very often questions become problematical simply because a vain attempt is made to construe certain data within a framework of thought into which they will not fit. Much of what I have said has been an endeavor to elicit such instances.

There is, for example, nothing particularly problematical to common sense in the idea that people sometimes have reasons for what they do, that they sometimes act with a view to achieving certain ends, that it is sometimes up to them how they go about realizing those ends, and so on. Such ways of speaking fit perfectly into the framework of everyday conceptions we continually apply to our dealings with men, conceptions we seldom reflect upon because they seem perfectly obvious. The study of philosophy and science, however, accustoms us to a rather different framework of concepts, one which we have learned to apply most usefully to the behavior of inanimate things. Accordingly, when men begin to philosophize about human behavior, they feel virtually compelled to interpret it within that very framework. Now in case human behavior should not fit into that framework, enormous and indeed insoluble problems must inevitably result. The host of philosophical and quasi-philosophical theories thus generated endeavor to represent certain apparent data as essentially different from what they appear to be. Thus, the seemingly purposeful behavior of men is depicted as not purposeful—or, if purposeful, then not so as to differ from the "purposeful" behavior of certain inanimate things. Again, the seemingly free actions of men are made to appear not free after all, or at least not free in any sense in which the behavior of inanimate things might not also be free. We are thereby led to suppose that the existence of such behavior is perfectly consistent with those deterministic presuppositions which are plainly derived, not from the study of men, but from the study of inanimate things. Then too, the reasons men sometimes give for their actions are, by the alchemy of philosophical thought, converted into desires, wants, and the like, which can easily be construed as the causes of their behavior—another instance of an unwarranted interpretation of human behavior in terms of the behavior of inanimate things.

Now it is fairly clear, I think, that by such familiar procedures nothing new is *discovered* about human nature. On the contrary, certain things which are already perfectly familiar to everyone are only represented in a radically different light. The sense of discovery is strong, though, and there are plenty of philosophers who declare, as if they were presenting certain discoveries, that men's free actions are "really" only actions that are caused in certain ways, that a man's thinking is "really" only a process in his brain, and thus perfectly describable by physics, that a man's purposeful behavior is "really" only behavior that is caused in certain ways, and so on. An enormous lot of contemporary philosophy has just this character, and some philosophers seem to imagine that the fruit of their study is certain discoveries hitherto unknown to the non-philosophical mind, which philosophy can present to the world as *new knowledge*. It should be quite obvious, however, that what is thus presented under the guise of new knowledge is nothing but what was already perfectly well known, but which we are simply exhorted to view in a new and unfamiliar light.

If we were confronted with a philosopher who professed to find nothing intelligible unless it could be construed within a teleological framework, we would undoubtedly regard him as naïve. Our reaction to his way of going about things would be similar to our reaction to certain of Aristotle's writings on scientific matters. If, for example, he professed to find no light in a complete causal explanation of some perfectly familiar phenomenon, such as that of a falling object, but insisted that there must be some explanation in terms of purpose or end—that there must be some reason *why* it behaves as it does, some end or goal that it accomplishes—then we would say, quite rightly, that he was trying to view everything in an anthropomorphic way—that he was trying to fit his experience into an arbitrary framework.

Now the question should be seriously considered whether we may not regard those thinkers who profess to find nothing intelligible unless it can be construed within a non-teleological framework as equally naïve. If, for example, someone professes to find no light in a complete teleological explanation of some perfectly familiar phenomenon, such as a man's heading for the pantry, but insists that there must be some explanation of this in terms of ordinary causes and effects—that there must, in that sense, be some explanation for his behaving as he does, some cause he is responding to—then I think we should say that he is trying to view everything in a non-anthropomorphic way, that he is trying to fit this experience into an incompatible framework of concepts. If the first man, who is so intellectually obsessed with purposes and goals, is arbitrary and naïve, then the second man, who is so obsessed with causes, seems on the face of things to be no less arbitrary and naïve.

What any man tends to regard as arbitrary, naïve, and implausible pretty much depends, however, on what conceptual framework he has already embraced. If the theme of this book were to be expressed in a single sentence, perhaps it would be this: that we should elaborate our theories and intellectual frameworks to fit what at least appear to be the facts of our experience, rather than adjusting these apparent facts to fit, well or ill, into such frameworks and theories as we happen to cherish.

In the second part of this book, for which Part I serves as an intro- duction, I have addressed myself entirely to certain fundamental questions about human nature. While a vast amount of contemporary philosophy concerns itself with "reducing" various concepts derived from our knowledge of men to those derived from our far more extensive theoretical knowledge of physical nature, my aim throughout has been precisely to extricate the former from the latter. Thus, I have *contrasted* agency with physical causation, reasons with causes, persons with things, freedom with chance, action with passion, final causes or ends with efficient causes, deliberation with speculation and in- ference, mechanism with purpose, and so on. Men find excitement in diminishing the differences between things, particularly the differences between those things that are and those that are not well understood, for it allows them to see otherwise baffling things in a much clearer light. But in fact, as I have kept urging, it is a borrowed light in which things are thus seen, and a light that distorts.

I have not in this book tried to build up any ideal conceptions of which I happen to be fond. If a certain conception of human nature has emerged, it is no result of a conscious purpose. It is only a logical consequence of taking certain considerations for what they are, and not contorting them into what they really appear not to be, however much we might wish them so.

But what is this broad picture? There would be no point in my simply summarizing what I have said, but if I may speak in loose and general terms, the basic conception of human nature suggested by my reflections is roughly this.

Men, unlike machines, sometimes have reasons, trifling or moment- ous, for some of the things they do, and this distinguishes them at the very outset as purposeful beings. For reasons are not causes, and cannot be construed as causes without the most violent distortion of both concepts. The idea of explaining behavior in terms of reasons rather than causes is a teleological idea, for no sense can be made of it except in terms of the concepts of means and ends. Typically, a man's voluntary behavior is the means to the attainment of something, behavior that has a point, intention, or goal—and this, of course, quite independently of whether such behavior is noble or even particularly significant. It is in any case distinctive, and utterly unlike anything found in physical nature. None of men's contrivances duplicate it, and when highly elaborate and sophisticated man-made tools and machines are described in teleological terms, or indeed in terms of any concepts of anthropological origin, the descriptions are throughout either metaphorical or meaningful only in a derivative sense.

Men sometimes cause certain things to happen, both in their own bodies and, by this means, in their environment. In thus causing certain things to happen, typically as means to the attainment or prevention of certain other things, they are active beings, or agents. This kind of causation—causation by agents—is so different from the kind of causal sequence found in events that it is unfortunate, and the source of much error, that we use the same word for both. Causation by agents remains, however, the fundamental idea of causation that all men possess. This is significant because it obliges us to view men as being sometimes the initiating or originating sources not only of their own behavior, but of all those events, sometimes events of the greatest magnitude, which are the causal consequences of such agency.

Now this idea strikes many as quite incomprehensible. And indeed in a way it is, for anyone who has a fondness for mysteries can find here a fertile source. Yet it should be noted that it is mysterious or incomprehensible *only* in the sense that it is not what a man having any familiarity with physical science or the general history of speculative thought would be led to expect. In another sense it is strange indeed to speak of some perfectly familiar thing—something so familiar as a simple act of moving one's limb—as being in any sense mysterious. If we find something in our daily experience, and if we also find that we cannot, without being led to absurdities, represent it as a special case of something else that is already familiar and well understood, there is surely no point in calling it mysterious other than to indicate that it is *not* a special case of something else that is well understood. In other words, there must be a sense in which the commonplace cannot be so strange, however badly it might fit into the philosophy and science we have learned.

Some philosophers, making much of certain observations of the sort that I have brought out, have leaped to a certain dualistic or Cartesian conception of human nature. Such an attempt I have not encouraged because, again, it seems to make things intelligible by. jamming them into what at least resembles the familiar. Thus, noting that men sometimes act and are not merely acted upon, that their actions can sometimes be represented as means to ends or as guided by reasons, that they sometimes deliberate, and so on, philosophers tend to suppose that men are not really what they appear to be, namely, physical objects, but are instead non-physical minds or "selves." This way of going about things, however, only circumvents the question by providing a receptacle for things that are in no way explained. It is as if a bill collector were to imagine he had collected all his debts as soon as he had arranged for a special pigeonhole for the bad ones and had given it a label designed more or less to conceal its true contents. If it is, in some sense, not quite clear how men *can* be the initiating sources of their own behavior, then it is made no more clear by saying that their "minds" or "selves" manage this feat for them; if it is not quite clear how men *can* act from reasons rather than causes, it is made no more clear by saying that reasons are transactions in their "minds"; if it is not plain how men *can* behave purposefully and sometimes even, as it seems, freely, no clarification is reached by asserting that it is really their "selves" that are purposeful and their "wills" that are free. At the same time I cannot forbear iterating that facts, and particularly commonplace ones, cannot really be *unclear* except in this sense: that they perhaps are not instances of other things that are clear. The real question, of course, is whether such things are facts.

Reflections similar in some ways to mine are often found in disquisitions on man's freedom of will. The concept of agency and the claim that human behavior is sometimes explained in terms of reasons rather than causes do certainly give comfort to anyone for whom the philosophical doctrine of free will is a dear one. I do not, however, suppose that any of my arguments prove freedom of the will, nor the contrary. In fact I have claimed that such a thesis can be neither proved nor disproved philosophically. There is nothing in philosophy that can show, concerning *any* action a man ever performs, whether or not anything caused him to do it. This is a perfectly factual question that can be asked concerning *any* action, one, moreover, which requires a unique set of data for each action, hardly to be found in philosophical argument. Much less will one find there data on which to answer every such question that might ever be asked concerning every action that will ever be done.

The question whether men have "free will" is really only the question whether men ever act freely. No special concept of "the will" is in any way needed to understand that question. And to ask whether a given man has acted freely with respect to something he has done is nothing more than to ask whether he could have acted otherwise. This, in turn, becomes the question whether, given that he did what he is alleged to have done, there was anything that rendered his behavior inevitable, or whether there was any cause, other than himself, of which his action can be seen as an effect. Now while I have not answered this question, I believe I have destroyed all the familiar philosophical arguments purporting to show that men never do act freely. If, as I have claimed, men are agents or the initiators of some of their behavior, and if, moreover, a man's behavior is sometimes understood in the light of his reasons, intentions, purposes, ends, or goals, then there is clearly no reason whatever for asserting that in addition to such reasons, intentions, and so on there *must* also be causes, and there is considerable reason for dismissing such an assertion as at least arbitrary and at most implausible. Men do sometimes suppose that they are not caused to do some of the things they do and are sometimes mistaken in their belief. It is logically possible that they are always mistaken. But it is also logically possible that they are sometimes quite right. To affirm that they *must* always be mistaken turns out always to be a rather different affirmation—namely, that a certain philosophical theory *must* (somehow) be true.

There is no need for me to mention again the implications of my observations upon the more or less speculative pronouncements on human nature we receive in such abundance from scientists, particularly psychologists and other anthropological scientists. I want only to stress that my reflections have not sprung from any polemical motive. I have no inclination to join sides in the defense of any doctrines whatever. I have only urged that certain concepts be given their due, that certain conceptions which are part of the very commonsense of mankind not be dismissed or distorted just on the ground that they do not accord with certain notions, no matter how much learning these latter may rest upon.

Index